The Body in Postwar Japanese Fiction

In the immediate postwar years, the body became an obsessive object of focus in Japanese fiction in both popular and highbrow novels. The freedom suggested in carnal hedonism and the representation of the body contrasted starkly with the political ideology of wartime Japan. In a time when bodily needs were often suppressed, the body became for writers and readers a symbol of physical toil and a celebration of individual identity and freedom that suggested a new way of living.

Through an examination of the work of a number of prominent twentieth-century Japanese writers, this book analyzes the meaning of the body in postwar Japanese discourse, the gender constructions of the imagery of the body, and the implications for our understanding of individual and national identity. Slaymaker discusses the ideological and historical conception of the body and *nikutai bungaku* (literature of the body) in general before analyzing more specific themes including:

- the body as revolution;
- the body as a tool to subvert militarist control;
- the adaptable nature of the body and its role in fashioning identity;
- the body in relation to protest and celebration;
- detailed analysis of the writings of Tamura Taijirō, Noma Hiroshi, and Sakaguchi Ango;
- an analysis of the differences between male and female writing in the period.

Concentrating on the literature produced between 1945 and 1960, this work highlights the varied uses and meanings of the human body in postwar Japanese fiction and its relationship to postwar and wartime society. It will be of interest to all students of modern Japanese literature, as well as students of this period in Japanese history, and anyone with an interest in the role played by the body in time of upheaval and change.

Douglas N. Slaymaker is Associate Professor of Japanese and Director of the Japan Studies Program in the Department of Modern and Classical Languages, Literatures and Cultures at the University of Kentucky, Lexington, Kentucky, USA.

Asia's Transformations
Edited by Mark Selden
Binghampton University and Cornell University, USA

The books in this series explore the political, social, economic and cultural consequences of Asia's transformations in the twentieth and twenty-first centuries. The series emphasizes the tumultuous interplay of local, national, regional and global forces as Asia bids to become the hub of the world economy. While focusing on the contemporary, it also looks back to analyze the antecedents of Asia's contested rise.

This series comprises several strands:

Asia's Transformations aims to address the needs of students and teachers, and the titles will be published in hardback and paperback. Titles include:

Opium, Empire and the Global Political Economy
Carl A. Trocki

Japan's Comfort Women
Sexual slavery and prostitution during World War II and the US occupation
Yuki Tanaka

Hong Kong's History
State and society under colonial rule
Edited by Tak-Wing Ngo

Debating Human Rights
Critical essays from the United States and Asia
Edited by Peter Van Ness

Asia's Great Cities
Each volume aims to capture the heartbeat of the contemporary city from multiple perspectives emblematic of the authors' own deep familiarity with the distinctive faces of the city, its history, society, culture, politics and economics, and its evolving position in national, regional and global frameworks. While most volumes emphasize urban developments since the Second World War, some pay close attention to the legacy of the longue durée in shaping the contemporary. Thematic and comparative volumes address such themes as urbanization, economic and financial linkages, architecture and space, wealth and power, gendered relationships, planning and anarchy, and ethnographies in national and regional perspective.

Titles include:

Hong Kong
Global city
Stephen Chiu and Tai-Lok Lui

Shanghai
Global city
Jeff Wasserstrom

Singapore
Carl Trocki

Beijing in the Modern World
David Strand and Madeline Yue Dong

Bangkok
Place, practice and representation
Marc Askew

Asia.com is a series which focuses on the ways in which new information and communication technologies are influencing politics, society and culture in Asia.

Titles include:

Asia.com
Asia encounters the Internet
Edited by K. C. Ho, Randolph Kluver and Kenneth C. C. Yang

Japanese Cybercultures
Edited by Mark McLelland and Nanette Gottlieb

Literature and Society is a series that seeks to demonstrate the ways in which Asian Literature is influenced by the politics, society and culture in which it is produced.

Titles include:

Chinese Women Writers and the Feminist Imagination (1905–1945)
Haiping Yan

The Body in Postwar Japanese Fiction
Douglas N. Slaymaker

RoutledgeCurzon Studies in Asia's Transformations is a forum for innovative new research intended for a high-level specialist readership, and the titles will be available in hardback only.

Titles include:

1 Chinese Media, Global Contexts
Edited by Chin-Chuan Lee

2 Imperialism in South East Asia
'A fleeting, passing phase'
Nicholas Tarling

3 Internationalizing the Pacific
The United States, Japan and the Institute of Pacific Relations in war and peace, 1919–1945
Tomoko Akami

4 Koreans in Japan
Critical voices from the margin
Edited by Sonia Ryang

5 The American Occupation of Japan and Okinawa*
Literature and memory
Michael Molasky

Critical Asian Scholarship is a series intended to showcase the most important individual contributions to scholarship in Asian Studies. Each of the volumes presents a leading Asian scholar addressing themes that are central to his or her most significant and lasting contribution to Asian studies. The series is committed to the rich variety of research and writing on Asia, and is not restricted to any particular discipline, theoretical approach or geographical expertise.

China's Past, China's Future
Energy, food, environment
Vaclav Smil

China Unbound
Evolving perspectives on the Chinese past
Paul A. Cohen

Women and the Family in Chinese History
Patricia Buckley Ebrey

Southeast Asia
A testament
George McT. Kahin

---

* Now available in paperback

The Body in Postwar Japanese Fiction

Douglas N. Slaymaker

RoutledgeCurzon
Taylor & Francis Group

LONDON AND NEW YORK

First published 2004
by RoutledgeCurzon
11 New Fetter Lane, London EC4P 4EE

Simultaneously published in the USA and Canada
by RoutledgeCurzon
29 West 35th Street, New York, NY 10001

RoutledgeCurzon is an imprint of the Taylor & Francis Group

Typeset in Garamond by
BOOK NOW Ltd
Printed and bound in Great Britain by
Antony Rowe Ltd, Chippenham, Wiltshire

British Library Cataloguing in Publication Data
A catalogue record for this book is available from the British Library

Library of Congress Cataloging in Publication Data
The body in postwar Japanese fiction/Douglas N. Slaymaker.
   – (Asia's transformations)
Includes bibliographical references and index.
   1. Body, Human, in literaature. 2. Japanese fiction – Shōwa period,
1926–1989 – History and criticism. I. Slaymaker, Douglas. II. Series.
   PL747.82.B65B63 2004
   895.6'35093561 – dc22   2003014997

ISBN 0–415–32225–1

Contents

Acknowledgments

No project like this reaches fruition without the aid and support of many people and agencies, across many years. I am humbled as I think back on the debts incurred along the way.

To start at the beginning, many of the ideas represented here were sparked in conversations and seminars at the University of Washington. John Whittier Treat III has been unstinting in his support across many years, reading early drafts and clarifying points. The intellectual ferment of Seattle at that time was enriched by Jay Rubin, Andrew Markus, Motoo Kobayashi, Chris Brockett, and Kaoru Ohta. The mark of each of them remains at different points in this manuscript. Fellow students have also added much to this, including Jim Dorsey and Jeff Johnson, in particular, who have shared much of the best and worse of this project: Rachel DiNitto, Davinder Bhowmik, Christine Marran, Mellek Ortabasi, and Bill Burton have been integral to the completion of it (much as they might wish to deny it).

My thinking has been honed across many conversations and much hospitality, in Japan, with scholars including Watanabe Kazutami, Karatani Kōjin, Katō Shūichi, Nishikawa Nagao, and Nishi Masahiko. Yone, Machiko, and Junko Kitagawa have provided much hospitality and support, a home away from home.

Financial support has come from a number of sources, including eighteen months of research supported by Japan's Monbusho, at Kumamoto National University, under the tutelage of Nishi Masahiko. One year of research at the University of Library and Information Science in Tsukuba was supported by the Social Science Research Council. Kuroko Kazuo provided much in the way of facilities and support, as did the university president, Yoshida Masayuki. In addition, I have benefited from financial support in the form of University of Kentucky Research Grants, North East Asia Council (NEAC) grants, a Indiana University Research Grant, and the Stanford University Research Grant.

This manuscript has been greatly strengthened by those who have read portions of the manuscript, in addition to those named above: Rebecca Copeland, Kevin M. Doak, J. Thomas Rimer, Ann Sherif, and Michael Molasky. The anonymous readers who have commented on the manuscript have given me much valuable advice. Colleagues at the University of Kentucky have given much guidance for which I am grateful, including department chairs Jerry Janecek and Ted Fiedler, who were unflagging in keeping things on track. Colleagues in various departments have given the support needed

x *Acknowledgments*

for such projects, particularly Jeff Peters and Jonathan Allison, having both read parts of the manuscript as well as offering emotional encouragement. Members of the Social Theory Consortium at the University of Kentucky have also contributed much – Wolfgang Natter, J. P. Jones, and Dana Nelson, including the works in progress series that provides a forum to discuss works in progress. Kevin Millham and Susan Janecek, with unsparing red (and green and blue) pencil, have cleared up many infelicitous sentences and prolix paragraphs.

Karen has been here for the entire project, and knows the full measure of the cost of this undertaking. It is therefore dedicated to her. And to Erika and Reina, who may someday know what it was all about.

Introduction

Within eighteen months of Japan's 1945 surrender to the Allies, Japanese devotees of Western art queued in lines rivaling those for food rations to see a "Living Picture Show" staged on the fifth floor of a Shinjuku Theater. Having finally reached the head of the line, they confronted a series of wall-sized picture frames draped with black curtains. These were drawn back for ten-second intervals to reveal semi-nude women posed in twenty recreations of Western art masterpieces. In this "picture frame show," spectators could ogle, for example, scantily clad women in a *Birth of Venus*, as well as other models posed in famous pastoral, picnic, and beachfront scenes. While not shocking by present-day standards, such eroticism characterized postwar Japanese culture, an eroticism of commercialized sexuality that garnered hand-wringing and media attention to these "scandals" (all the while filling theaters and selling publications). One of those scandals centered on the famous scene from the 1947 stage adaptation of a Tamura Taijirō novel – a woman being strung up, stripped to the waist, and flogged – and filled Shinjuku's Kūkiza theater to capacity.[1]

Isoda Kōichi reports the case of a certain Nakamura who "chose a decadent lifestyle following his shock at the loss in the war." According to Isoda, Nakamura and his wife engaged in sadomasochistic sexual acts in the main hall of Shinto shrines so as to perform their transgressions "in front of the gods." There is much suggested by this act, highlighting a level of disgust with the tradition of state Shinto, the Imperial system, and the repressive nation-state it represented.[2]

Many Japanese transgressed the boundaries of state and religious authority, redefining conceptions of the body, during the upheavals of postwar Japan. Writers such as Tamura Taijirō (1911–83), Noma Hiroshi (1915–91), and Sakaguchi Ango (1906–55) offered images and narratives that led the way in those redefinitions. This book focuses on the body as represented in Japanese fiction after what in Japan is called the Asia-Pacific War.[3] (For my purposes, "postwar" refers to the period between the 1945 surrender and the early 1960s.) The body became an obsessive object of focus in the years following Japan's defeat for a complex of reasons. First, this resulted, at least partly, from the sheer physicality of everyday life – the demands of bodily needs – which, for urban populations in particular, was given over to securing food and finding shelter. Concerning the shortages of food, Tsurumi Shunsuke notes, for example, that the Department of Welfare had decreed in 1941 "that a male adult engaged in normal work would need 2,400 calories per day . . . In 1945 [this figure] was further lowered to

1,793 calories. As a natural result, the health of the nation deteriorated." These lowered caloric standards represent an attempt to correlate need with availability. It is a statistic that suggests just how bleak were the war years.[4] Yet, in many ways, the postwar years were even more desperate. Allied bombings had destroyed virtually every major city and with them internal transportation networks, and daily necessities were in chronically short supply. Inordinate amounts of time and energy went to procuring food, via the black market or other illegal means.[5]

For a second reason, the body offered antidotes to the bankruptcy of the traditional and military values which characterized the previous fifteen years of war. The desecration of Shinto shrines by Nakamura and his wife is an example of this. Their celebration of the carnal body (*nikutai* 肉体 "physical/carnal body") suggests a punning contrast to the national polity (*kokutai* 国体 "national body"), the focus of their desecration. This binary of individual and state helps to structure the writings I examine, yielding imagery of liberation-through-carnality that suggests carnal hedonism as a corrective to the political ideology of wartime. Such physicality was a response to the failure of political ideology in the imagination of society, and was especially resonant given the postwar shortage of goods.

Third, this obsession with the body was also, in part, a response to the wartime censorship that made it extremely difficult to write of the erotic, of the political, and of wartime deprivations. Governmental press censorship of writing that criticized wartime politics prevented narration of the war experience during the war (where "war experience" means the drudgery and dreariness of the battlefield). In result the experience of soldiering was only narrated in the postwar years: "postwar" writing is often a literature of war.

The confluence of these circumstances – wartime and postwar privations, the reaction to an individual-denying social order, and the constrictions of censorship – fostered the ubiquitous concern for the body in postwar Japan generally, and in postwar writing particularly. Many writers responded to this postwar situation with imagery that was heavily focused on the physical/carnal aspects of existence. Such a characterization is true of writers active both before and after the war such as Nagai Kafū (1879–1959), Tanizaki Jun'ichirō (1886–1965), Dazai Osamu (1909–48), or Kawabata Yasunari (1899–1972), writers known for their treatment of sensuality and sexuality.

In the chapters that follow, I will explore the imagery of the body from a number of perspectives because the eroticism of the postwar writers marks a quite different approach to the body. The initial chapter of this study outlines the discourse of the body known as *nikutai bungaku* or "literature of the body" that was ubiquitous in the immediate postwar years. Succeeding chapters focus, in turn, on the fiction of three representative postwar writers that I call "the flesh writers": Chapter 2 on Tamura Taijirō, Chapter 3 on Noma Hiroshi, and Chapter 4 on Sakaguchi Ango. The flesh writers' articulation of the body in the literary imagination of the postwar years is integral to the development of postwar discourse on the body. They were widely read authors: Tamura the more "lowbrow" and "popular," Noma the more "highbrow" and "literary," while Ango appealed to middle- and lowbrow audiences, in their contemporary receptions. Together, they have been referred to collectively as the "flesh-group" or the "body-school" of writers (*nikutai-ha*). Much of their imagery responded to the increasing militarization of the populace that began in the 1930s, intensified through the Pacific War, and came to an official end only in 1945. They wrote with an eye of protest towards the nation, itself predominately imaged as male during the war years, to suggest alternative constructions of society. Expressions of the protest had been repressed by militarist censorship but burst forth in a torrent under the relaxed censorship of the Occupation. The writers' compulsion to describe the wartime oppression once publication became possible suggests a continued sense of immediacy.

Tamura Taijirō is usually credited with introducing the literature of the flesh – *nikutai bungaku* – with his "Nikutai no akuma" ("Devil of the Flesh") in the October 1946 issue of *Sekai bunka*, and "Nikutai no mon" ("The Gate of Flesh") in the March 1947 issue of *Gunzō*. Tamura, in particular, is thought of as a writer of the body (*nikutai sakka*), but has only recently been included in "serious" considerations of postwar writers.[6] Tamura's assertion about the issues and the place of the body is critical:

> "Thought" [*shisō*] is, at this time threatening to push us down; it does nothing else. "Thought" has, for a long time, been draped with the authoritarian robes of a despotic government, but now the body is rising up in opposition. The distrust of "thought" is complete. We now believe in nothing but our own bodies. Only the body is real [*jijitsu*]. The body's weariness, the body's desires, the body's anger, the body's intoxications, the body's confusion, the body's fatigue – only these are real. It is because of all these things that we realize, for the first time, that we are alive.[7]

He reacts to the ideology of the militarist state and proposes that militarist control will be subverted by an emphasis on the body. Tamura conceives of the body in terms of revolution, a violent opposition.

Noma was sometimes linked with the *burai-ha* (the "decadents") and also the *nikutai-ha* ("carnal writers"), but wrote a Marxist-influenced literature, focusing on the individual body as the source of identity and liberation. Widely credited with having introduced or discovered the style now associated with "postwar writing," Noma Hiroshi is, in Honda Shūgo's words, "the first voice of the postwar writers and his is in a sense, the first voice of the entire body of postwar literature."[8] In Noma's fiction, it seems that one must jealously protect one's body in the face of a military that attempted to extend its reach into all the nooks and crannies of society, threatening to destroy the individual while doing so. Kitayama Toshio, a character in Noma's important story, "Kao no naka no akai tsuki," has learned this lesson as well: "He had learned in violent battle that a man preserves his life with no power but his own, he eases despair by himself, and must watch his own death. Each man, like the water in each canteen, must hold himself in that canteen."[9] The struggle for wholeness is located in the body.

Sakaguchi Ango employs imagery similar to Tamura's:

> I ask, what precisely is humanity and mankind? It is unabashedly to desire what one desires, it is forthrightly to declare unpleasant that which is unpleasant. In essence, that is the whole of it: to proclaim forthrightly that which one finds desirable, to proclaim one's affections for the woman one is drawn to. It is to cast off

the sham garments and the [wartime] slogans we wrap around ourselves: "doing all to preserve proper relations between subject and superior," "to forswear illicit relations," "to uphold the proper balance of duty and emotions." We must strip off these robes and bare our souls.[10]

Ango[11] admonishes unrepentant prioritizing of the physical as a countermeasure to militarist control and as a means to achieve his ideal society. In 1946 he paired the recently available translations of Jean-Paul Sartre with Tamura's writings and suggested that together they constituted a "literature of the flesh," because they share a representational strategy of the individual that appeared independently of one another, in different countries.[12] Ango, who rocketed to prominence in 1946 with works such as "Darakuron" ("On Decadence") and "Hakuchi" ("The Idiot"), provided the fuel, with his iconoclastic images and powerful prose, for this postwar emphasis on the body.

The intertwined strands of protest and celebration so pervasive in postwar Japanese society come together in the flesh writers' conceptualization of individual identity. The mutually constitutive skein proves resistant to sharp delineation. This understanding of individuality and identity supports, however, the construction of the body that is the central imagery of post-1945 fiction. The flesh writers protested the centralized organization of culture that had marked the militarist decades, and celebrated the possibilities of a new "democratic" age. They imagined a male identity that could adapt to and function in this new reality. They were convinced that the mistakes of the past war were attributable to the wartime state's undervaluation of the body. Establishing a proper respect for the individual body promised a new start. The flesh writers suggested that renewed emphasis on the physical could offset the disastrously mistaken focus of the militarist past and help avoid another lapse into militarism.

The sense of purpose and possibility in these years prompted many male writers to write of liberation and utopia. "Democracy" itself, even though it had been brought by the agents of Japan's defeat, possessed a utopian aura, promising freedom and liberation that often overlapped with the "freedom" imagined in their fiction. For the flesh writers, the body marked the source of this freedom, and they imagined a male identity that could adapt to and function in this new reality. Anxieties concerning masculinity and attempts to forge one anew, however, led these male writers to an identity most often imagined as a sexually aggressive male: to fall back on, that is, the conceptualization they ostensibly decry.

This male discourse of liberation through the body is dependent on the Other of a female body. The concomitant imagery of women reworks older ideologies in an attempt to form a new, "appropriately" postwar, body. While new, it draws from such older, prewar conceptualizations as described by Nina Cornyetz: the "literary productions of a coming-into-being of a phallic, national subject through the intrinsically polysemic establishment of woman as Other and the repository of literary nativism and the coterminous establishment and naturalization of idealized maternity as female vocation."[13] The flesh writers would consistently denounce the literary trends that precede them, but the imagery that Cornyetz describes concerning the prewar writings of Izumi Kyōka (1873–1939) – nativism, woman as Other, woman as maternal caregiver – is reiterated in this writing, albeit to different ends. Many prewar concerns are denounced by these postwar writers even as, we find, they are reworked.

The flesh writers were propelled by the heterosexual assumptions of narrative that Peter Brooks has so cogently mapped – consistently "masculine" in Brooks' "epistemophilic" sense, "scoptophilic" in the system of knowledge and representation that Luce Irigaray describes[14] – where the pursuit of sex offers greater knowledge, itself a form of liberation. The experience of empire is never far for these writers: the body of a woman, actual or metaphorical, becomes terrain to be explored and subjugated. Further, the telling of tales is a desire to "know" or, in the related sense explored by Anne McClintock, a desire to conquer and tame.[15] The men hope, through sex, to learn more of the world, to learn more of themselves, to change the world, and, usually, to enter some Edenic primitive space, a womblike space that is protective and comforting, a place of cleansing and rebirth. The sexual body of a woman becomes Other in every sense, a paradisiacal locale where the quest for comfort, solace, nurture, and peace culminates, a place of liberation. Such "freedom" was often associated with democracy: in result, freedom (and democracy as well) came to be thought of in terms of carnal liberation.

While my primary focus is the imagery of the body that these three "flesh writers" employ, in the final chapter I will discuss the writing of women such as Sono Ayako (1931–), Hiroike Akiko (1919–), Nakamoto Takako (1903–91), Shibaki Yoshiko (1914–91), and Saegusa Kazuko (1929–), whose contemporary writings elucidate the issues implicit in the men's writing. The fiction of women in this period is striking for its counterdirection: we find women writing of the details of daily life with no sense of such imminent liberation; they were evidently impressed more by the degree to which old structures had not changed. Their counterimagery system provides many points of departure, as I will elaborate in the concluding chapter, including insight into the gendered particulars of the male writers' vision.

Women also wrote of sex workers and slaves, and of identity after the war, but they expressed none of the men's liberating optimism. Rather, their writings underscore the masculinist-gendered assumptions of male writers. Their plots suggest that the place accorded women in the male visions was not particularly rewarding, let alone ideal. They found none of the (putatively) liberating possibility expressed in men's fiction. For their characters, little had changed since the war and women remained subservient in power structures whose sole change goes no further than the hue of men's faces and the color of soldiers' uniforms. Thus, these female contemporaries of the flesh writers help us to see that the masculinist visions were not as monolithic as often assumed. Though many of the women's works have been relegated to obscurity, re-reading them is to discover anew the power of the narratives because they highlight the possible configurations of the body in the context of the destroyed, demoralized, and democratizing postwar Japan. We also discover their applicability to the gendered nature of narrative in general, and of postwar experience in particular.

When was the "postwar"? The issues only become murkier with the passage of time. Given the drawn-out experience of Okinawa, for example – not "returned" to the mainland until 1972 – one cannot simply declare that the "postwar" began on 15 August 1945.[16] The term also has a prewar history: "postwar" had first been used to mark the important societal changes following the Russo-Japanese War of 1904–5. Prior to the Pacific War, this is what "postwar" referred to, and in 1946 this "postwar" was still within living memory.[17] Nishikawa Nagao writes provocatively on this, noting how "postwar" could be pushed all the way back to the beginning of the Meiji period if one wished.[18] Positing an end to the "postwar period," and with it "postwar literature," proves particularly contentious and has been variously and animatedly debated since the early 1950s. No consensus has been reached and the debate continues. For the purposes of this study, I am looking most closely at the years between 1945 and, roughly, 1960.

However "postwar" is defined, national identity has been tethered to this historical event in a complex network of remembering and forgetting that fuels a continuing public debate in the process of Japanese society's self-definition. The end of the war seems to signal a moment when the whole world changed, to mark the point from which society would never be the same and daily life could no longer be constructed in the same terms.

The radical change associated with the end of the war masks continuities from prewar society. Most of the writers considered "postwar" – including those I will focus on – were in fact active before the war. For example, Noma Hiroshi's *Kurai e* is always discussed as "postwar literature" – it appeared in 1946 – even though it was written during the war and was set in and reflected his experiences of the late 1930s.[19] Tamura Taijirō first published a short story in *Shinchō* in 1934. Sakaguchi Ango was likewise an established writer before the war, with such prewar works as "Kaze hakase" ("Professor Sneeze" 1931) and "Kurodanimura"("Kurodani Village" 1931). Yet their most representative work appears after the war, with a new feel, exhibiting a style and a sensibility that had not appeared in Japanese literature to this point. Critic Nakamura Shin'ichirō also notes that writers like Noma and Shiina Rinzō (whose work is outside the scope of this study) wrote in an entirely new style, yet were nonetheless writing against the traditions that characterize the prewar.[20] Noma Hiroshi characterized "postwar" this way:

> Postwar literature is a literature that asks, through [the filter of] the war, what is humankind, what are the things that envelop us? Up to that point [of the war] a cup was a cup, and a table was a table, things that do not change. With the war we realized that "it is there" is not the entire reality because what is there can immediately disappear. The war was that sort of experience. Likewise, friendship was friendship and love was love – choose whatever you like – we were accustomed to thinking that it was "there." All of that, during the war, you see, took flight. That was the war experience. On the political front, say, the one who was beside me until yesterday has been hauled off to jail, has disappeared. Or they were sent off to the front and their existence snuffed out.[21]

This sudden loss of surety introduces doubt and disillusion about all that came before, and that extends to previously accepted literary styles and truths. The writers that I discuss here write as though accepting Noma's characterization, for the war is immediate referent and a key to understanding humanity. Further, the flesh writers are representative of postwar writing, particularly because of their emphasis on the body: an individual and erotic body that has long been a central component of the intellectual and literary tradition of Japan.

As groundwork for the discussion of individual writers in Chapters 2, 3, and 4, the first chapter explores the discourse on the body that comprises *nikutai bungaku*. The setting is postwar Japan, but the discourse incorporates a reaction to the repression and oppression of the militarized 1930s and 1940s. For this reason, I consider next the ideological and historical conception of that body.

1 The discourse on the body

The "body" of this literature

Nikutai is the name of a short-lived journal that began publication in 1947. Its title, *The Body*, and its date immediately connect it to my discussion and to the postwar interest in the carnal body. The "body" discussed in this literature is the *nikutai* of the journal title, a term that gained new currency in postwar Japan. In the postwar era, *nikutai* signified the expressly carnal and physical and was posited as the ground for individual identity.[1] *Nikutai* (肉体) operates on three semantic axes: first, within a set of works which explore the physical body; second, in the context of the personal and physical which contrasts with the non-physical, roughly equating to the meanings of "spiritual"; and, finally, on the social/external level, it operates in contrast to the *kokutai* (国体), the body politic. *Niku* (肉), meaning meat, muscle, or flesh, paired with the character for body, the *tai* (体), connotes the physical carnality of the body and operates on the second axis of body meanings. The postwar usage reflects a group of meanings that builds on a long history of usage to contrast to other words for "body," such as *karada* (体) or *shintai* (身体). Iwaya Daishi recalls *nikutai* being a loaded term (*gokan*) at this time, noting that "before the war we would not have used *nikutai* but *shintai* [when referring to the body]."[2] While this accurately captures the nuances embedded in the writings I consider here, it seems slightly too schematic given that a number of earlier examples argue against Iwaya's assertion. For one, the authoritative dictionary of Japanese usage, the *Nihon kokugo daijiten* gives, as definition, "the body comprised of meat/muscle (肉)" and offers *karada* as one synonym, although qualifying *nikutai* as "the body [*karada*] of sexual desire." At the same time, *nikutai rōdō*, or manual labor, emphasizes the physical muscle necessitated by construction work. For another, and these reach back to much earlier usages, the authoritative dictionary of Japanese, the *Nihon kokugo daijiten* cites examples of *nikutai* from Samuel Smiles' *Self Help* (translated into Japanese as *Saikoku risshi hen*) of 1877 and Fukuzawa Yūkichi's *Bunmeiron no gairyaku* of 1875. The nineteenth-century usages associate to the English-language backgrounds of these two works (in that Fukuzawa is drawing from his travels in the West), where the negative associations of the carnal and the sexual resonate. The same connotations appear in other contexts, as well. *Nikuyoku*, as "carnal desire" (肉欲) is accompanied in the *Nihon kokugo daijiten* by citations of late nineteenth-century and early twentieth-century works by novelists Morita Sōhei and Arishima Takeo.

Older citations in the dictionary include the classical *niku byōbu*, or "flesh screen," where a man is surrounded by beautiful women who screen him off from the cold. Hirabayashi Taiko gives *nikutai* another nuance in her fiction of the 1930s, consistently using *nikutai* when she discusses the (female) body in sickness, weakness, pregnancy, and childbirth, which is far from the sensual body imagined by the flesh writers. These contrasting examples show that Iwaya's statement, which seems commonsensical at first encounter, elides the historical usages propelling these postwar invocations.

Shintai (身体) is also a synonym for the "body" and it is often included in dictionary definitions of *nikutai*. It refers to the physical and material, rather than the carnal and sensual, body. *Shintai* is the word preferred in philosophical discourse, for example in phenomenology.[3] The distinction arises in the overtones of baseness and carnality that *nikutai* incorporates, as opposed to the use of *shintai* as a more clinical term in philosophic writings. Whereas *shintai* gives the sense of a solid object as in physical science usage, *nikutai* generally refers to the subjective and emotion-laden response of a living object. *Shintai* often corresponds, subjectively, to a more "refined" register of discourse than *nikutai*.[4]

The sinified compound *shintai* also overlaps with the native Japanese word *karada* (体), perhaps the most straightforward equivalent to English "body." *Shintai* in its philosophical delineation refers to the phenomenological body, the body as material object, as thing, in a society of individuals where each is aware of the other and thereby aware of the self. The idea of an individual "self" incorporates the Japanese *seishin* (or spirit, 精神), a concept often functioning as a synonym for *seikaku* (性格, or personality), but which also includes the sense of soul or spirit. This is because the individual person is more than a lump of flesh – *nikutai*, *shintai*, *karada* – but a complete person, a human being, comprised of both fleshly body and spirit (*seishin*, *seikaku*). Thus, *karada* (which Iwaya referred to as the word of choice in the prewar years) is commonly used to discuss the material body. *Shintai* incorporates both body and spirit, for to be more than material object, one needs awareness of the Other, and this is the work of the personality, the *seishin*. *Seishin* may be closest to the various senses incorporated in the French *esprit*. *Seishin* does not represent the soul (of Judeo-Christian tradition), but is close to "personality," i.e. that which complements the physical to make a person whole. As set off from the physical and concrete, it also accords with the abstract and ethereal. A person is not complete without the *seishin*, which is like ether, clearly "there" but only containable in an individual body, the element that gives identity to the individual. That is, *shintai* seems an amalgam of *nikutai* and *seishin*, combining the material and the non-material. *Shintai* is the physical body incorporating both spirituality and essentiality, the physical and the personality.[5] The flesh writers focus on the carnal physicality of the *nikutai* and eschew the *seishin* which they associate with the propagandistic usages of abstract "spiritual" values.

This is the second axis of meaning, where *nikutai* appears as the opposite of the *seishin*, which represents the immaterial and abstract in existence and personality. The *Kōjien* dictionary offers the initial definition of *seishin* as "in contrast to matter, body [*nikutai*]." *Seishin*, whether invoked directly by the flesh writers or obliquely as the Other to *nikutai*, forms a chain of meaning linked to the abstractions of wartime ideology. The body stressed in the flesh writers' works opposes wartime ideology and is strengthened in the lexical items and the imagery itself. In Japanese, *jidai no seishin* can refer to "the spirit of the age," a personality of sorts that goes beyond the individual and incorporates the whole: a "national consciousness," perhaps, that downplays the individual in order to elevate the group or societal experience. *Seishin* was also a term used with numbing frequency in wartime propagandist clichés such as *gunkoku seishin*, "the spirit of the military nation," or *kōkoku seishin*, the "spirit of the Imperial nation."[6] It is precisely such references to the undifferentiated mass that writers like Tamura and Ango resisted in order to emphasize and glorify the individual. *Nikutai bungaku* registers the reaction to this emphasis on the *seishin*, a reaction many readers shared. The flesh writers, by assuming that the body is central to individual identity, and by extension to a national identity, reflect the attempts in the postwar years to come to terms with the war years by both repressing the body through disavowal, and expressing it through carnality.[7]

The opposition of *seishin* to *nikutai* is an ancient one. Critic Saeki Junko cites a nineteenth-century example of the terms in relation to the development of an ideal of "love" in Japanese society. She cites Tsubouchi Shōyō's Meiji-era categorization of love (*irogoto*) in which the pleasure of the flesh (*nikutai*) and physical enjoyments (*nikutai no kairaku*) ranked the lowest. Tsubouchi likened pursuing the external only – i.e. physical attraction – while ignoring or not caring about internal attributes, to the sexual attraction of animals, base and uncivilized. Likewise, in Tsubouchi's scheme, the "love" found in barbarian societies was physical and carnal; only in the "progress" towards civilization does lust pass to affection, to true love. That is, a "civilized" and modern society valorizes the spiritual – the abstract and cerebral, as it would seem to the flesh writers – and downplays the physical. It also avoids the simply platonic, the exclusively *seishinteki*, while striving for a balance between the physical and the spiritual, the internal and the external, in an attempt at balance still operative after the war.[8]

Finally, on the third axis, *nikutai* contrasts with *kokutai*, the body as nation, or national polity. The organic imagery of body-as-nation was not newly emphasized in the postwar years; rather it is a reworking, and at times an attempt at recuperation, of prewar and wartime discourses. As Yoshikuni Igarashi writes in the context of analyzing the body imagery that arose in the construction of postwar memory, "Japanese bodies had already been at the heart of nationalistic discourse before 1945."[9] The contrast between an individual body and the national body had increased resonance in the postwar years precisely because, it seems, of the way the distance between them had been collapsed during the war and prewar years: "the distance between mind and body was collapsed in wartime efforts to create a nationalistic body. What was regarded as 'unhealthy' – unproductive and unreproductive – was branded as threatening national interests."[10] A heightened sense of the physical seemed so unremarkable, and the appearance of a "literature of the body" so emblematic, in the postwar years, that Maruyama Masao doubted there was any need for a term such as *nikutai bungaku* ("body literature") at all. He found carnal, physical concerns – of an erotic sort – sufficiently pervasive to label all postwar fiction "carnal" or "bodily." Maruyama clearly considered this obsession with the body a negative trend in literature and not at all representative of the majority of the populace, noting that "people often argue that the state of postwar sex life itself is characterized by irresponsibility and that literature is only reflecting a real situation. Of course this might be true if we were considering only one segment of present-day society," but not all of it. He feared that, in the future, observers "would get the idea that in about 1949 the Japanese people had their heads filled constantly with the business of coitus."[11] Tsurumi Shunsuke, in a more political approach, explains it this way:

> The concept of *kokutai* or "national structure" derived from the fundamental insularity and isolation of the Japanese. The concept served as a powerful linguistic weapon for both attack and defense in the political arena of the period 1931–1945. Although the expression "national structure" disappeared with Japan's defeat in 1945 and a new style of political argument was initiated by the United States occupation, the concept, if not the term, is still alive in a submerged form in Japanese politics . . . After the Meiji Restoration, "national structure" was used to signify the uniqueness of the existing government of Japan.[12]

In wartime talk and propaganda, the individual body (*nikutai*) was set in opposition to the national (*kokutai*). A great wealth of material exists concerning the concept of the *kokutai*. George Wilson reflects much that energizes the idea as I am referring to it. In the Tokugawa period, he argues, the Imperial realm was holy; the Meiji Restoration replaced this realm with the nation-state. Even though the nation-state had political power, it could never attain the moral authority of the realm, much as it might wish to. Thus,

> When twentieth century Japanese "ultranationalists" championed the *kokutai*, they were nostalgically harking back to the notion of the realm. Its function was central and it was "religious" in character, so it is appropriate to the sense of metaphor to follow George Elison in translating *kokutai* not as "national polity" but as "the mystical body of Japan."[13]

The *kokutai* became something of a state religion, with the mystical emperor at the apex, and it transformed in the war years into a particularly formidable edifice that brooked no dissent.

Such explicit connections between concerns of the body and authoritarian governments are a feature of the twentieth century: the "histories of the body" that have emerged since Michel Foucault's groundbreaking work have often stressed just this relationship. This physical body carries specific political meanings; emphasizing the body, carnality, and sexuality functions is explicitly counterhegemonic because it defies the primacy of the national body: such characterizations have applicability for contexts much wider than the flesh writers only. Refusal to subordinate individual desires to national projects serves as revolutionary act and protest. In earlier periods – eighteenth-century France is a notable example – the king's body symbolized the state, and punishment for treason was, correspondingly, excruciatingly physical, as indicated in the detailed description of a man being drawn and quartered that begins

Foucault's *Discipline and Punish*. Treason was imagined as a physical offense against the physical body of the king, and the appropriate punishment was physical.

Foucault has written of the body that it "is also directly involved in a political field; power relations have an immediate hold upon it; they invest it, mark it, train it, torture it, force it to carry out tasks, to perform ceremonies."[14] This understanding of the body and its direct relation to political realms illuminates much in the postwar Japanese context. As Dorinda Outram reminds us, "Modern histories of the body originated during the same era as the high point of European Fascism. The 1930s and 1940s saw an intense focus in many of the social issues which fed into historical enquiry on the social functions of the human body."[15] The chronicling, control, and categorization of bodies focused seemingly unlimited energies in the early decades of this century throughout the world.

The *kokutai* was synonymous with the government but it was also an all-pervasive system of imagery that, even if submerged, persisted in postwar political society, still resonant with mystical, spiritual overtones. This normalizing force that was (and is) the *kokutai* was established vis-à-vis and opposed to the individual body, which was severely punished for any dissent. Thus,

> After the defeat, and after the Emperor's proclamation that he was only a human being, the idea of national structure also fell off like another layer of dandruff. Then all that finally remained was the body [*nikutai*]. This was the basis of what was called "bodyism" [*nikutai bungaku*],[16] rampant in the period after the war and persisting in various forms to this day. To be true to the needs of the body was proclaimed the supreme aim in the postwar literature of Sakaguchi Ango, Tamura Taijirō and Tanaka Hidemitsu [1913–49].[17]

Conflating the national body with the physical – that is, using the imagery of the physical body to discuss the state – has a long lineage as well. The late Edo scholar Aizawa Seishisai (1782–1863) imagined a national body as *shintai*. Aizawa explicitly discusses the *kokutai* in terms of the body's five limbs, claiming that unawareness of the five limbs of the country's body is tantamount to unawareness of one's own five limbs. Aizawa goes on to draw a parallel between the physical body's limbs and the physical attributes of the Japanese archipelago: Heaven is the top (head), middle is the earth (ground), East is neck, and West is feet. He then draws parallels to each limb and each part of the archipelago: "[Aizawa] construed kokutai, or what is essential to a nation, as the spiritual unity and integration that make a territory and its inhabitants a nation."[18]

Constructing the national body

While Japanese textbooks of the first two decades of the twentieth century show an increasing emphasis on Confucian-based ideas of filial honor and respect, the concept of the *kokutai* (the national body/polity) and with it the sense of the *kazoku kokka* (the nation as family) never diminished. Indeed, they comprise the common knowledge about Japan by the Japanese, and an image system that contrasted individual body to national body was completed with ever more robust colorings. "*Kokutai*, then, with its mixture of Confucian and distinctively Japanese elements, was the mainstream traditional view of the Japanese polity, the backdrop against which Western ideas were introduced into Japan."[19] The ideology of wartime Japan, which subsumed individuals to a national body and which these postwar writers so vehemently opposed, had been established in Japan long before the war.

At an anecdotal, but poignantly relevant level is the experience that led the young instructor Inoue Hideaki to consider these issues while teaching in England in the 1960s. Inoue was reminded of the visceral power of the word *kokutai*, which he "doesn't hear much anymore," when a student discussed the concept in an essay on Japan. Inoue had given no previous thought to the *kokutai* being literally the "body of the state" (*kokutai no shintai*), a literal physical body, although this is what the characters comprising the word signify. He was reminded of the spiritual and mystical connotations of this word and idea in Japan, of the nation as a body-space (*shintaiteki kūkan*) that contains the people of the nation. Further, the system functions as a parallel to the family *ie* system, the extended patriarchal family system. He concludes that this patriarchal extended family structure is part of the wartime ideology that made (makes) Japan so insular. Threat comes from outside. The enemy/Other threatens the body space, threatens to come straight into the house (*ie*) of individuals and of the Japanese nation. Since one cannot enter the body space, by definition, without inflicting some sort of wound (*kizu*, also blemish), intrusion from outside is especially fearsome. Thus, "the *kokutai* is not simply a sociological political structure, but it is a body [*shintai*] fleshed out as a biological organic space."[20] The body being breached in this image system is that of Japan, in a subtle coding of Japan as feminine. The postwar flesh writers rework the tradition in response to new situations. For one, they felt much more keenly the uses to which the body had been put by governmental agencies; they wished to posit the means to attain individual autonomy and freedom. Their emphasis on the body was part of reestablishing that freedom.

The journal *Nikutai* was important for focusing these issues and appeared while Tamura Taijirō, Noma Hiroshi, and Sakaguchi Ango were publishing their postwar work. This period immediately following surrender prompted many to rethink their lives and that of the nation in the terms of this *nikutai*; it seemed to them the historic moment for clarifying meaning and planning a future liberating course. The body focused such considerations. Freedom, for these writers, refers most often to the ability to forge individual identity and agency following years of abstract propaganda and calls to self-sacrifice. Subsumed, because less conscious, in these concerns is a reaction against militarized wartime society and an anxiety about the reconfigured male in postwar occupied society. Reaction against the bureaucracies and regulations led to a view of "liberation" which, at times, however, seems little more than the desire to be freed of all external demands. In the wartime and postwar context, many associated liberation with satiation and imagined it as the fulfillment of individual desires, and these seemed to be physical: sex, food, housing. The freedom even to pursue these desires is often portrayed as a liberation as well.[21] We find in this writing, then, a two-pronged approach to this freedom: the flesh writers protest the bankrupt goals of the previous militarist decades and celebrate the possibilities of a new "democratic" age.

Second, we find the need to recuperate a male identity operative behind these images of liberation. Anxieties about masculinity are subsumed in the obsessive concerns about sexual freedom (often, itself, an obsession with and fear of women), a so-called "freedom" that is "male." When Alan Wolfe writes of the potential for change in the midst of defeat, he describes "the synchronic and diachronic as an interlocking nexus, grounded in the obdurate reality of the US Occupation. The problematic is related to the paradoxical perception that the agent of defeat is also the agent of liberation."[22] The sense of purpose and possibility in these years prompted many male writers to write of liberation and utopia.

The discourse of the flesh writers' fiction thereby conforms to what Foucault has termed the "repressive hypothesis" wherein the proclaimed repression, being proclaimed so loudly, leads us to interrogate this need to "repress." There is, as we find here, a repressive organizing power structure that is deployed and ultimately supported by a discourse of protest. The liberation the flesh writers propose looks very similar to the society they decry. Their liberation is gendered, dependent, as it is, on a sexualized woman's body-as-object discovered by a virile man-as-actor. Much of this, I will suggest, was motivated by the writers' own sense of marginalization, and, in particular, their anxiety over emasculation during the crisis of male identity accompanying defeat and occupation. And while these writers do not make such connections explicitly, the next generation of writers would: I am thinking of works such as Kojima Nobuo's "Amerikan sukuuru" ("The American School," 1954), *Hōyō kazuko* (*The Enveloping Family*, 1965), and Nosaka Akiyuki's "American *Hijiki*" (1967) among others.[23]

In the image system of the fiction examined here, a woman's body serves as an object, a means, via sex, for male characters to achieve a variety of goals: utopia of communality, connection with fellow human beings, a guide for the path to another level of existence, or liberation from current oppressions. Tamura's idea of a "liberation from the body by the body," shared to some extent by all the flesh writers I discuss, proves to be a liberation of *male* bodies (rather than all bodies, as they seem to assume) towards, via, or from, a woman's body.[24] As a result, bodies are not re-imagined. Rather, the characterizations focus on interactions between a virile angular man and a soft-edged sexually available woman. Sex marks communion with another and this promises an end to radical loneliness. In this image system, the body is gendered in particular ways that reveal much about the postwar milieu. Likewise, an understanding of an individual self, rooted in that body, is not questioned. The goal of liberation for the body was to be a liberation of selfhood as well. Folded into this is a desire for liberation towards self-determination and liberation from restraint. Liberation from the constrictions of a militarized society is often portrayed, while an insistent strain is desire to be liberated from *any* demands, whether national, domestic, or individual. The Other of a woman's body is not, for example, a domestic woman freeing men from these constraints as well, but sex workers.

Isoda Kōichi contends that the "uniform culture" of militarist Japan constitutes the historical moment when the individual and private became the public, when national and individual bodies are most completely conflated. Here the national body attired itself in military uniforms, just as do the citizens of the realm. The public sphere – the military-controlled social space – as well as what might be called the private sphere, was completely taken over by, co-opted by, the militarist government.[25] He contends that, simultaneously, the taboos surrounding sex were being strengthened; thus in this time when the uniform was intended to suppress and control individual bodies in the interests of the national body, "sex, which corresponds to that most physical [aspect] of the individual body [*nikutai*]" was constricted by the general taboos against the private. The public space extended into the private; even sex was conscripted (a pun that Saegusa Kazuko would appreciate, as we will see in the final chapter). "The military uniform is inseparable from the stoicism of the times because it was used to cover and adorn the *nikutai* for the purpose of the state [*kokka*]."[26] Thus, the postwar change from uniform to individual adornment marked a liberation for that *nikutai*, the physical body. The haunting, damaged portrait of a soldier in uniform that unifies Yoshikuni Igarashi's study of postwar history also brings light to the simultaneous repression and expression of these images in postwar discussions of wartime loss. The emphasis that Tamura, Noma, Ango, and others place on the physical is not unrelated to their experience as soldiers and citizens in an authoritarian regime.

As I have noted, the flesh writers wrote, in the postwar years, against the military and authoritarian state of the war years. In their representation of the individual, they make carnality central and reject the nation, variously conceived as *kokka*, *kokutai*, or *kazoku kokka*, its referential Other.[27] Togaeri Hajime's focus on the body as a means of escape from wartime oppression is similar to his friend Tamura's, although Tamura's focus on the material body takes place in a search for a transcendent value. As Alan Wolfe notes in this connection, the *kokutai*, functioning as an Other, is also a transcendent value. The flesh writers pursued the material body in a search for the transcendent, a way out of the postwar impasse, and this also takes them beyond "decadence." As we have seen, the *nikutai* of this fiction was most often the flesh-and-blood material body, the body of muscle and blood that fights, struggles and bleeds, survives and dies. As depicted in postwar literature, the soldier's body experienced the horrors and deprivations of the battlefield, only to return to the horrors and deprivations of postwar Japan. Rationing and shortages of basic human requirements – food, water, shelter – caused civilians to focus on their bodies and its needs. Much postwar fiction reflects writers' reactions to the manipulation of bodies by the wartime state, and this motivated their postwar call for physical, carnal liberation. Through a celebration of the body they removed themselves from the arena of state control. While the individual and erotic body has long been central to intellectual and literary traditions of Japan, these writers, finding that fresh images and descriptive styles were needed, reworked the tradition. The loss of autonomy and freedom prompted a reaction, which emphasized the body as a way to take back that freedom. Framing that loss of autonomy as Japan's, the flesh writers also spoke to their own loss of masculine identity, in the arena of the national identity.

Reaction to the wartime authoritarian state's manipulation of bodies motivates the postwar call for physical, carnal liberation that I am mapping here. The Japanese writers of the postwar era felt keenly the state systems of control inscribed on the body; even in the immediate postwar years when many controls had been loosened, this celebration of the body in order to protest state control still had resonance. For most of the population after the war, day-to-day survival needs were insistent; furthermore, the disillusion felt by many prompted the violent rejection, by postwar writers, of anything that smacked of the cerebral and the abstract, i.e. the propagandistic discourses that supported the war.

Individual identity within a national body

While much of the postwar discussion of these issues was framed in terms of *kokutai–nikutai* (national body vis-à-vis the physical body), a number of integral issues are subsumed under this linguistic dualism. I will concentrate on the meaning of individual identity and agency in the construction of the national society (as body). A complex interdependence between ethnic, individual, and political identities was so tightly woven with the strands of the nation that even the most iconoclastic of Japanese found themselves tempted by nationalistic/essentialist identities. For many, to criticize the nation/ethnic group "Japan" was to destabilize the powerful marker of individual identity integral in the ability to enunciate "I am Japanese." The knotty interaction between nation and individual plagued postwar writers, complicating the relationship between one's radical individuality and one's inextricable identification with Japanese society. (Such identification is not a priori, although the fiction often treats it as such.) Thus, while the flesh writers focused on individual identity, national identification is fundamental to them as Japanese and constitutes the intellectual topos. The difficulty these writers have in distancing themselves from national identification in order to assert a rebellious individual identity means that the most radical of them can, with little difficulty, be found to be articulating nationalistic understandings, as they are tempted by essentialist configurations. (As noted, we find that the object of protest and that protest collapse into a single entity.)

The flesh writers articulated an image system of the body that reflects their desire for "liberation." For these writers, the liberating body was the sexualized body of a woman: Tamura's women form an ideal community that men emulate; Noma's male characters use sex with women to try to connect with the rest of humanity; Ango's women promise the complete knowledge of enlightenment, but they destroy everyone in the process. Further, I will explore how the anxieties about masculinity after the surrender are articulated in these attempts at fashioning postwar agency via sexuality and exchange with a woman. Following a period when soldierly activity provided the definition for masculine behavior, what does it then mean to be a man in a defeated country, especially under a United States-led Occupation that is actively dismantling "aggressive militaristic" tendencies?[28] The reconfigurations of society that followed upon surrender and occupation redrew gender roles while increasing the pressure on existing stress points. The occupation period introduced concepts of freedom and "democracy," but for many men the loss of sanctioned roles in society threatened their masculinity and therefore their identity. This upheaval fueled much of the flesh writers' fiction, and, I think, much of their obsession with the female body as they were casting about for gender identity, and with it an understanding of the "self" in relation to society and nation. While they conceived of a body opposed to the prevailing structures, their images are firmly entrenched within a masculine and often a patriarchal construct that fails seriously to challenge the structure of society. The freedom they describe, far from freeing the women in their works, rearticulates and reproduces structural hierarchies.

The liberation hoped for in the postwar period was expressed in stories located on the battlefield. Establishing a proper respect for the individual body promised a new start following the conviction that the mistakes of the past war were attributable to the wartime state's undervaluation of the body. The flesh writers suggest that renewed emphasis on the physical could offset that tragically mistaken focus. The result, however, often proved to be a circularity where an ostensibly liberating ideology replaced a constricting one; this circularity – and the inescapability of all ideological constructs – is an insistent undercurrent in this fiction. The energetic responses of readers suggest that these ideas were convincing to many contemporary readers even though the flesh writers offer, in the end, an ideology as constricting as that which they hoped to overthrow.

Isoda Kōichi makes a pertinent observation on this subject of national identification.[29] He suggests that if we talk about the "form" of culture as "style," and then consider clothing (as a mark of civilization) in opposition to "Nature" (the naked and unclothed), then prewar and wartime Japan can easily be discussed as a "uniform culture." This allows a play on words in English not available to Isoda's Japanese, for the "unvarying" meaning of "uniform" is not reflected in the Japanese words; nonetheless, it accords with his intent. What is not visually obvious in English is the "literal" meaning of uniform (by which I mean the Sino-Japanese lexical item – *seifuku* 制服 – when over-read according to the Chinese characters with which it is written) as the "clothing of the establishment," or "organized clothing." Not only was Japanese society being orchestrated to be increasingly unvarying and conformist – uniform – by a militarist government, but the uniform of soldiers and citizens at war was itself emblematic of military culture. In the prewar years the uniform – military especially – was ubiquitous in Japanese popular culture. The military attire gained symbolic referential power in that uniform – unvarying – culture. Further, Isoda continues, this was a time when the personal and private aspects of individuality were transmuted into the social and the societal in ways more intentional than before, and issues of sex, the most private and personal (*shiteki*) realm of the physical (*nikutai*), were treated as a societal taboo. The private was made public, and vice versa. Thus, when individuals covered their bodies (here representing "Nature") in unvarying, uniform clothing styles, the state was able to complete the project of formalizing and standardizing its reach and control. With the reforms of the Occupation, uniform dress was done away with in favor of individual styles (*seifuku* for *shifuku*, 制服 for 私服). That is, to the extent that sexual liberation was a societal phenomenon, it was reflected in this move to cast off the robes of the establishment and don those of the individual. It was a move to make orthodox the right to wear whatever one wished.[30] Liberation was not, however, complete: Occupation censorship allowed for the uncovering of certain body parts and activities, but staunchly prevented it for others.

The editorial board of the journal *Nikutai* (mentioned in the opening sentence of this chapter) made explicit its desire to participate in a move "back" to something more fundamental in Japanese culture, a physicality they felt had been lost to over-spiritualized and insubstantial wartime discourses. Nothing is trustworthy in the current situation, they wrote. The body is the starting point:

> We begin from the body [*nikutai*]; we do not start from ideals nor from matter. In the midst of all that is suspect in the current moment, the only existence that is not suspect is the here-and-now of the *nikutai*. We take this as the starting point for thinking.[31]

While this journal ran for only four issues, it featured the writers and topics discussed here: the first volume carried Sakaguchi Ango's masterpiece "Sakura no mori no mankai no shita" and also Hino Ashihei's "Haikyo," Volume 2 was devoted to the poetry of Rimbaud and the third was a special issue devoted to "literature and the body" (*bungaku to nikutai*) with most articles focusing on D. H. Lawrence. The final volume was devoted largely to articles on Existentialism, an important thematic connection, as I discuss later.

Within this postwar context, portrayals of masculinity were problematic under an occupation that was especially sensitive to expressions of aggression and militarism. Male roles and identity were destabilized following the discrediting of wartime ethics and soldiering. The ideal of an aggressive, in-control male soldier was discarded along with the militarism of the previous decades, fused as they were in the consciousness of many Japanese men. Under Occupation, Japanese men were further emasculated because power was located in foreign men. Thus, while the flesh writers' characterizations of women are often the most striking aspect of their work, imagery relating to their own masculine bodies emerges as a powerful force. Their fiction suggests that gazing at others (women) may have been an attempt to deflect gazing at themselves and their situation. The flesh writers valorize the sexual female body as the Other providing liberation, and the basis for identity and relationships (sex) vis-à-vis women anchors their proposed "new" identity.

Issues of masculinity and identity are firmly rooted in the sensibility of the "postwar." The flesh writers discussed in this study are unified in valorizing carnality to oppose and overcome military–governmental–cultural structures of oppression. The carnal sexual body suggested a place from which to reconstitute and rediscover the individual (and the masculine) destroyed during the war. Thus, Tamura could write, "The physical body that has been buried for ages is finally being unearthed. We must dig and search to the depths to uncover the entire body. This is the age of liberation for the body."[32] While "liberation" is multifaceted and amorphous in their fiction, the flesh writers consistently image and locate it in the (female) body.

In addition to seeing the body as a means of liberation, the flesh writers also highlighted the individual physical body as the complement, and at times the opposite of the national body. As I have already noted, the *nikutai* (肉体, carnal body) contrasts linguistically and graphically with the *kokutai* (国体, national body/polity). Tamura Taijirō, in particular, privileges the *nikutai* to discount the Other, the *kokutai* (nation). In the wartime formulations, the individual body (civilian, soldier) was suppressed and pitted against the cause of the national body; the individual's concerns are subsumed to the demands of the greater, the national body. In the postwar years, and portrayed in Tamura's writings, individuals that had until now been repressed and taken advantage of, suppressed for the ideological needs of an abstract, national, body, reacted by glorifying the physical body. These writers' intentional opposition of individual body

to corporate/national body is of special interest and gives the postwar writing a particular potency. Kamiya Tadataka writes of this emphasis on the physical:

> Concerning literature of the Shōwa [1926–89] age, we can speak of an art-for-art's
> sake [i.e. Shiga *et al.*] aesthetics that pursued as far as it could a spiritualism [*seishin
> shugi*] that sacrificed the body [*nikutai*]. We can alternatively speak of Proletarian
> literature looking for a way out of an idealized "self-consciousness." Both ended at
> a dead end, however. This was the time when the *nikutai* appeared as the extreme
> conceptualization of the spiritual.[33]

That is, one finds that the idealized writing that seemingly banishes the physical in
the end forces the discussion full circle, back to the physical. I find here a return of the
repressed: in highlighting one side of this dialectic, the writers focused attention on its
dialectical Other; writing to oppose one ideology they only establish another.[34]

   In addition, key to the differences within these image systems is the relationship
that war and soldiering establish between individuals and the nation. Identification
with the nation was not only possible, but expected, of men because they represented
the nation and, however forced, supported its goals as soldiers, in many cases even to
death. Attempts to dismantle the militarism and distance themselves from the dominant national culture notwithstanding,[35] the assumption remained that men could
effect change in society. Hence, even after the end of armed conflict, the possibility
of changing postwar society for the better motivates men's writing. Additionally, a
temptation toward essentialist understandings of the state cuts against some of their
more radical pronouncements, perhaps a result of this overly easy identification with
the state. Women, however, are much less likely to exhibit this fundamental assurance
of effectiveness in greater society or the temptation towards essentialism.

   Soldiers returned in defeat from the battlefield, the classic stage for male performance: action, valor, bravery, etc. However, many found just the opposite, for the battlefield also highlights how easily the male body can be violated by bullets, and this
vulnerability of the body constitutes one more way in which the "masculine" military
experience carries overtones of the "feminine." Fear of such violation of the body's
borders is but one of the soldiers' anxieties. After the war and under Occupation these
men were also imagined very differently, as marginalized and powerless, heightening
anxieties concerning masculine identity in postwar sexual economies. Moreover,
Occupation policies actively repressed articulations of "masculinity" with one result
being that men (in an occupation replicating colonial relationships) were encoded
as effeminate by the occupiers. The sense of postwar emasculation was layered atop a
wartime experience that was, for most, as a subordinate soldier whose relationship to
power already suggested similarities to the experience of women. Noma imaged this
most powerfully as the soldier (writer) viscerally opposed to the regimented power
structures of the military, yet denied any and all power of action, protest, or even voice
within that system. Noma's soldiers thus found post-surrender society eerily similar
to the battlefront. Noma's fiction suggests that, in both situations, men feel feminized
in that they have no choice but to follow numbing demands, in a constricting society,
determined by male superiors. The common soldier (along with most of the female

population) was placed in a subordinate and powerless position vis-à-vis superior officers, regarded as objects by commanders. (I do not mean to suggest that these experiences are equivalent, only that parallels would have been especially poignant.) We find, even so, that the male writers tend to (re)construct similar power structures in their fiction, perhaps in a doomed attempt to recreate the older order in which they were afforded autonomy and power, a nostalgia for the valorized male, embedded though he is in the militarist culture they criticize. This suggests important differences of experience: the bodily violence done to women in these systems, focused on sex and genitalia as markers of difference, is qualitatively different: men suffered oppression; they were not raped. Even so, the parallels of experience in relation to power overlap at points often overlooked and fuel the imaginaries of the flesh writers, just as war colors postwar descriptions.[36]

The flesh writers insist so strongly on the body that it takes on not only material, but also transcendent, characteristics. Interest in the physical body is evidenced in Proletarian literature of the prewar years, but, as Kamiya argues, the extreme emphasis on the physical does not come to the fore until after the surrender. In this view the *nikutai* was repressed, but ineffectively, for in the end it was the physical that asserted itself, and this while the state – which constructed an ideology that abstracted the individual body for use in national abstract projects – was complicit with the spiritual-izing tendencies of mainstream literature. Nonetheless, ideology remains: the ideology of the insubstantial is rejected only to be replaced by an ideology of the physical. Each ideology misses what it refuses to accept, but in the end there is no liberation in any ideology that overlooks one half of the individual's constituent parts, whether it is the physical or the spiritual.

The disillusion, despair, and anger at the outcome of a war to which so much had been sacrificed and which proved to have been for naught left many Japanese with a keen sense of angst, anxiety, and the absurd. This spiritual despair was compounded by a day-to-day existence that had likewise been reduced to the basest of basics, the body's materiality in a struggle for survival. The calm at the end of the war quickly became one of physical and emotional desperation for civilians and soldiers alike. It is remem-bered and recorded in ways important in their difference: Noma and Tamura drew on their own war experiences and wrote largely about soldiers and the war; Sakaguchi Ango never served as a soldier, but neither did he leave the very dangerous Tokyo for safer havens in the countryside.[37] Sone comments that one of the aspects that separate Tamura's writing from that of writers such as Oda Sakunosuke (1913–47) and Ango is his experience of the war – "an existence of nothing but sleeping, eating, and fighting" in Tamura's words[38] – an experience that carried over into the postwar period. Tamura returned from the Chinese battlefield in 1946 after nearly seven years at the front. I suspect that the anxiety in his characters reflects his own, where "wartime" concerns continue to impinge on the freedom of the postwar era, especially as the returning soldier discovers a burnt and wasted Tokyo landscape differing little from the scorched battlefields he has just left.

Noma's characters also reflect this confusion, exhibiting the symptoms of post-traumatic stress syndrome[39] as battlefield experiences consistently intrude on their everyday experiences. His fiction is poignant in reflecting no perceptible change in lifestyle from wartime to the immediate postwar period, where the primary concerns of life are still "eating, sleeping, and fighting." Noma conveys this forcefully in works such as "A Red Moon in her Face," in which flashbacks of battlefield experiences and memories continually intrude on the present, making postwar civilian life impossible. In Noma's fiction, the radical loneliness of the battlefield results in an obsessive desire to connect with other individuals, most often via physical union with a woman. This postwar fiction reflects a reaction to the wartime suppression of the body; inexpressible during the war years the reactions flow forth after surrender. And since, in many ways, civilians found the postwar years a time marked by more severe material shortages than the war years, the material needs of the body continue to be central to their existence. Furthermore, previously censored wartime complaints link thematically with postwar privation, and can now be published. In this context, the pairing of "liberation" (*kaihō*) with "the body" (*nikutai*) to form *nikutai kaihō*, takes on special relevance. In Tamura's conceptualization, and reflected in the other flesh writers, we find a physical "bodily" liberation *from* the physical body, but only *through* the body, via carnality. Against this background, the body marked one site for a liberation focused on the individual. As Honda Shūgo was to write:

> The ultimate goal of the search by the Postwar writers, if we are to give it a name, was human freedom. "The realization of the self," or "the realization of individualism," has a similar meaning, but most Postwar writers did not think of human freedom within the framework of individualism. Freedom itself was the ultimate goal.[40]

Freedom and liberation persist as unformed ideals, and Honda is right to stress that individualism is not the goal. We will find, however, that creating a place for the individual to act is a project subsumed in the writings of men and women. Out of the depths of postwar difficulties surfaced "liberation" (*kaihō*), a word invoked repeatedly in these writings. Liberation from the restraints of the body proves to be one of the most representative of postwar phrases. As a result, we find that the limitations of the body, of which the war and postwar period made so many aware, can be overcome only by being transgressed.

There is more to all this, as Kimura Yoshinaga describes: in the years following the war, physical limitations were all too obvious:

> During the war years, "to live" simply meant finding enough food to get by. If one did not find sufficient food, it meant death. Now when peace finally returned it was no longer sufficient to simply get by. One was constantly drawn to find the meaning of existence, to find why one was living.[41]

When survival was uncertain, metaphysical questions seemed, somehow, especially compelling. The imagery reflects the satiation of bodily desires while the discourse invokes transcendent ideals in the search for identity. And so one ideology is invoked to displace another; the transcendent is desired but is wed to the physical. The flesh writers located those transcendent ideals in a woman's body.

Intimations of the body before the war

Given the bleak realities and eventual hopelessness of wartime and postwar Japan, a postwar backlash is hardly a surprise. The disillusionment and cynicism following the defeat – in many ways an even more desperate time than the war itself, for most Japanese – prompted many to reject the nation's calls for selfless sacrifice and conversely to revel in individual goals and desires. The emphasis on the physical body in the years following the war represents, in large part I think, a frustration with the wartime sacrifices demanded by the government. I find important links between these postwar and prewar concerns in Proletarian writing. For Japanese writers and thinkers, the body as disposable object was intimated in the prewar years, in the grand treason trial of 1910, in the death by torture of the Proletarian writer Kobayashi Takiji in 1933, in the mass arrests and imprisonments of leftists (many of whom were Proletarians) and freethinkers throughout the 1930s. Kobayashi Takiji's death at the hands of police interrogators could be seen from the postwar vantage point as "the action of one who sacrifices the body [*nikutai*] to preserve the spirit [*seishin*]."[42] Kobayashi's death contributed to the angst (*fuan*) and general malaise felt by intellectuals as the physical body was continually assailed by the state. His death was metonymical. The state expressed its cavalier attitude towards bodies during the war years by sending them off as cannon fodder. This attitude is mirrored in the almost universal portrayal in tales of the Pacific War of an "enemy" that is not the Chinese or US troops, but the ranking officers in Japan's own military who imposed harsh physical demands to be borne by the bodies of the soldiers, now writers, who recount these tales (such as Noma Hiroshi and Hino Ashihei (1907–60)).

The postwar writers' condemnation of the abstractions in much prewar fiction continues Proletarian literature's emphasis on the body. Nakamoto Takako, whose work I touch on in the final chapter, is but one whose Proletarian concern for the individual body in prewar works carries through to postwar writing. The postwar flesh writers are vehement in their criticisms of the "confessional novelists" such as Shiga Naoya for over-valorizing the *seishin*. Proletarian literature is itself, in many ways, a reaction to the "spiritual" aura of the *watakushi shōsetsu* (confessional fiction), which is also a fictional form ostensibly anchored to a self. These early twentieth-century writings take for granted a discreet individual with full agency, a philosophical assumption shared by the male writers under discussion here. The individual self of the *watakushi shōsetsu* is the body in its immediate surroundings of bar, geisha, and domestic squalor (the works of Iwano Hōmei, Shiga Naoya, and Kasai Zenzō come to mind).[43] In this fictional practice, the self in flight from external pressures – society, bills, employment – retreats into the internal; structurally, this flight resembles the flight of a male from the public sphere to the private and domestic, inhabited (and usually signified) by the woman and her sanctioned space.

The abstractions and self-referentiality of Shiga and others in the *watakushi shōsetsu* tradition seem even further removed from the concerns of the living in the wake of Kobayashi's death. Confessional writing was castigated, eventually, not only for being ineffectual in the face of state oppression, but for tacitly supporting that structure with its interiority. This retreat from the public to the personal prompted the distrust of the abstract notion of "self" and a concern for the concrete and tangible "material" body. In Horii Ken'ichi's discussion of this aspect of Proletarian literature, he stresses the interest in the body that is integral to this writing and identifies in it a mind–body dualism (*seishin* contrasting to the *shintai*, *nikutai*) that is conveyed in the emphasis on physical labor and the worker's body. Horii continues:

> On this point of there being no way to be free in relation to the State [*kokka*], the soldier's body [*shintai*] was more like that of a slave than a commodified body [*shōhin toshite no shintai*]. It seemed the whole purpose for this body was to be harmed.[44]

Proletarian literature highlighted the radical separation of body from spirit, and this sense of separation became accentuated in wartime as the state used bodies for their fighting value, seemingly only to bring them harm. The body was then little more than an expendable and replaceable resource. Thus, when Proletarian writers began to write fiction set in the war years – the stories of Kuroshima Denji (1898–1943) and Hayama Yoshiki (1894–1945) set in China, for example – one finds soldiers, like laborers and comfort women, who are merely commodities, bodies only of value for labor and not freed even in death.

Commodified, objectified, valued only in exchange: these descriptions of soldiers on the battlefield apply equally to sex workers. Noma Hiroshi is most articulate on this point, although such connections were not his goal: soldiers share many of the everyday, material realities that define a woman's marginalized place in society. Nakamura Miharu also notes this overlap:

> In the most noted cases of the Proletarian arts, bodies took the brunt of [both] the nation's authority and monopoly capitalism, and were placed in a situation where the individual [*kojin*] was established between the repressed body [*shintai*] and the oppressive system.[45]

Thus, the body so central to Proletarian literature was intentionally opposed to that expressed in the *watakushi shōsetsu* tradition. While the Proletarian writers were concerned with the "mass" as the working class, Proletarian realism nevertheless attempted to describe the mass in order to describe the many individuals who comprise it.[46] The body was also of central concern to the state in that it was a crucial commodity in whatever endeavor it undertook, especially for wartime Japan, a nation in great need of bodies to send to the front.

Wartime ideologies of national identity (stressing ethnic and racial purity) demanded that individual Japanese concentrate their energies on state projects while decrying individual desires (*messhi-hōkō* in the contemporary phrase). The momentum established by these pervasive militarist admonitions of the war still resonated through the immediate postwar years. Individual desires inexpressible during the war years tumbled forth in a deluge in the years following. Wartime militarism reinforced a compelling national ideology fostered during the Meiji era that endures even today, given the foundational relation this conception of the Japanese nation brings to bear on individual identity. The legacy of samurai values cannot be dismissed here, enveloped as it is in a militarist imagery of the soldier/male who embodies valor, loyalty, and prowess.

To continue this historical placement, a different sort of physicality also gained credence in the late nineteenth century, that of the Naturalists. Isoda Kōichi, for example, identifies the scientific gaze in their project and their treatment of the individual and the body:

> Thus, it seems that the Naturalists, when they looked at their characters as "animals who crawl upon the earth," had in mind the desire to posit a Nature that was in opposition to that represented by a traditional ethical order.[47]

I take this to reflect a motive similar to Tamura's: that in the old order and understanding of mankind (i.e. the established order) is an abstracting and idealistic desire, one that overlooks the physical. In reaction, both the Naturalists and the postwar writers, albeit at different times, wished to posit a vision more attuned to individual physicality. Tamura was very critical of the results of the Naturalists' vision, however, for he finds that the scientific gaze only estranges them from physicality. As Tamura sees it, the Naturalists' scientific approach and emphasis on a physical description ultimately led to an empty cerebral understanding. Reading this back through the frightful descriptions of men/beasts crawling over the nightmarish earth that begin Noma's *Kurai e* gives an added poignancy to this "scientific" gaze.[48] Isoda goes on to quote Hanada Kiyoteru (writing about Mishima Yukio) on this point:

> Despising the fetters of the spirit one finds in opposition the body, the fetters of which are loved. Within that desire is another spirit. At the end of a line that begins with Tayama Katai is Tamura Taijirō. In the space between Ōgai and Dazai is a clear break.[49]

That is, there is an important lineage in the understanding of carnality in Japan that begins with Tayama's *Futon* and stretches to Tamura's "Nikutai no mon"; more precisely, as Isoda words it, a lineage of literary representations of the carnal is contained here, leading him to write that "we should properly call Tayama Katai the forerunner of *nikutai bungaku*."[50]

The Sartrean body

This current of interest in the body in postwar Japan was joined and enriched by a stream coming from another place far away: the fiction of Jean-Paul Sartre flowing in from France. Sakaguchi Ango, when he praised Sartre's short story "Intimité" (translated as "Mizuirazu" in the October 1946 issue of *Sekai bungaku*) for the manner in which it was "thinking through the physical,"[51] marked the point at which the two streams convergence. Ango's comments established a tie between Sartre's work and the carnality of postwar Japan. When Togaeri Hajime, writing early in the 1950s, discusses the *nikutai* in postwar Japan, he references Sartre's recently available fiction to explain how it came to hold a new meaning in the postwar years. *Nikutai* (by which Togaeri means "body" in the broadest sense) was a topic of concern to critics and thinkers before the war. Nonetheless, the manner in which it was discussed and the degree of interest varies greatly in the prewar and postwar periods. As Togaeri argues, a "literature of the body" (*nikutai bungaku*) before the war corresponded to the sensuous carnality he finds in Tanizaki Jun'ichirō's fiction, "but this *nikutai* is constructed only from a carnality and does not treat the issue as one of *nikutai* versus *seishin*," as did postwar writing. Moreover, the postwar instance of *nikutai* is a discourse of physicality in broad relation to, as well as in conflict with, the spiritual and psychological, a distinctly different conceptualization.[52] That is, this postwar *nikutai bungaku* differed qualitatively from prewar eroticism by its explicit political edge and the concern for the essential (registered by its opposition to the *seishin*).

In Ango's important short essay entitled "Nikutai ga shikō suru," he praises Sartre's "Intimité" for its focus on the carnal body and for doing away with the cerebral. The thrust of his argument is succinctly reproduced in his title: "The Body Thinks." Ango wrote of Sartre's short story as though it were *nikutai bungaku*, cut from the same cloth as the fiction of Tamura (and his own). His characterization of Sartre as a writer of the body was to set the tone for subsequent readings, by others, of Sartre's fiction in Japan. This reading established Sartre as a writer of carnal erotic fiction. Ango suggested that Sartre's characters think only through their bodies, that they are only *nikutai*, displaying no abstract spirit at all, and he praises "Intimité" for accomplishing what other postwar writers had unsuccessfully attempted. With Ango's compelling essay, writers in Japan felt they had found in Sartre a comrade engaged in a common project. Ango – although, or because, he professes no philosophic interest in nor even understanding of Sartre's philosophy – read Sartre's "Intimité" very much as erotic fiction, as a "literature of the body":

> ["Intimité"] does not preach one moral word. It is, simply, the *nikutai* that thinks, the *nikutai* that tells the story. Lulu's body, strangely enough, loves the body of an impotent man. Through the words of her body the story is told.
>
> In ethics we have come to think of the spirit thinking through the body, but people have forgotten that the *nikutai* itself thinks and speaks. People don't know this. They've never thought about it.
>
> Sartre attempts, in "Intimité," to narrate thoroughly and completely through the thoughts of the *nikutai* itself. At first glance this is nonsensical, but in fact it is a wisdom beyond sense, and this is its revolutionary meaning.[53]

This praises "Intimité" as the accomplishment of what Ango and other postwar Japanese writers, particularly the flesh writers under consideration here, had been attempting: to write the postwar body. Sartre's fiction was extremely important to postwar Japanese fiction because it was read as displaying this concern for the body and its carnality, and for its impatience with abstractions. Writers would read Sartre with an eye to the erotic for some time to come. That is, Sartre seemed less European philosopher and more a writer solving a common fictional project, a correlation reflected in Sekine Hiroshi's earliest readings of Sartre:

> The first thing I read of Sartre's was the translation of "Intimité" that appeared the year after the war. Sakaguchi Ango had [also] published his fevered response to it. It appeared that Sartre was the new master [*kamisama*] of erotic literature.[54]

This Existentialist fiction expressed a humanity based on the carnal and reflected a sensibility and feeling pervasive in the postwar years, a decidedly physical response to the war experiences.

The body took on this representational energy at precisely the moment that Sartre's fiction became available in Japan, reinforced by Ango's associations: indeed, without the correlation that Ango drew, a very different history of reception may have resulted.[55] Sartre's philosophical writing would have great impact on Japanese intellectuals, but never proved as dramatic or explosive as the fiction. The Sartre first encountered in Japan, therefore, was a writer of fiction, and within that rubric, a writer of the body. Many of the themes associated with Existentialism – loneliness, *angst*, purposelessness, waiting, and enduring – also described the postwar for many. To the writers at this time and to many who write of those years, a strong link exists between war, postwar experiences, and Existentialism. More to the point, postwar writers took Sartre's (prewar) writings as a way to express in fiction the (postwar) issues they were facing. Thus much of the literature of the postwar years, while often referencing Sartre and Existentialism, was not "philosophical" at all, but only tangentially related to Sartre's writings and thought.[56] While postwar writers often invoked Sartre, the immediate referent was not his philosophical treatises but his short fiction, and because it suggested solutions to the novelistic and technical issues faced in a time of difficult intellectual and physical choices. Issues of physicality, individual freedom, and responsibility became prominent, as Ishizaki Hitoshi notes when outlining this history of postwar Japanese writers, and "translations of Sartre, along with the fiction of such writers as Noma Hiroshi and Shiina Rinzō, then hold a place in postwar literature as being contemporaries."[57]

Postwar intellectual issues in Japan overlapped at many points with the issues raised by Sartrean Existentialism. Shirai Kōji, Sartre's first translator, wrote that the basic query of the Japanese after the war was "What does it mean to be human?"[58] The pertinent questions that derived from this included: "What does it mean to exist?" "What does it mean to act?" "How does one undertake responsible action?" Existentialism highlighted the impotence of existing categories to decipher these issues. Kikuchi Shōichi had noted already in 1947 that "It is a fact that an interest in *existenz* [*jitsuzon*], or phrased differently, an interest in understanding the phenomenon of humanity by an Existentialist means, continually grows."[59] Existentialism garnered great interest, although Kikuchi doubted that the attraction lay in anything that could properly be called "Existentialism." He was not himself sure what "Existentialism" meant, and Occupation censorship – which prevented access to Western language materials – made it no easier. It seems likely that much of the attraction was precisely because its definitions were not solidified and this existed as an undefined category, to be made of as one would wish. Iwakami Jun'ichi echoed these concerns writing, in 1948, that concepts associated with Existentialism such as unease and hopelessness (*fuan* and *zetsubō*) were more than themes in fiction; rather, they were guiding principles, a framework, for postwar writing. Senuma Shigeki noted in 1949 that Sartre's writing was of a piece with that of Ango, Shiina Rinzō,[60] and Noma Hiroshi in the sense that they all showed the bankruptcy of previous conceptualizations in the face of contemporary issues.

Sartre's introduction in Japan was essentially after the Pacific War, and in a curious turn of events his fiction was translated and introduced in Japan before his philosophical work – i.e. according to a different chronology than in France and not contemporaneous with the appearance of his fiction in France, largely due to the vagaries of wartime censorship and restrictions on "enemy" languages. This translated fiction was understood to represent "Existentialism." Further, given the themes of Sartre's early fiction and the interest in the erotic in Japan, this "Existentialism" was read as a literature of the body. Sartre's fiction appeared to be similar to that of Tamura and the other postwar flesh writers.[61] Japanese readers of the late 1940s were especially struck with Sartre's marked concern for the material body and, particularly after Ango's response to the story "Intimité," found Sartre's fiction to be *nikutai bungaku*. This reaction to Sartre's work is quite different from that in any other country. Sartre's paradigm was paralleled in much Japanese fiction, meaning that many postwar writings often appear "Sartrean." Postwar Japanese fiction even seems to anticipate Sartre's imagery, suggesting similar historical developments, perhaps even spawning two similar movements in countries separated by space and time.[62]

The "decadent" writer Oda Sakunosuke, closely associated with Sakaguchi Ango, commented on these connections, but with less enthusiasm. According to him, the intellectual ground was less well prepared in Japan than in France, where Existentialism was all the rage and one could even hear it discussed in the subways – in short, it had penetrated to all levels of French society. In Japan, the only thing that moved people to line up outside bookstores was the promise of something in one of the *bundan* (academy) publications. The counterestablishment tendencies in France were not in evidence in Japan: "Both Japan and France are physically sick, buffeted by waves of despair and confusion. The young generation especially has embraced doubts concerning traditional ideals wrapped in a veil of establishment thinking, and are overcome with *angst*."[63] Existentialism was born, Oda claimed, as a system of thought in this situation, with a goal of tearing apart the veil of tradition. Its proponents confronted the negativity of existence, finding in it the only means for an ultimate freedom for humankind.

Oda claimed that "Intimité" was not all that interesting to him, certainly not enough to prompt him to write about it, but when the label of "Existentialist" was applied to a handful of Japanese writers, himself included, he could not decide whether to react with thoroughgoing anger or simply regard it all as a joke, as journalistic overstatement. For example, he claimed, Japanese writing lacked the structure to support a true Existentialism. Even when writers attempted a pessimistic description it was through the Japanese tradition of lyricism. Oda suggests that, although Heidegger and Kierkegaard, say, did appear in Japan, there is no foundation to support the literary movement of Existentialism because Japanese writers have always stuck to confessional fiction. Thus,

> For example, even while trying to portray the carnal body [*nikutai*], the only body that comes to [*Japanese writers*] is an ideal physical body. Fiction that describes this

carnal body is not, thereby, carnal. The grip of the [lyrical, confessional] tradition in Japanese fiction is so extensive that a new form cannot be initiated.[64]

He claims that Sartre is not really writing the "physical," at least not in the sense of Japanese *nikutai bungaku*. Oda writes that Japanese writers influenced by Sartre describe the possibility of humanity by pushing to a moment when the ideals of spirituality (*seishin*, the non-physical) are abandoned in order to pursue the elemental aspects of human experience. Sartre may provide a model to young Japanese writers in that he does not begin where his French predecessors – Stendhal, Gide – left off, but rather at a place they could not even imagine. In this sense, the *nikutai* found in Sartre's "Intimité" may serve as an apt model to young writers:

> When calling for a new literature there must first be a strategy to attack the established ideal of the "human." The armor that envelops the stubborn medieval ideals must be rent apart. It is with the description of that body, newly rendered nude, that the structure of the *nikutai* can be portrayed.[65]

He thereby finds, in imagery that echoes Isoda Koichi's description of "uniform culture," that this "new" writing harkens back to Ihara Saikaku's (1642–93) carnality hundreds of years earlier: its intended audience are the townspeople – lowbrow – and firmly within the limits of accepted morality and ideals. (Aono Suekichi had made a similar comparison in 1949. Aono, a premier Marxist theorist, was most concerned with the class issues invoked in the postwar works and in Saikaku, as well as the readers of those works.[66]) Oda charges that the descriptions in Saikaku's fiction fall entirely within the parameters of what is acceptable to society; if it is revolutionary, it is only slightly so. That is, for all its revolutionary rhetoric, this "literature of the body" offered little that was new. The various eroticisms of his fellow writers contain a search for a salvation, and this is its problem, he continues: "Sartre liberates, but does not search for salvation."[67]

This is a creative reading, as creative as Ango's, but ultimately no more helpful in getting at the heart of Sartre's thought or even Existentialism in Japan. It does register, as does Ango, the degree of interest – here by an impassioned disavowal – in Existentialism in the postwar years. I suspect as well some internecine bickering, given the closeness of Oda, Ango, Tamura, and others being discussed here. But even for Oda, the fundamental issue of concern is the *nikutai*, i.e. the body and the individual in postwar society.

Sekine Hiroshi, writing in 1966, quotes from Ibuki's afterword to the Japanese translation of Sartre's *Complete Works* to note how Existentialism was taken to be eroticism after the war: "Reflecting on that now it is complete nonsense, but it was the fact in the postwar years [that Existentialism was taken to be an eroticism]. In the midst of the suppression of 'carnal literature' [*nikutai bungaku*] the oddest pairings were possible." For, at the same time, he goes on,

> Taking Sartre's "Intimité" as *nikutai bungaku* is not that unreasonable either. It was a time when mere mention of a word like "naked body" caused a sensation.

For those unaware of the regulations on speech before this time, they cannot imagine how this could be . . . In that environment then, a work like "Intimité" that opens with a description of nudity caused no little explosion. It was quickly taken up as an erotic novel. I was one of those who took it as such . . . I thought to myself that this thing called Existentialism was a great thing, even though I understood it to be nothing more than [the product of] another of the carnal writers [*nikutai-ha*].[68]

The erotic physicality found in Sartre's work attracted many. Noma Hiroshi's work, particularly his theorizing of the "total novel" (*zentai shōsetsu*), reflects this attraction via a literary dialogue with Sartre. Noma is quite pointed in an essay that accompanies volume 5 of the Japanese-language edition of Sartre's *Complete Works*. He wrote that only Sartre was able to adequately grasp the *nikutai*:

For example, Gide, in order to extricate himself from the introverted universe of the Symbolist's pursuit of consciousness, searched for a restitution of the physical [*nikutai*] as liberation from desires. While Gide did in fact realize [this] he had no grasp of method or language for handling the *nikutai* . . . Now Sartre, on account of his bringing about the birth of a language by which to grasp the *nikutai*, could clarify the internal description of an individual where the consciousness and the physical [*nikutai*] are unified. Sartre could accomplish this because he turned inside out the language of the Symbolists and their hold on the internalized consciousness and pushed on to a place where he could grasp the *nikutai* internally.[69]

The intersection and chronology in Noma's understanding of Sartre's movement from Symbolism to Marxism offers parallels to Noma's own development as a writer. Noma praised Sartre for overcoming the possibilities and traps of Symbolist language (traps which Noma struggled with), and for uniting the internal with the external. Symbolism and the physicality of the *nikutai* were concerns that remained with him throughout his life. Noma's "total novel" (*zentai shōsetsu*) attempted to unify the spiritual and the physical, whereas in his earliest stories the intent, like Tamura Taijirō's, was to posit that physical as an antidote to the overly spiritualized atmosphere of the war years. Noma finds that Sartre starts from the body:

This is how Sartre is able to give form and shape to gratuitous acts originating within an individual and then makes clear the connection between that person and the action. Sartre could place the gratuitous act in the midst of everyday activity, situate it and give it substance, that is, give it flesh [*nikutaika suru*] . . . Sartre's new method comes in his pursuit and grasp of freedom without excluding the physical [*ningen no nikutai*].[70]

We find in all this that the Japanese reading of bodiliness in Sartre is entirely appropriate, although unorthodox, in the Western tradition.[71] In particular, as a result of the fact that the initial Japanese introduction to Sartre was via the fiction, contemporary writers understood Sartre to be participating in the same nexus of issues that they were. Their reading of the body corresponds to Sartre's in which, stated rudely and summarily, consciousness proceeds from an awareness of the body as thing, as physical object. The *nikutai bungaku* of the 1940s, which included Sartre's fiction, quickly developed in the 1950s, and deepened in the 1960s, into a more sophisticated philosophical conceptualization. (This development is perhaps most evident in the writings of Ōe Kenzaburō (1935–), Kurahashi Yumiko (1935–), and Abe Kōbō (1924–93).) These writings all built on the understanding of the body that was read out of Sartre,[72] especially as writers tried to delineate the two Japanese words that are used, as we have seen, to signify "body," *shintai* and *nikutai*. Hazel Barnes suggests that the bodiliness of Sartre may in fact have been downplayed in Western discussions, and she notes how basic the body is to Sartre's philosophy:

> Two other psychological positions, original, I believe, with Sartre, are of particular importance in connection with his views on the For-itself's relation with other people – the For-Others. These are his ideas about the nature of the body and sexuality. In one sense, of course, the body represents man's facticity, his Being-there in the world. It determines certain physical limits to what the For-itself can do within or to the world . . . Without a body the For-itself could have no relation whatsoever with what we call the world . . . The For-itself does not *have* senses. It is present to the world *through* the senses, and the world spatially has meaning only with the body as center of reference.[73]

She calls attention to the central position that the body holds in Sartre's thought; it would seem that the Japanese (male) readers understood this at the start, where the body is a limit and also the location for action. Barnes continues, "While the body is that through which the Look is experienced, it is sexuality which just as much as in Freudian psychology – though in a far different way – lies at the origin of all human relations."[74] This philosophical conception is described in fiction such as "Intimité" to fictionalize a body that "lies at the origin of all human relations" precisely as read by these Japanese writers.

The male flesh writers reacted to the ideology of militaristic and fascist totalitarianism, a system that actively managed culture to support the war. For Maruyama Masao the contradictions are economic and structural: "The stress on 'idealism' and 'spirituality' as against materialism in the fascist ideology [of Japan's wartime government] signifies in reality an attempt to divert the eyes of the people from the fundamental contradictions of the social structure."[75] The flesh writers I discuss, and others as well, were responding to the same attempt by the state to divert attention from the material, physical body through forced compliance to an ideological system that they found insubstantial, bodiless, and lacking an essential core. (As I will explore, they do not challenge the assumption that some essential core exists.) Against this background of militarism and of devaluation of the individual and the physical in the writings I examine in the following chapters, the body will be given precedence.

2 The (gendered) discourse and a (woman's) body

The woman's body of this literature

A vision that places so much weight on the saving power of a woman's body renders her an objectified commodity in a sexual economy, and most of the women in these writings are sex workers and temporary lovers. This erotic construction of the body inevitably intersected with the political since the erotic body both animates and disrupts the social order, particularly in a time when the state is actively manipulating the individual. Carnality was offered as both critique of and antidote to the ideological system set in place during wartime, even though the system was ostensibly dismantled with Occupation. Such reactions to state projects had been previously repressed, but now, being permitted, pour forth, meaning that many wartime reactions are expressed in a wartime imagery.

The flesh writers equated liberation and masculine identity with heterosexual union and the ability to "perform" in a variety of roles and registered much anxiety about the performative nature of identity. As Peter Brooks writes:

> In modern narrative literature, a protagonist often desires a body . . . And that body comes to represent for the protagonist an apparent ultimate good, since it appears to hold within itself – as itself – the key to satisfaction, power, and meaning . . . Desire for the body may appear to promise access to the very *raison d'être* of the symbolic order. Thus narrative desire, as the subtending dynamic of stories and their telling, becomes oriented towards knowledge and possession of the body. Narrative seeks to make such a body semiotic, to mark or imprint it as a linguistic and narrative sign. If the plot of the novel is very often the story of success or failure in gaining access to the body – and the story of the fulfillment or disillusionment that this brings – the larger story may concern the desire to pierce the mysteries of life that are so often subsumed for us in the otherness of other people.[1]

Brooks' description of narrative maps exactly to what is found in postwar writings. The men write of women who structure the universe and who hold the key – indeed, *are* the key – to the symbolic order Brooks here identifies; they are the guide and the location for unraveling the mysteries of life, they are then transcendent, and a relationship with the woman yields access to that universe. The woman's almost mystical body takes one to the source of universal power and knowledge; to master and possess the woman's body would then provide the key to the universe and to oneself. Since the quest is for a transcendent value, we find here an attempt to make the body transcendent as well, to establish its place beyond conventional semiotic markers. The grail that motivates this search is self-knowledge and understanding of one's place in the symbolic order coded as liberation.

The masculinist constructions of the flesh writers are thrown into relief by women writers who clarify the plastic, constructed nature of their "liberation" and ridicule it in their fiction. Such "liberation" is not coveted by the women writers. When women write of sexuality during the "liberation" of postwar society, one encounters an entirely different range of concerns. Women's fiction focuses on individual women and their environment without attempting to construct an ideal environment. Few characters display much hope of escaping, being liberated, or changing their surroundings; most struggle alone to keep their heads above water. Women writers who have made careers writing about issues of the body and sexuality – Hirabayashi Taiko, Hayashi Fumiko, Uno Chiyo, and Miyamoto Yuriko, for example – do so in a different sphere from the male writers. Hirabayashi Taiko, in but one example, consistently uses *nikutai* in her fiction of the 1930s when discussing the (female) body. While she refers to the *nikutai* as physical female body, it is not the sensual carnal body found in the flesh writers. The mother (womb) often marks domestic home and family for men,[2] perhaps, but in Hirabayashi's case, it also marks the point from which to explore flight away from that same system. Novelist Kuroshima Denji (1898–1943) wrote, in 1928, that Hirabayashi Taiko wrote "the body" (*shintai de kaiteiru*) in her fiction,[3] in what may be an early example of *écriture féminine* in Japan; nonetheless, her writing of the body is not motivated by the concerns of the flesh writers. Hirabayashi writes of a bleak physical reality integral to a woman's experience – in this instance, childbirth – compounded by experiences often recounted by women writers – abandonment, alienation, and poverty. She emphasizes the female body, drawing on her experiences in prison and of childbirth in the politicized environment of colonized Manchuria, alone while her partner – rarely mentioned – is himself in prison.

The shock of much women's writing, like Hirabayashi's, at least in its contemporary reception, was perhaps precisely a result of their focus on the sexuality of the everyday rather than the bracketed areas of prostitutes and waitresses – the focus of men. Women tended to write from the realm of personal experience and place a female protagonist within intimate relationships. We find that the choices available to these protagonists are limited (rather than expanded) by physicality. Women writers seem to construct, or reflect, women's situation(s), rather than to construct an ideal, utopian situation. They portrayed individual experiences of women, describing them in the midst of work and the struggle for survival. The portrayals are more tightly focused as we are introduced to their workplaces and the power struggles therein, where they are caught in both lateral and vertical relationships reflecting hierarchies among themselves, all governed by societal structures. The most critical representations implicate Japanese men who do not stand allied with Japanese women in the face of Occupation authority, but who prove to be more authoritarian, demeaning, and hierarchical than the Americans. The "enemy," for all his condescension and sexual threat, in the fictional imagery often displays more respect to the female characters than do their countrymen. Thus, while both the male and female writers I discuss here wrote of women and sexuality, they wrote of entirely different realms, marked by different borders.

Powerlessness in post-surrender, Occupation society is a central theme in much writing by both men and women, yet while disenfranchisement and desperation are real in the womens fiction, they are rarely expressed in the imagery of impotence or conquest. For the women writers I examine, sexuality does not constitute individual identity, even in situations where the possibilities associated with sexual/gender identities are expanded. Men seem to fear the loss of their sexuality and with it their identity as men; the women's fiction does not establish so close an identity between women and their sexual identities. Nonetheless, sexual exchanges between men and women were accentuated because, in Occupation society, sexual roles gained primacy and had political ramifications.

Further, the imagery of individual freedom in the flesh writers was sexualized, portrayed in terms of relations of men with women.[4] A wartime legacy of hyper-masculinity – the male as soldier – continued in the postwar years, even during an occupation intent on squelching aggressive ("belligerent" in the terminology of occu-pation censorship) tendencies. Most consistent is the anxiety expressed by men as their roles as soldier and provider were altered radically under this occupation. Occupation policies severely constricted expressions of masculinity (i.e. of the warrior/soldier ideals or experience), a practical result being that reactions and articulations of their soldier experience needed to be repressed. Possibilities to explore publicly the meanings of masculinity in this society were thereby foreclosed. Furthermore, over-sexed US GIs, objects of fear and awe, haunt the Japanese men in postwar fiction. Expressions of their anxieties and doubts vis-à-vis these newly arriving soldiers, particularly any reference to the recent military experience of Japanese men, were largely forbidden by Occupation authorities who were obsessed with suppressing expressions of a "Japanese militarist spirit."[5] It seems that in response the Japanese men then turned their gaze towards their countrywomen. As Michael Molasky observes, the very meaning of being male was threatened:

> In men's writing of the occupation of Japan and Okinawa, it is not only women who are rendered defenseless before the foreign troops. Male characters are also depicted as powerless, especially when they prove incapable of protecting the women around them from unruly occupation soldiers. These literary depictions of powerless men commonly rely on sexual metaphors of castration and impo-tence, metaphors that represent the men as "feminized" and thereby equate men's social powerlessness under foreign occupation with that of women under suppos-edly normal social conditions.[6]

I am arguing that the flesh writers manage to establish an ideology even as they wish to do away with all ideology. In their imagination of liberation, while attempting to articulate a new place in postwar society, we find the reassertion of male dominance over female bodies. In the face of this sense of male powerlessness – "male authors

[who] so often appropriate the female body to establish male victimhood"[7] – the flesh writers imagine a subjugated woman as the key to liberation.

The war brought changes for women as well, as they moved out of their homes and into the various occupations during the war as never before,[8] yet the fiction of the women noted above shows no hopes for long-term change and restructuring of society following their changed roles within it. The body that the flesh writers describe does not prove liberating for women, however, because it reinscribes older structures of oppression; the women's fiction will highlight what has not changed.

The characterizations of individual identity are quite different as well. These women writers do not equate individual identity with social roles formed by work, nor do they go on to attempt to restructure postwar power relationships. The flesh writers, as I have argued, equated liberation and masculine identity with heterosexual union and the ability to "perform" in a variety of roles and registered much anxiety about the performative nature of identity. The changed relationships between men and women are reflected in the women's writing, but sexuality does not appear as a key to freedom. Judged from their fiction, the war and postwar milieu register only externally as changes in the nationality and uniform of the male oppressor, for the system of male dominance and oppression does not change. Their fiction does, however, reflect specificities of post-Surrender society: the women work as maids and *pan-pan*, American GIs are ever-present, and shortages and disruptions are commonplace. Domestic employment in foreign households may have changed, and the *pan-pan* may be strictly a postwar phenomenon, but the expectations regarding domestic labor and sexual availability have not. Women still survive in different and subordinate economies based on a commodified sexuality.[9]

Another striking difference in women's fiction of this time is the lack of images of sexual impotence. Emasculation is a key theme in the writings by men, and while disenfranchisement, role-anxiety, and desperation are central themes in the women's fiction as well, the imagery is not sexual. Loss of power represents a newly articulated problem for men, and many find compensation in a woman's body. For women, the experience of powerlessness has hardly changed; only the external situations and boundaries are configured differently. That is, the women articulate no expectation that liberation from postwar oppressions will be achieved through carnality. The body serves in an entirely different mode. "Living by their bodies" (i.e. sex work) is usually the only choice available – a forced choice, the one they must make the best of.[10]

I have noted how the postwar experience brought clarity of purpose to many. Not all, of course, found renewed possibilities; postwar fiction often focuses the writers' own disenfranchisement from society. As Nishikawa Nagao suggests,[11] the contemporary interest in Tamura's "Nikutai no mon" and its prostitutes is also related to postwar writers' feeling that they, like the sex workers, were not fully accepted in society's power structures. The sex workers and slaves victimized by the war embody the sexualized humiliation of an emasculated Japan, while also displaying a sexualized freedom. That is, they double in the imagery of writers – *male* writers, that is – who fear being marginalized, stripped of power and authority, and their fear becomes gendered in these anxieties about emasculation. The wartime sex workers (*pan-pan)* come to embody the humiliation of postwar Japan, even while embodying the freedom of that time, particularly in the fiction by men. The *pan-pan* was a paradoxical figure symbolizing both a desperate marginalized existence and unrestrained liberation at those peripheries.[12] Both images energize postwar fiction.

While women were afforded greater mobility and access to Occupation power structures, that access often proceeded from the sexualization of their bodies. Male writers described an Occupation society wherein they were feminized – i.e. powerless and subordinate, unable to care for and provide for their women and families. Furthermore, the role of protector and provider had been usurped by women able to negotiate this new societal order. Men were marginalized while women had direct access to the American GIs, and thereby to the source of wealth and supplies. That access was suspect and produced great anxiety in the men, as it undermined the arena in which they could act.

The antidote offered by the flesh writers was to live by the body, according to a logic that is not cerebral. This assumption conforms to a long history wherein the body is understood as the term opposite to the mind, representing the base and the emotional, the non-rational and non-thinking. Such characteristics overlap with those often associated with women, continuing a traditional tendency to associate the body with the female. The body has traditionally served as the border between the subjective inner self and the objectified external world, contrasting emotions and feelings (bodily/female) with objectivity and rationality (clear thinking/male): "The body, notoriously and ubiquitously associated with the female, regularly has been cast, from Plato to Descartes to modern positivism, as the chief enemy of objectivity," write Susan Bordo and Alison Jaggar[13] in answer to the question "What *is* the body?" In their essay – a consideration of the body in Western rationalism, Cartesianism in particular – we read: "Within our dominant traditions, the very concept body has been formed in opposition to that of the mind. It is defined as the arena of the biologically given, the material, the immanent."[14] The tradition Jaggar and Bordo analyze is the Western one, but the definitions and practical results hold true in the image systems invoked by the flesh writers.[15] Further, associations of the body and the female are multitudinous in the Japanese literary tradition of the pleasure quarters, of the nineteenth century and earlier. As Ann Sherif states, "many authors of earlier demimonde literature had evinced a primary interest in sex and romance. A voyeuristic fascination with the women of the quarter – as objects of desire and consumption – became orthodox in the texts they produced."[16]

These images of this genre conform to a poetics, i.e. a set of rules, invoked even as it is changed in depictions of the postwar demimonde of the *pan-pan*, and reflected in the linguistic dualism suggested by the word *nikutai*. The flesh writers do not write of elegant geisha but do write of female bodies in an economy of consumption. The attributes ascribed to women – immanent identity, sexual liberation, sensuality based not on rational principles but natural ones – draw from this lineage. The momentum of past genres organizes these postwar narratives; older ideologies prove inescapable even as the flesh writers attempt to transgress them. The assumption that women are naturally more in tune with unmediated desires serves as the grounding for the freedom the flesh writers describe, but also draws from the older tradition that entraps them even as they intend to overturn it.

Sharalyn Orbaugh suggests one reason why men's fiction is fundamentally different from women's fiction on this point. While "the integrity of the body and its boundaries is, for both men and women, a powerful metaphor for the integrity of personal identity," she goes on to paraphrase Nick Fiddes to the effect that "in normal everyday life, the only activities that involve the breaching of the body's apparent boundaries are eating and sexual intercourse." (Orbaugh rightly adds other activities such as childbirth and pregnancy.) Such breachings are gendered, for the facts of breaching those bodies are qualitatively different for men than for women. Childbirth and pregnancy transform body boundaries in ways available to women only, and even, in the heterosexual intercourse suggested in these works, only the woman's boundaries are violated.[17] I find that many male characters in postwar fiction affirm their identity via agency and transgression under the gaze of the Other; insisting on their agency in sexual relations, they thus re-assert an inviolate identity (precisely what they are anxious about) through heterosexual agency, an act that violates the boundaries of a woman. The flesh writers display an assumption (which I suggest is male) that founds the identity of the thinking individual on an agency coded as liberation; the agency they image violates the integrity of the woman.

Stated another way, and this seems to me to be the crux of the matter, women's fiction displays no sense that liberation from the postwar oppressions and difficulties will be achieved through physicality. Sexuality and intimacy were compelling themes for women writers as well, but for men the body (especially of a woman) was the place to work out relationships, to carve a place in the world, marking a foundation from which to root the project. The women writers were more inclined to portray the situations of their women characters, the postwar background that has placed them in very difficult situations, and the forces that propel their bodies to the forefront of exchange, of identity and sexual politics, rather than celebrate their autonomy in the situation. For example, Tsutae, of Shibaki Yoshiko's "Susaki Paradaisu" ("The Susaki Paradise," 1954, which I discuss in the final chapter) registers conflicted responses as she sits at the bar and watches a couple that has just arrived. The woman has wrapped her arms around her date, nibbling on his ear. Tsutae feels herself looking in a mirror when she sees this scene and is filled with sadness, feeling "for those of us who can only get partners with our bodies [*shintai*], and the sadness and irritation that arises when the body is not sufficient to retain the partner."[18] To live by the body, so valorized by men, is unstable and pathetic in much of the writing by women. Theirs is a much more somber vision, with more attention paid to the environment than to the freedom implicit in their bodies. Their bodies are not a source of liberation, but rather simply the bodies they possess, the bodies they must live by.

Relatedly, women, in men's fiction, form a countersociety, or at least a different society, one largely inaccessible and inexplicable to the male characters who nonetheless desperately desire access to it. As a countersociety that exists alongside the dominant society, it forms a photographic negative of the existing positive. The resulting differences between these two "societies" are not then fundamental, even though the author's posit them as such. Julia Kristeva has written of the trap presented by this strategy of building a countersociety. I think the "female society" of which she speaks is an ideal one; in that way it parallels the utopian visions of the flesh writers of my discussion.

The more radical feminist currents . . . make of the second sex a countersociety. A "female society" is then constituted as a sort of alter ego of the official society in which all real or fantasized possibilities for *jouissance* take refuge. (This conforms to the *nikutai–kokutai* dualism established in the flesh writers' fiction.) Against the sociosymbolic contract, both sacrificial and frustrating, this countersociety is imagined as harmonious, without prohibitions, free and fulfilling. In our modern societies the countersociety remains the only refuge for fulfillment since it is precisely an a-topia, a place outside the law, utopia's floodgate.[19]

Any countersociety "is based on the expulsion of an excluded element": this also explains the structure I have outlined in this postwar fiction, for while the flesh writers may appear to write of a feminist utopia, they do not, and they fall into the trap that Kristeva has here identified. That is, just as many feminist movements replicate the power structures they try to supplant when imagining a utopia, even more so do these men. The community they envision is a parallel image of the predominant society, imagined as the "only refuge," a "place outside the law" and society, in another turn on Foucault's "repressive hypothesis," mentioned earlier. As an alter ego of official society, it replicates its structure. Following this logic, the flesh writers do not backslide from utopia into suppressive structures and practices; rather, the oppressive power relation is written into the structure from the very beginning.

The dearth of publishing outlets for women after the war meant fewer numbers of works by women were printed, leaving the treatment of (female) sexuality in the years following the war to male writers, suggesting that a different conceptual framework was in operation.[20] The relative silence of women hints at a different set of priorities and only amplifies the obsessions of the men and highlights the aporia in men's writing. Exploring these differing obsessions reveals much about the construction of war memories and of sexuality.

Kristeva's identification of the falsely utopian countersociety explains the structure of the men's failure to portray all aspects of women's experience, a structure that Mizuta Noriko explains from the Japanese context.[21] She has cogently outlined the foundational structures that gave the masculine obsessions their shape. Looking back to (and beyond) the organizational logic established in the Meiji era, she outlines the organization of privacy from the industrialized nineteenth century, in the realm of politics and company/office, where male work becomes marked as the "public." The opposite term is the home, the place of privacy and of refuge. Andrew Barshay has also explored the development of these two spheres in his study of the development of the modern nation-state in early Shōwa:

Owing to the heavily bureaucratic character of Japan's political and institutional evolution, however, "publicness" soon ramified into positions distinctly "inside" and "outside." Public life pursued in large, especially official, organizations was accorded greater value and prestige; independent (and dissident) activity, while public, did not enjoy such approbation. Indeed, *public* tended to be identified with the state itself.[22]

The man escapes from the demands of the public workplace by withdrawing into a private place, the home, the place of the woman.[23] Desire for escape to the private – and "liberation" in the work I review – equates with a desire to inhabit the woman and her space. The private space of home is often associated with women. Her space – and with it her body – are then equated with salvation and release, the private space of refuge. The home cannot thereby serve as a private sphere of refuge for the woman because for her it is a public space, the place where she carries out her socially sanctioned roles. The man's "private" space is her "public" arena and no truly private space remains for her. While the Meiji "ideology made the family an integral part of this state apparatus for exercising power – contrary to the notion in civil society that the family is a 'private' institution" – important changes had occurred by the early Shōwa years.[24] With men needed in the colonies and as soldiers, the nurturing roles of women were being emphasized in order to preserve the inherently patriarchal family system. Thus, "according to these [wartime] documents, woman's role in preserving the family system was a crucial analogue to the male role of soldier fighting the 'sacred war' for the Japanese family-state."[25] Women are central to this system, but the realm wherein they are placed is marked as public. Further, this establishes the ideal woman as married and maternal, not the single woman of most fiction under discussion here. Some men escape from the public towards the private and the woman (the home), others escape from the home, which often functioned as an organic imagery for the public (i.e. the *kazoku kokka*) towards the woman of the pleasure quarters, the sensual woman. By locating this freedom in unmarried, un-domestic women, the men locate their freedoms outside the official realms of family and state.

Such dichotomies destroy the ideal woman because she is constructed as a fiction which can never exist. The men imagine a metaphorical woman, signified by the space she inhabits and her sexuality. They expect to discover a richly satisfying interior space via this imagined sexuality, and are disappointed with the "actual" physical woman. They never find this ideal woman: their search has been thwarted by the woman's physical body, which now proves to be a barrier. This, we will see, is the trajectory of many of Noma Hiroshi's characters and their relationships with women. The men then direct their anger and frustration at the woman they do find:

> The men of contemporary Japanese literature are unable to envision an internal space without a connecting [relationship] with a woman. They search for a salvation of their own internal [space] in such a metaphorized woman. She does not exist and they are refused, and they find real women hopeless and agonizing. Thereupon they flee.[26]

If the ideal woman does not exist in the "real" person before him, she must be deficient (goes the men's logic). This establishes the recurring pattern of interaction with a "woman": desire for her, flight from her deficiencies, followed by a renewed search for her in a different woman. Finding her lacking (as she can only be), he flees again and the pattern starts anew. The home thus marks the no-place of Japanese women, leaving them a "volume without contours," to borrow Luce Irigaray's words. Irigaray's descriptions (which inform Mizuta's essay) of the situation of Woman capture the structure replicated in this fiction:

Woman remains this nothing at all, this whole of nothing yet where each (male) one comes to seek the means to replenish resemblance to self (as) to same . . . She must therefore wait for him to move her in accordance with his needs and desires . . . The unstitched sex . . . through which he thinks he can repenetrate into the interior of her body, hoping at last to lose his "soul" there.[27]

Quite literally too: nearly all of the work I discuss in this study involves men trying to burrow into a woman's body for release. Woman represents the place where he hopes to lose himself in order to be found. She marks the location of liberation and reconstitution. She is a metaphorical and utopian marker of space wherein the man wishes to abandon himself, as Irigaray further explains:

If . . . woman represents a sense of place for man, such a limit means that she becomes a thing . . . She finds herself defined as a thing. Moreover, the mother woman is also used as a kind of envelope by man in order to help him set limits to things.[28]

The men find that she marks a space that is empty; furthermore, the impossibility men find in crossing the boundaries leads to the women's disappearance, dissolution, and death. The woman signifies the maternal, here in profound imagery that reminds one of the womb, that also overlaps with the domestic space of home and family, as Mizuta comments in the Japanese context,

The men, by submerging themselves in (metaphorical) women, even though they desire a retreat to the truest and private area of the individual, and to go deeper into themselves, find in her not a savior, not even an insightful guide, but simply a disconcerting and inexplicable Other.[29]

The valorization and (ostensibly) objective treatment of personal experience – the *watakushi shōsetsu* tradition – that has had such a strong appeal to Japanese writers, was at the same time the object of opprobrium for the male writers I discuss here, partly for its perceived weaknesses, lack of action, and inattention to larger social issues. Tamura cast it as weak and contributing to the abstractions of wartime – in a word, effeminate. The men who disparage that tradition as self-centered nonetheless continue self-(and male-)centered representations of experience, for experience continues to be valorized as opposed to thought. Continuing from Mizuta Noriko's insights, I propose that the inability to jettison this style is structural. The internal had been feminized, for home was the place of sanctuary for the Japanese male. Literary men experience in this structure a double bind. Since literature is already equated with the private, marking what is of no use and no value in capitalist society, it also marks the place of the feminine and the marginalized. Anxiety concerning gender roles in society is reflected here as well. Mizuta writes,

There has been an overwhelming number of fictional works in contemporary Japanese literature in which the central character is a man who has been refused by a woman. Men suffering under romantic love, men suffering in relationships with their wives, men drowning in their infatuations, men searching for their ideal woman. Men afflicted by "women troubles" in this way have created this world in the representative genre of contemporary Japanese literature, the *watakushi shōsetsu*.[30]

These hierarchies of space and personal experience lead, intimates Kamiya Tadataka, to the work of writers such as Shiina Rinzō, Noma, Ango, and others whose fiction often resembles *watakushi shōsetsu*, and may even be *watakushi shōsetsu*, because they are narratives of an individual self that is hemmed in and under siege by an outside delimited by public society. Kamiya paints with a broad brush, but the landscape that emerges is enlightening: before the war both the solid, material individual of Proletarian fiction and the protagonist of *watakushi shōsetsu* who is retreating into individual interior space presume a self that is stable and whose borders defined the area of a solid and unassailable reality. The individual marked a solid kernel of knowable reality and "truth," and, although under siege by various external forces, was still secure, concrete, and identifiable. In the fiction of Noma and Ango the individual may still seem to be in a final safe area, but that safety is no longer assured and cannot be taken for granted. The material reality of the individual was in doubt as boundaries were unclear and borders proved fluid. The force that impinges on that terminal space, threatening to collapse the borders entirely and crush the self, was, in both prewar and postwar articulations, the state that killed Kobayashi Takiji. One motivation for the writers' obsession with a carnal physical being may have been to shore up the threatened physical body. The increased emphasis in the postwar years on the concrete space of the individual seems a last-ditch effort to offset the onslaught of the state and its power into the realm of the personal.

The woman has consistently been constructed as the guide to the ideal place of release: Tamura's women lead the way to utopia; Noma's characters search for a "Beatrice of the Flesh"; Ango's men are led to the dissolution of a questionable enlightenment. She is disconcerting and does not deliver this promise. She then bears the brunt of his anger and frustration.

The imagery of the *pan-pan*

In the heady postwar context, in the image systems of carnal physicality, sex workers obtained singular representational power as a locus of possibility and autonomy in the despair that characterized postwar society. They marked a site for protest against the preceding militaristic era. In particular, the sex workers known as *pan-pan* – themselves a postwar phenomenon – embodied the freedom and excess promised by the postwar changes. These women were invoked repeatedly by the flesh writers as embodiments of the newfound liberation-in-carnality. The representations of these women, especially the freedom ascribed to them by writers like Tamura, contrasted greatly with the bleak but sympathetic portrayals of oppression recorded by women writers. The apparent free agency of the *pan-pan* – apparent to the male writers, that is – with their access to foodstuffs, their bright clothes and swagger, attracted much imaginative energy. They represented a liberation and freedom from care and seemed to exist outside constricted society. This representative imagery is so persuasive that I want to look closely at it here.

The very name of the *pan-pan* seems tied to the colonial and wartime experience. A range of etymologies is available for the origin of *pan-pan*; although none can be taken as authoritative, most of them carry sexual connotations. Kanda Fuhito has it that the word *pan-pan* originated from the Indonesian "perempuan," the word for "girl" (Japanese transliteration being "puromupan"), which in some Indonesian dialects can be construed to mean "one who sells/prostitutes oneself for bread [*pan*]."[31] Another explanation suggests the word originated in the sounds of Imperial Japanese seamen on temporary shore leave in the middle of the night, knocking on the doors of the prostitutes' quarters to wake them. Alternatively, it may represent the cry of young women in what is present-day Vietnam requesting food ("pan," i.e. bread) from the Japanese soldiers. After the war, young Japanese women engaged in essentially the same activity, motivated by the same near-starvation. It is also suggested that *pan-pan* is onomatopoeia for the sound made by women in New Guinea who would slap an open hand on a closed fist in a vulgar representation of sex. Yet a final possibility is that *pan-pan* is taken from the "pom-pom" guns used by the English navy, noted for their piston action, which in Japanese transliteration becomes *pan-pan*.[32] All of these come from areas colonized by the Japanese army during the war years.

Regardless of the origin of the term, the *pan-pan* denoted a powerful set of images. In his discussion of the *pan-pan*, Michael Molasky captures many of the stereotypes:

> These women embraced not only the occupiers themselves but also American mannerisms and fashion. Decked out in brightly colored dresses, strutting around in high heels and puffing on Lucky Strikes, the *panpan* elicited ambivalent responses: admiration and disdain, pity and envy, fear and desire . . . Yet the *pan-pan* was above all a survivor of the postwar chaos, and in this regard nearly every Japanese who lived through the war could identify with her.[33]

Prostitute-as-survivor very likely was an image that most Japanese, both male and female, could identify with after the war. Prostitute-as-liberation seems to me, however, the point where this imagery divides along gender lines. The flesh writers find in sexually available women the means to a fuller existence, an assumption entirely lacking in the fiction by women. Tamura's women, in particular, carry this imaginative charge. For him and other flesh writers, the *pan-pan*'s border existence carries all the romance of the free agent and transgressor.

Whether or not these stereotypes reflect the reality of the *pan-pan*'s existence, they certainly elide certain aspects of their postwar lives. Sone Hiroyoshi suggests that one of the most glaring historical flaws in a "realistic" representation of the world around postwar Yūrakucho, in central Tokyo, is that Tamura's *pan-pan* do not attract clients from among the ranks of the occupying servicemen, but from Japanese office workers, black marketeers, and factory owners. He quotes Tamura to the effect that "realistic" representation was not the goal and that these characters were purely imaginative creations, but he also corroborates Isoda Koichi's point that this may just as likely have been to placate the US censors who would have cut out references to fraternization between Japanese women and US servicemen anyway.[34] Although *pan-pan* were made available to American GIs at the beginning of the Occupation, it was not long until MacArthur's GHQ declared the red-light districts off-limits in an attempt to counter the spread of sexually transmitted diseases.[35] That is, the "recreation" facilities organized under the Occupation forces (the Recreation and Amusement Association, RAA) and staffed with *pan-pan* were closed down by GHQ because they were seen to harbor sexual diseases (replicating an old pattern of placing blame on the women as impure and unclean).[36]

Harada Hiroshi, who rode with the American Military Police as interpreter and liaison in occupation Japan, recounts that pressure from women's groups precipitated this change in official policy. (I take his reference to be US women's groups, or perhaps the women's groups attached to the Occupying forces.) He comments dryly on the effects of these arbitrary regulations on the women involved: recruitment was at first an official government activity; the sanctioned facilities were disbanded shortly thereafter, and public solicitation by prostitutes was then made illegal; thereupon many of these women were forced to solicit on the street. The irony, of course, is that these women, enticed to be "the new women of Japan" by advertisements that disguised the sexual nature of this employment, were just as callously turned out from those jobs, when the jobs were declared illegal. Saegusa Kazuko (discussed in the final chapter) will make much of this irony in her imagery, for example, as characters note the obscure wording of advertisements that apparently promise office jobs but actually are recruiting for sex work. The high rates of sexually transmitted diseases discovered among the *pan-pan* then prompted the "*pan-pan gari*," literally "*pan-pan* hunting," the roundups, and mass arrests of suspected prostitutes, all to protect the troops, as it was worded. Harada reports that sometimes the police "overdid it somewhat" (*yarisugita*) and arrested a number of unaffiliated "regular" young women, who were then subjected to the forced medical examinations – the result of which, he reports without apparent irony, was that a number of them then went on to actually become involved in prostitution.[37]

3   Tamura Taijirō

Tamura Taijirō and "the literature of the body"

For all practical purposes, Tamura Taijirō invented *nikutai bungaku*. He gave prominent place in his titles to the physical and carnal body represented by the *nikutai*; he almost single-handedly introduced both the term and the idea of the postwar *nikutai*. The contemporary reaction to his work was explosive: "It was simply amazing how Tamura Taijirō's "Nikutai no mon" ("The Gate of Flesh"), appearing in the March 1947 issue of *Gunzō,* sent shock waves not only through the literary establishment but through the general readership as well," recounts Okuno Takeo. He goes on to note that only Ishihara Shintarō's 1955 "Taiyō no kisetsu" ("Season of the Sun") known for its scandalous scene in which the protagonist pierces the paper of a *fusuma* with his erect penis, came close in its "societal repercussions."[1]

The sensation invoked by publication of "Nikutai no mon," Tamura's story of sex workers in postwar Tokyo, was only intensified through various stage and screen adaptations. Its 1947 dramatization by Ozawa Fujio proved widely popular and broke numerous attendance records; it was staged over 1,000 times in a three-year period, and more than 700 times in 1947 alone. The volume of collected stories in which it was later released sold over 700,000 copies and has been produced numerous times on screen. The first film version appeared in 1948, directed by Makino Masahiro, and the most recent in 1988, directed by Gosha Hideo.[2] The popular appeal of the work may be attributed to its erotic portrayals of the young women, especially in the more sensational theater and movie versions, all in the spirit of the 1940s eroticism I outlined in earlier chapters. Okuno Takeo recalls seeing the dramatization in Shinjuku as a student: "There were no strip shows at that time. This play became notorious as 'sadistic theater' because of the scene [in which one of the prostitutes] is [stripped to the waist,] tied up and beaten."[3] Tamura's work was thus associated with postwar eroticism – albeit a masculine version – from the very beginning.

Tamura writes of the landscape of war and postwar, the burned-out and desolate landscapes where individuals have been reduced to the most basic elements and drives – food, water, shelter, sex. "Nikutai no mon" is set in the bombed rubble of Tokyo's burned ruins (*yakeato*), while the 1946 "Nikutai no akuma" ("The Devil of the Flesh"[4]) is set in the brutal expanse of the wartime Chinese continent. In both wartime and postwar societies, in both Chinese and Japanese locales, the individual confronts the limits of survival and therefore of the physical body, the *nikutai*. Tamura invokes the *nikutai* to represent the physical, carnal body and to concentrate on the individual, with a subversive political agenda to overturn the collective and still-resonant *kokutai*. Tamura erected an ideological framework and image system wherein emphasizing the physical was subversive to the reigning ideology. It was also part of a historical moment when, with the Occupation, the focus of censorship changed, and private sexuality could again be discussed in public.[5] Even so, his work would land him in trouble with postwar Occupation censors for its allusions to fraternization between GIs and Japanese and for references to Japanese imperialism in Korea.[6]

In writing this fiction, Tamura created a version of the postwar male. Alan Wolfe suggests that "the word '*nikutai*' offers an instance of language trying to become its own referent," which is the desire to render the women transcendent, as noted earlier.[7] This, I think, explains the imagery of the women living together in their "den" in "Nikutai no mon." The community exists to strip away the layers and get to the essence; this unity would make the language equal itself. This, however, is an attempt to bind essentialism with transcendence: "What is perhaps specific to the postwar is the effort to focus on the body as a metaphorical vehicle for philosophy."[8] Tamura envisioned a liberation, a freedom, allowing the individual to be "truly free," but he roots that freedom from the body in the (male) body. This pairing ultimately introduces contradictions in his project, as his later work suggests. In Tamura's explication, the inordinate attention given to the nation undervalued the *nikutai* and led the nation into the disastrous war and its attendant postwar aftereffects. John Dower writes:

> In celebrating *nikutai*, or the carnal body, Tamura was engaging in a potent act of linguistic demolition, for his choice of language amounted to sacrilege bordering on outright lese majesty . . . From the mid-1920s on, criticism of the *kokutai* was a major criminal offense. Glorifying *nikutai*, as Tamura did with spellbinding effectiveness, amounted to a complete repudiation of *kokutai*, a shocking inversion of the body (*tai*) to be worshipped.[9]

Tamura also makes this point in the title of an influential article, "The Fleshly is Human" ("Nikutai ga ningen de aru"), as well as in the phrase that becomes something of a rallying cry in his work, "The body is everything" ("nikutai koso subete da"). These coalesce and focus his opposition to the ideology of the state (body) by highlighting the existence and needs of the individual (body). We find that Tamura stresses the body and its carnality to provide a counterdiscourse to the hegemonic state and to posit a base for individual subjectivity.

Victor Koschmann notes that in "Nikutai no mon," "Behavior is governed by instinct rather than conceptual reasoning, and animal life provides the most compelling similes with which to describe it . . . Tamura portrays life without a guiding Logos." The body is a "form of subjectivity as the will to fight, but only as a dependent variable, an extension of the biological need to survive."[10] I would clarify that the characters of "Nikutai no mon" act in accordance with bodily desires to posit an ethic, a way of living. Koschmann places Tamura's short story in its rightful place as integral to postwar debates concerning the nature of the individual self, and the *shutaisei* debates.

Tamura portrays the lack of a Logos even as he searches for one and attempts to equate the actions of the women with a transcendent guiding principle. Here is where "*nikutai* becomes its own referent," as Wolfe suggested. This is because, in the attempt to posit a way of living, Tamura imagines a way to live with agency. Ultimately, I think, the circularity is too heavy for the image to bear, even though the optimism and suggestion of a method to posit agency provides a counterweight to postwar bleakness and nihilism. Yoshikuni Igarashi discusses Tamura's fiction in his study of the politics of memory in postwar Japan and concludes, "The body was to Tamura the basis for a critical understanding of history" and "Tamura claims the body is the sole site where one can encounter the historical reality of defeat and confusion."[11] Tamura emphasizes the body, again, as the site of an ethic appropriate to postwar realities. Thus, I do not find Tamura "claiming" that the body is where one can face the reality of defeat, but suggesting that it is the place where one can forge an identity built upon the foundational experience of war, defeat, and postwar society. Tamura's work participates in the wider forces that Igarashi plots, organizing the memory of the war and facing the ensuing trauma of loss and, therefore, holds an important place in the history of memory that Igarashi describes. Tamura suggests the body will provide the means to get beyond not just the trauma of defeat, but also the limiting materiality of the body. This is where Tamura's project trips over itself, however, for he suggests that the focus on the material will provide access to the transcendent.

At the same time (and in contrast to the tone of his essays, as we shall see below) Tamura is also writing escapist fiction, not of engagement but of withdrawal. His project is stymied by structural constraints, not least because his focus on physicality belies the desire for transcendent value. Wartime co-option of the *seishin* rendered suspect any terms and ideas associated with the transcendent. His argument comes to resemble the one he wishes to deny; concentrating on one (for Tamura, the body; for society, the *seishin*) only devalues, while putting under erasure, the other (for Tamura, ideology; for the state, the body), leading to the contradictions in his fiction. The attempt to excise one ideology leads him to erect another.

Tamura expressed surprise at the initial reaction to these early stories. Some years after their publication, he wrote:

> It is odd for me to say this about this work of mine, but it called forth explosive reactions not only from literary critics but also from society as a whole. I must say, I was quite surprised by the force of this response. As I think back on it now, no one had made the *pan-pan* and their milieu [*seitai*] the subject of fiction until then.[12]

This is not strictly true, and Takami Jun, for one, claims to be the first to characterize the *pan-pan* in fiction.[13] Nonetheless, the pervasive metonymical power of the underground world of sex workers seemed new, at least in the mainstream fiction of the postwar *bundan* magazines. Tamura's surprise at these public reactions suggests that his intention was not to heighten the erotic, but to write something philosophically rigorous.

Although "Nikutai no mon" is his most famous work, it was his "Nikutai no akuma" that brought him initial recognition. Together, these works welded his name to *nikutai bungaku*. "Nikutai no akuma," set on the Chinese continent during Japanese military incursions, is the story of mutual infatuation between a Japanese soldier and a female Chinese prisoner of war. She and the narrator share an undeniable intensity and desire for each other in the face of mutual incompatibilities: she never denounces her Communism nor lets go of her hatred of the Japanese, for example. Nonetheless, her Communism, like his Japaneseness, seems essential, a defining characteristic, innate, and incontrovertible. The mutual attraction, in spite of these basic differences is, the story suggests, the "demon of the flesh" of the title, the inexorable quality of the physical that cannot be overlooked, that cannot be suppressed even in the face of wartime ethnic and political boundaries. Physical desire asserts itself in the face of differing ideologies as a carnality that cannot be dismissed even in the midst of war. This is Tamura's point: the physical had been stifled and now it is time to resurrect it, to return it to its central, proper place, so that the Japanese may know a fuller humanity, not least because carnal desire is irrepressible.[14] The enthusiastic contemporary response to "Nikutai no akuma" by such figures as Masamune Hakuchō, Aono Suekichi, Yokomitsu Riichi, and Niwa Fumio as well as a wider readership may also suggest that these fictional portrayals resonated with readers' own experiences and feelings about the war and the postwar years.[15] Its place in wider discourses, as discussed by Igarashi, Koschmann, Isoda Kōichi, and others, rightly attests to its broad significance. Before exploring the structure of this physicality in his fiction, I want to discuss his expression of the ideas governing his writing.

Tamura's philosophic goals

Tamura summarized his idealistic and philosophic goals in a 1947 essay where he stated that only with a "liberation of the bonds that constrict the body can we be truly free."[16] The narrator of "Nikutai no mon" sympathizes with the *pan-pan* and their aboriginal community replete with taboos, rituals, and social codes. This community of sex workers has abandoned the chains of society to establish a society that follows the logic of the flesh. The narrator stresses with much animal imagery that they have developed this community to ensure survival; all else is superfluous. This utopia where all live according to the logic of the body and resultant codes of their own making is Tamura's antidote to the numbing ideology that has structured their lives:

> Rather than young female humans, the women resemble wild animals. Small of frame like bobcats, they were fearsome creatures. These mountain lions would roam the nighttime jungle with their prey in sight, prowling the dark streets of the vacant city, frantic to survive no matter the cost. Whether businessmen in suits, demobilized soldiers turned black marketeers, old factory hands well-supplied by under-the-table commerce, all were fair game for these carnivores.[17]

Morals and other idealistic concerns have no place in this primitive and physical community. This story provides, in Mori Eiichi's words, "a description of the *pan-pan* who, in the tumultuous postwar years, existed by using their bodies [*shintai*] as their sole business stock."[18] The body becomes central, and more properly, the *nikutai* has become central because it serves as a commodity. Further, the women have chosen without remorse, in Tamura's telling, to use their bodies this way, divorcing their identities from the exchange value of their sexualized bodies. Thus, to call them "carnivores" is intended to be positive, natural, and primitive, even as it treats the women as objectified commodities. Much of the contemporary power and attraction of this work came from such putative freedom to choose one's own lifestyle, one that had not been decreed from above and seemed free of wartime and postwar constrictions. This portrayal is not a value-free statement, however; it betrays a masculinist economy that will become increasingly clear. When women writers portray the *pan-pan*, we find more "authentic" treatment of physical violence, poverty, and discrimination. Women write of women in postwar Occupation society functioning in an economy that is not determinate of identity and personality, not essentialist, not trying, that is, to ground transcendence in sexual activity.

Tamura expressed his aims in the above 1947 article, which is something of a manifesto for him:

> "Thought" [*shisō*] is, at this time threatening to push us down; it does nothing else. "Thought" has, for a long time, been draped with the authoritarian robes of a despotic government, but now the body is rising up in opposition. The distrust of "thought" is complete. We now believe in nothing but our own bodies. Only the body is real [*jijitsu*]. The body's weariness, the body's desires, the body's anger, the body's intoxications, the body's confusion, the body's fatigue – only these are real. It is because of all these things that we realize, for the first time, that we are alive.[19]

Tamura placed the body in opposition to thought (or ideology; *shisō* is emphasized in the original). To oppose the government's complete organization of society and culture for the purposes of the state, Tamura (and others) will concentrate on the individual, carnal body, and its desires and cruelty, usually relating to sex. By "thought/ideology" he refers to the constricting policies and ideology of the wartime government that encouraged the populace to subsume individual desires for national goals. In opposition and reaction, he would now have the body be the focus. As I have suggested, these portrayals contain anxiety about changing masculine roles. Tamura writes of the individual body to protest an obsessive, controlling national body, but driving that depiction are the patriarchal and masculine systems in a society undergoing change after the war.

Tamura makes use of the powerful postwar term "liberation" (*kaihō*) and suggests that liberation for the body (these bodies) is in, and only in, an emphasis on the individual body. Physical survival is now the first order of business, a situation that demands an emphasis on the body because ideas and abstract moralizing are meaningless. Tamura describes a populace weary of the idealizations of wartime and for whom a physical reaction is the only proper response, given that in the name of ideology the nation had fought, starved, and died to no apparent purpose. "The 'lie' that Japanese writers and thinkers embraced during wartime had to be demolished by the body," he wrote.[20] Wartime ideology proved meaningless, and the only thing left is one's own body. The postwar period offered the chance to demolish such abstracting tendencies. Liberation is from the body, yet by the body; freedom is for the body, and through the body.

Tamura began his *Gunzō* article by noting that his recent work had been criticized for its lack of thought (again, *shisō,* which I translate as "ideology"). He suggests that thought/ideology had existed in abundance, and look where that got us – following blindly we were led into a disastrous war. A work that lacks such "thought" (ideology) is then to be lauded. There had been more than enough of the selfless sacrifice encouraged by the state during the war and it had been rendered meaningless by the surrender, the lies it exposed, and the postwar disruption of society. In his words:

> The "ideology" that the Japanese have up to this point taken to be ideology was an ideology unable to prevent this war. Further, it is an ideology that was dismembered and lost with the advent of battle . . . Thus, the high place [I accord] this *nikutai*, which denies "ideology" still existing in Japan following the defeat, is to bring us back to the situation of freedom, which is the original form of humanity.[21]

And again,

> An ideology that forgets the *nikutai* has held a monopoly and from this has arisen the discourse [*setsu*] of a deified emperor; from this has arisen the ideology of the kamikaze, and also the idea of the holy warrior. The fragility of the Japanese view of mankind that forgets the *nikutai* has been fully blown open to exposure by this last war.[22]

Since the ideology and morals of Japan to this point have been proven entirely bankrupt by the war, he proposes exactly the opposite approach with a focus on the carnal, for the body is now "everything."[23] "No more of the ideological," is his message; "now it is time to focus on the individual." If Japanese do not relearn what it means to be physical, he writes, the sad history of the war will be repeated.[24]

Since the body is the correct focus of interest, it will of course be the correct focus of literature. As always, Tamura discusses the physical as a base from which to establish knowledge about individuals, the only foundation from which to truly grasp humankind, the beginning point for self-definition. Thus, the preexisting status quo understandings of humanity in Japan have been (in his imagery) so many baseless castles built in the air, so many plants without roots. He also writes that it is not his goal simply to portray the carnal and the physical, but insisting on the physical is to grasp the entire person, the gamut of humanity. The fiction provides the base from which to construct this inquiry, the place from which to proceed.[25]

Given the lofty goals he had in mind, one finds in Tamura's essays an undercurrent of frustration as to how his work was, in fact, read. He was not consciously writing pornography or erotica, even though that is what readers and critics focused on. He wanted to restore the dignity of the individual, which seemed to him to have been lost in the war. He would insist that he was not merely providing titillating portraits from the (under)world of the prostitute, but offering a picture of free individuals possessing agency and dignity. Togaeri Hajime is quick to note, however, that Tamura did not retain this high-minded distinction for long. His popularity had him associated with the erotic and sensational. Togaeri insists that while Tamura is certainly partly to blame for these associations, because he was responding to all the requests for work and offering up ephemeral pieces as a result, blame is also found in a publishing industry that increasingly hounded its commercially successful writers to produce as much as possible in order to stay in the public eye, no matter what the quality. Tamura became a commercial commodity and wrote quickly to capitalize on his popularity.[26] (If this is so, I would add, he has suffered the same inversion as the women he portrays: apparently in command of his own body, he is actually subject to the same commodity forces that take that "freedom" and make it theirs. The subjects – *pan-pan*, returned soldier, or popular author – merrily proceed according to their own rules when they are actually being played by larger forces.)

When Tamura explains *nikutai bungaku*, however, we find he intends something more than scintillating portrayals. Having come through the experience of the last war, he writes, we Japanese no longer have any confidence in the things we once took to be facts and reliable truths because we realize that our own powers of thinking and judgment were insufficient:

> All the established ideals have been stamped unworthy. The only thing we can now place our trust in is our physical desires, our instincts; in short, we can only trust those things we have experienced ourselves through our own bodies. The only things that really exist are those desires that fill our bodies – the desire to eat when we feel hungry, to sleep when we are tired, the desire to be physically close to another.[27]

Tamura iterates this line of thought in various postwar essays. For example, he recounts a conversation overheard among ex-servicemen: the recent regulations concerning black-marketeering have become so strict that it is difficult to get on any more, one complains. He asks, What are we going to do? We could join the special forces set up to reconstruct the country, responds another; it is either that or grand larceny, he continues, to great laughter. Rebuilding the nation or larceny: those comfortable with jobs will soon think that this is an unethical bunch, writes Tamura, while he thinks no such thing. He would like to see this spirited and uninhibited pursuit serve as an image of the Japan of the future. Given the available choices, these men will pursue that which ensures their survival. They will follow the dictates of the flesh – to eat when they are hungry, to sleep when tired, to be physically close when feeling alone. This makes one human, and this is the basic meaning of *nikutai bungaku*:

> It is not just some fooling around with an idea but the creation of an image of mankind based on subjective experience. It is this "body" that has arisen from various experiences that I wish to expound into the literary world . . . There are those critics who have charged that *nikutai bungaku* has no thought [*shisō*]. It seems to me, who have been trying here to place the *nikutai* as the primary item of concern

while negating the thought of the past, that there is nothing to be said to those critics who persist in the desire for the sort of thought that we had in the past. If that is the sort of "thought" that we are pursuing, there is more merit if it were not to exist. The sort of "thought" that Japanese have come to regard as thought was a system unable to prevent the recent war, it fought and then cleared out . . . . To place the stamp of mistrust on this "thought" is to begin to free ourselves from the feudalistic bands with which we have been bound for such a long time. The exaltation of this "body" that negates the "thought" we found in Japan after the war will bring us back to the original human condition of freedom.[28]

We encounter Tamura's characters in lives freed from the bonds of the past, from feudalism, from the false constructs of a society that limited people's movement and limited their choices. His ideal community would be free of such constraints.

Tamura offers the *nikutai* as the opposing term to prewar and wartime tendencies and as an antidote to the spiritual values pressed into service by the national polity, the *kokutai*. He reacts to the codes of conduct (as *shisō*) that divorce the individual from basic human instincts and drives. This ideology, to borrow from H. D. Harootunian's wording (borrowing in turn from Foucault), corresponds to the claims to knowing enveloped in structures of power.[29] What can be known, who can know it and, especially in this context, how knowledge and reality are determined and presented are organized in state power structures.[30] Tamura reacts against such organizing ideology, in his case contained in a government that presumed to present reality and thereby stripped the populace of their connection with their individual production of reality. Ideology (I borrow from Althusser) also presents a reality that in turn constructs individual subjectivities. When Tamura places the individual body in a situation facing the state, which is a restrictive dominating body, the image conforms to the state envisioned by Althusser, who defined ideology as "the system of the ideas and representations which dominate the mind of a man or a social group."[31] In this construct, the state is a system of apparatuses to produce a proletariat (in the literary context, subjects) that will unquestioningly carry out the desires of the ruling (political) class.

In one example of how this works, Tamura, in "Nikutai no mon," ridicules the ideology which lauds the fishmonger who advertises bargain prices because he has cut out the middleman, while at the same time disparaging the free-agent *pan-pan* who can offer her wares at "bargain" prices because she does not rely on a pimp or a madam. Tamura is at pains to point out that only the community of women in "Nikutai no mon" is "natural," i.e. primitive and pristine, authentic and true, a community that is wild and natural like feral cats (to which they are often compared). This ideal community exhibits no pretense but forms a network ensuring mutual survival, a mode of life in which the individual is in close relation to basic desires for food, sex, shelter, and companionship. He portrays a community of women whose physical needs are satisfied without external interference, without artificial rules, allowing its members liberation; such a community forms his antidote to the governmental ideologies that promoted an over-spiritualized body during the war years. It was an age when the spiritual was over-emphasized, when "higher" ideals were stressed in the most strident voices, but divorced from everyday physical experience.

Those ideologies denied the body while in fact, in the struggle for survival as a result of government policies, the body was everyone's primary concern. This imbalance, intimates Tamura, produced the sterility of the war years. Tamura writes of those years as primarily physical, a struggle to maintain bodily survival, but this aspect of experience received no official support because the rhetoric and ideology denied the physical. The state offered no help, no assistance, no support, for the people in their daily physical struggles. In that dehumanized time the reigning ideals of government and society were useless. The ideology of the state was, after all, the very cause of that dehumanization. As he says at the end of the article "Ningen ga nikutai de aru," it is only by exploring the carnal that we will know what it is to be human. In the carnal we will find liberation.

Tamura wants to restore this physicality to the individual so that the abstracting tendencies of the national body can no longer structure society and its subjects. Without an emphasis on the individual, no opposition to the totalizing desires of politicians exists. A society of liberated individuals is, in his mind, the best insurance against a reoccurrence of the war years. Tamura fears that the prewar proclivity for abstraction is being resurrected in the postwar period and that even while many are trying to overturn the oppressive militaristic tendencies, the people will again lose touch with their true natures, as it were, and Japan will again lean towards the insubstantial. In Tamura's mind the emphasis on abstract spiritual purity at the expense of physical needs leaves his compatriots susceptible to the militarists who led them into war. Tamura wants his readers, like his characters, to value the physical. Part of his urgency is the timing: given the postwar deprivations, he argues, an awareness of the physical is now unavoidable. He hopes to maximize the postwar experience of physicality and initiate a tradition of the physical. He wishes to push individuals toward an existence wherein they can live according to their own volition, according to a logic of the physical.[32]

That is, Tamura anticipated that during the postwar years Japanese would learn, with the body as a text, a more authentic way of life. Thus, he conceived of "Nikutai no mon" being as much a "Schooling in the Carnal" as a "Gate of Flesh," as the Japanese allows:

> The title "Nikutai no Mon" [refers to] the need for [spiritually] maimed Japanese who have been long constricted by a tradition of spiritualism [*seishin shugi*], which is, in a related sense, a medieval worldview. In order for them to become fully human, that is, to become modern, they must, at least once, make their way to the gate that leads to their own bodies [*nikutai to iu mon*]. I was thinking of this when I gave this story this particular title. My "gate of flesh" carries the meaning of "gate leading towards modernity."[33]

A number of issues are submerged in this pronouncement. His equation of advancement, civilization, and progress notwithstanding, it is clear that he has in mind a utopian goal where "fully human" equals "modern" in the conceptualization of stories such as "Nikutai no mon" (or, more accurately perhaps, he ascribes these concepts to earlier writings).[34] The entryway to a complete humanity is marked by the body, itself the entrance to this school of learning, this way of the flesh.

Kamiya Tadataka, in a discussion of Tamura's place in postwar literary history, connects Tamura's fiction with the eroticism of earlier writers such as Nagai Kafū and Dazai Osamu by equating the *nikutai* with a "physical/actual comprehension" (*jikkan*). He offers a compelling analysis of Shōwa literature that accounts for what is consistent through both prewar and postwar literary production, although nuanced slightly differently than my discussion in the previous chapter. Kamiya plots a lineage that develops between the poles of liberation (*kaihō*) and oppression (*yokuatsu*) and that culminates in the works of Tamura and Ango.

Kamiya identifies in this lineage a pressure driving writers to a very small area that allows individual action, an area demarcated by the physical body, the *nikutai* that Kamiya identifies as the *jikkan*, "real" understanding or actual sensitivity. In addition to the source of oppression we expect, the militant state, Kamiya also discusses the pressure that writers exerted on themselves in the form of an oversensitive self-consciousness. The suicides of Akutagawa Ryūnosuke and Arishima Takeo in the 1920s are understood as one result, where the psychological focus resulted in a severely constricted area for individual movement. Similar pressure emanated from the state in the 1930s and forced writers in on themselves. A martyr to this cause is Kobayashi Takiji, as I suggested in the previous chapter. In the prewar years there had been a growing interest in and literary treatment of the physical as the base for grasping the individual, but the censors had quashed this tendency. Following the war, Kamiya continues, Tamura, Ango, Dazai, Ishikawa Jun, and others focused on the *nikutai*, because this was the writers' sole remaining foundation of knowledge. This provides Kamiya with an explanation as to how Tamura came to equate the pressure of the state with the "pressure" exerted by the *seishin shugi* of prewar confessional "I novelists" such as Shiga Naoya. Kamiya echoes Tamura in characterizing this earlier literature as "over-spiritualization, and thus impotent to provide any moorings or direction for the people in their distress."[35] One also finds in the prewar period the sort of eroticism associated with Tanizaki Jun'ichirō, wherein "eroticism, exoticism . . . [and] the yearning for the maternal" organized the literary imagination.[36] Tamura thus takes his bearings from these prewar imaginative signposts in a fiction appropriate to, and marked as, "postwar." Again, it is in this flow that we come to realize just how Tamura's writing is linked with the earlier traditions, even while postwar writers deny it.

Tamura published "Nikutai no mon" in 1947. He had been writing fiction even before he entered the French department of Waseda University in 1926, and the influence of Joyce and Valéry in his writing was so profound that he had been called an intellectual writer, an appellation few would now attach to his name.[37] His shift from the art of the intellect to the art of the flesh is demarcated by his seven years as a soldier on the Chinese continent. Togaeri Hajime has argued that since Tamura had been writing for some time about Shinjuku and Ginza, areas notorious for cabarets and coffee houses, *nikutai bungaku* is not a product of the postwar situation but was already established with the aura associated with 1930s.[38] This is a minority opinion; I note it here to underscore how images of prewar and postwar have become dichotomized in discourse, when, in fact, many themes continue unbroken through these periods. Tamura decries all prewar tendencies, however, as examples of a debilitating spirituality, gathering all of them under the heading of *shisō,* the "ideology" that organizes society. Nonetheless, we find in his writing the issues initiated by Proletarian writers, and other "prewar" literary issues that continued to figure significantly in the postwar years.[39]

These two stories, "Nikutai no akuma" and "Nikutai no mon" propelled Tamura into the literary limelight. I want to turn now to a closer reading of those stories to trace the development of the philosophical ideas I have outlined above. Tamura also published "Shunpuden" ("Biography of a Prostitute") in 1947, a work I will discuss below because of its treatment of these themes. "Shunpuden" also introduces concerns that will structure the final work I will analyze, "Inago" ("The Locusts") from 1964. This later work provides a provocative tool to reassess Tamura's earlier stories and the issues I have identified. There are many other works I could analyze, of course; these four have been most often reproduced in story collections, and thus the most widely read. "Nikutai no mon" has received numerous screen renditions, as I noted at the outset. Director Suzuki Seijun produced two major films from Tamura's texts, "Nikutai no mon" in 1964 and "Shunpuden" in 1965, for example, making the works known to a wide audience.

"Nikutai no akuma" ("The Devil of the Flesh")

I begin with a discussion of "Nikutai no akuma" because this work garnered Tamura initial attention and led to commissions for the essays and stories in which he developed the thinking on the *nikutai*.[40] It is the first work that featured the term "nikutai" so prominently and begins his exploration of the term. Harada, the soldier of this story, like many in Tamura's works, is a sympathetic figure because he is not an unreflective member of the Japanese political machine, but a soldier who retains a critical distance. Even though unwilling to categorically demonize the enemy, he is ultimately a part of the military organization. Tamura's soldiers are in potentially compromising positions because of their implicit, and sometimes explicit, criticisms of the Japanese political configuration, and also because of the empathy they show for the Chinese prisoners and the Chinese cause. The uncharacteristic story development – a Japanese soldier who falls in love with a Chinese Eighth Route Army soldier, a woman prisoner of war, in contrast to his more common stories of soldiers and their relations with Japanese women – sets it apart.

The story opens with descriptions of a particularly brutal battle between the Chinese and Japanese forces. Among the Chinese prisoners of war taken after the battle is a small group of women, one of which is a particularly striking tall woman of "exotic" features. She, of course, becomes the sexual interest of the main character, who is attracted to her striking features and strength of resolve and personality. Even when he comes to distribute rations of dry bread – as if to animals – she is the only one who remains at a distance, who refuses to grovel. At that moment he catches her eye, and, as though addressing her, we read,

> I felt myself beginning to blush, embarrassed, feeling your contempt. It was at that time that I saw your eyes, saw the contempt and hostility in your eyes, the way they glittered with suspicion. And then I became aware that something that I had been searching for through long periods of battle was there [in your eyes]. I knew in that instant the painful truth of why I was so drawn [to you].[41]

The "why" is not clearly stated, only that he finds his destiny in her eyes. As I suggested earlier, this seems to hint at the title's "Devil of the Flesh," the irrational and inexorable quality of the physical body. Her contempt and the manner in which she seems to retain control most attracts him, creating an almost sadomasochist desire, such that:

> At that moment my entire body was struck with all the weight and gravity of fate. I felt a physical shudder. I was left dazzled. I feared my chest would explode; tears came to my eyes. Then I quickly realized this could be nothing more than self-serving conceit because between us there existed many objective reasons that rendered any relationship impossible.[42]

The first of these "objective reasons" is that in their battles with the Chinese army, the Japanese army was faring badly, and it did not seem that they would last much longer. Second, he realizes that, even if he survives this situation, he will remain "but a low level soldier bound by all the army regulations that limit my freedom."[43] The third reason, he suggests, is the most definitive of the three: she is Chinese and he is Japanese. They are of two different races (*minzoku*), unable to mix any better than oil and water. Further, he is fully aware of the "things the Japanese army has done to the Chinese," and this precludes any possibility for real interaction between them. The essential political identity that proves more powerful than the physical individual will be encountered again in his work.

We encounter a statement made two or three times in this short work, a comment that, while written in the voice of the narrator, seems to reflect the voice of the author as well, raising questions about this fictional enterprise: "A Chinese woman who loves a Japanese man, *even though one often finds this in fictional or movie worlds*, in the real world there is not even the smallest fragment to hint that this could actually take place."[44] This irony is found throughout Tamura's work and suggests a rift between the stated and the known, a rift that could be plotted along any number of planes – internal and external, public and private, *omote* and *ura*, *honne* and *tatemae* – but most fruitfully along the one that Tamura makes a foundational trope: the dichotomy between physical body and spiritual reasoning. The soldier insists a number of times that the two races could not possibly interact, but in the end they are attracted to each other at some human level. That human level is, for Tamura, the *nikutai*, which wins out over the rational. The physical body carries individuals into these complicated situations, with no regard for political realities. This ridicule of transparent fictional structures is powerful enough to dismantle his entire enterprise because it discounts the scene he has constructed in his own fiction, rendering it unlikely precisely because it is so obviously fabricated. The reader wonders how he approached his own relationship between the two realms here seen as divided and separate. At what point do "reality" and imaginative fiction overlap?

Some of Tamura's assumptions about progress and modernity also become clear in this early story, as well as when Harada addresses the Chinese prisoner: "There is one thing I can say with conviction: your body and its passions are feudalistic, while your thinking resides in the present."[45] She lectures him on the issues of women's rights within Mao's society, while he points out that even for one as strong of will as she, the desires of body ultimately win out over cerebral ideals. For example, since Mao allows romantic interest only between two persons at the same level of understanding of Socialism, she is that much more decadent for falling in love with a Japanese. She shows herself an enemy of the country, outside of the Party. The narrator suggests an extreme decadence in all this – the word is in English – which is heavily nuanced for Tamura. Decadence structures their romantic interest, as one body desires another and (borrowing from Togaeri again) "Includes a desire for consistent opposition and destruction of prior regimes and establishments, and a wish to tear down the old systems."[46] As to irony:

> In the space of a single evening you have fallen from revolutionary soldier to traitor. The body of one soldier of the invading army and the body of one anti-war [Chinese] patriot desire each other and become entwined. What a cruel irony.[47]

(The decadent "fall" in a spatial imagery will be encountered again in Sakaguchi Ango's work.)

Isoda Koichi, in his discussion of uniform culture that I referenced in the previous chapter, cites "Nikutai no akuma" as one important example of the overlap between eroticism and the uniform. This story exemplifies the revolutionary aspect of eroticism, the power of individual desire to overturn national ideologies by placing personal needs over those of the state, the radical power of the individual body. A Japanese soldier is attracted to a Chinese revolutionary, a prisoner of war, one of a group of women he is to guard. When the private and the public overlap in this way, the erotic has the power to disrupt erected partitions and render meaningless the very uniformity signified by the military uniform. Isoda notes, in this case, that this pairing not only has the power to rend the uniform policy of Japan but also implicitly critiques Mao Zedong's ideology of society, of love and marriage. The Chinese revolutionary soldier claims fidelity to Mao's teaching, but the complications of the heart and body reveal the artificial nature of that ideology; this parallels Tamura's critique of the structures of Japanese society and his hope that the affairs of the individual body – the "devil in the flesh" – will overturn official government ideology.

Isoda reminds us that the uniform ideology that Tamura critiques was set up in the 1930s in order to clothe the primitive and natural: that is, to civilize the populace and unify disparate groups in a modernizing nation-building project. Tamura's critique, especially in "Nikutai no mon," and the attempt to dismantle that uniform culture by a return to the primitive, brings the argument full circle. He suggests that the populace needs to move towards modernization and civilization, but at the same time he valorizes premodern modes of existence as integral to the individual identity necessary for this goal. This returns us to the situation that the military government exploited in the first place, for modernizing forces were the most efficacious in the ordering of society. Once again we see Tamura attempting to destroy one system of ideology but only managing to establish his own. Returning to Isoda's reading, Tamura not only reestablishes an ideology, but also resurrects conceptualizations that originally nourished prewar militarist structures.[48] Moreover, I would add, when "Nikutai no akuma" is read together with "Nikutai no mon," one finds that the liberation of the individual body, while having the ability to restore the individual (as above), also contains the power to restore a sense of the group (as in the *pan-pan* in their underground lair). The result is a different communality (*kyōdōtai*) but, given the power that imagery of the group has in Japanese society, and the goals to which such imagery has been harnessed, invoking this group mentality takes Tamura back to the structure he ostensibly dismantles. By resorting to something as basic as individuality, and with it a primitive participation in the group, Tamura has brought us one step closer to the prewar political situation that prompted his reaction. That is, for all Tamura's critical stance towards what he calls the feudalistic manners remaining in Japanese society, one soon realizes he merely reestablishes them. What Tamura criticizes as feudalistic in one scene is praised as pristine and primitive in another. Even the characters we are to emulate use women to their own advantage. The men in his stories retain the feudalistic attitude he criticizes, and reestablish masculine and statist structures of society. As Igarashi phrases it, "Japanese male subjectivity thereby used female bodies to confirm its historical continuity from wartime into the postwar period."[49]

The Chinese prisoner is at times cast as the perfect wartime lover, for when the soldier returns from an expedition – out hunting her compatriots! – she welcomes him back like the Japanese woman of melodramatic wartime songs and stories, with open arms, pliant and warm, wanting to hear his stories of adventure. This is so incongruous as to be ridiculous, especially against the background of the nationalistic projects that commit them to be mortal enemies. It also highlights Tamura's inability, at least in these early stories, to get beyond stereotypical gender roles for his characters. When viewed as part of the contemporary Japanese palette of images,[50] his women present a resolve and decisiveness that is unusual, "masculine" even (by which is meant decisive and confident), but from another perspective we find here little more than a rein-scribing of traditional structures by recirculating existing images, already clichés, of nurturing women. This presents the ultimate hindrance to Tamura's project. The kind view would be to consider it the flaw of an immature work. This would explain much and forgive much; it would not explain the reoccurrence of this structural failure in the early works of this stage of his career. The final work I analyze in this section, which is from much later in his career, comes closest to handling these concerns satisfactorily.

In a key scene of "Nikutai no akuma," the Chinese prisoner attempts to escape the prison camp. Harada searches for her, runs outside in time to see her fleeing figure and her attempt to scale the cliffs that encircle the encampment. Caught in extreme conflict of interest as both guard and lover, he raises his pistol (she is at thirty meters), he releases the safety (she is forty meters away). She then turns around and looks at him. In this moment of suspense she runs to him in tears, sparing him the ultimate difficult choice. She later offers the explanation that she intended to die by his bullet: "I knew that you would shoot me. But then I had to ask myself, why did I want to die? I was fully aware that you hated me; even so, were I to die by your hand I knew how badly you would feel and how you would miss me."[51] If she were to have died, she would never set eyes on that kind face full of such feeling again, she says, continuing the melodramatic and stereotypical language. This statement builds on an earlier comment: "This body of mine [*nikutai*] must seem to you to be the existence of the most hateful of demons,"⁵² an image reflected in the title. Harada then relates that when he imagines how she must hate his very existence as a Japanese, he finds her that much more beautiful; it incites his passion and he finds that he desires her even more. This seems to be Tamura's colonial fantasy: the unsubjugated women from the wild terrain have finally been broken.

The story ends with a final battle in the spring of 1944. The Japanese have been routed and all the members of Harada's unit – he lists all those who figured in the story – have been killed. And then, "the following August, Japan surrendered." The Chinese prisoner returns to her village, leaving a multitude of issues unresolved. For example, he never questions the difficulty of her position, the power relations and sexual politics that prevent this relationship from being mutual. He never considers that she may be leading him along for other purposes, for intelligence gathering, or the possibility of escape. The end result is a story that ends as rather simplistic melodrama.

In the final analysis, this work is long on diction and short on action. For one, the actions and thoughts of the characters are prosaically recounted for the reader. Nor does it deliver the eroticism promised in the title and by Tamura's reputation. For another, this is a very cerebral work, one that underscores one of the difficulties Tamura gets himself into: he is a cerebral writer calling for a physical existence, appealing to the particular while motivated by the transcendent. Ultimately, he offers a cerebral system of masculinist and power relations that varies little from those he criticizes. He is often tempted by the romantic, melodramatic tricks of a popular writer, which erodes the subversive potential he suggests in his essays. On the other hand, while "Nikutai no akuma" may not have aged well, the contemporary response was very positive and led to the commission for the following, now more famous work, "Nikutai no mon." The contemporary (male) readers found freedom and possibility in "Nikutai no akuma." The anxieties about male identity following defeat and then under Occupation would seem to have attracted those first reading these works. Those are the qualities that make Tamura's work crucial to understanding postwar discourses of memory and identity.

"Nikutai no mon" ("The Gate of Flesh")

"Nikutai no mon," the best known of Tamura's stories, was published in 1947, on the heels of "Nikutai no akuma." The story that shocked the literary establishment and became an even more popular play sets up an erotic sensuality in its very first lines:

> When Omasa no sen and the self-named Asada sen are unclothed, their breasts do not yet swell in mature fullness. They are nineteen but their skin lacks the glow one expects, their muscles lack a healthy plumpness. The paleness of their bodies [*shintai*] seems a trifle sickly.⁵³

Omasa no sen is getting a tattoo in a cramped two-room shack along the river; one room is a famed tattooer's shop. The burned-out and crumbling buildings of the *yakeato* line the banks. She is having her name emblazoned on her upper arm as a totem to scare off *pan-pan* who would dare encroach upon her territory. These inscriptions on her body establish her identity and mark her role and territory. It is the opening of a trashy novel, replete with prostitutes, gangsters, tattoos, fighting girl gangs, and the underworld. Often read as pulp fiction, a reading Tamura resisted, the story line and imagery invite such readings.

Here, too, an anti-establishment bias is readily apparent. We encounter a community of women in a society we know to be controlled by men. The opening scenes present the male-dominated criminal underworld that preys upon the established "society" of bureaucrats and police, reflecting the topsy-turvy nature of postwar Tokyo. These men are soon dispensed with, having appeared only briefly with the gangsters and black marketeers who are at this shop, in this milieu. The professionals mix with the amateurs in a confusion of professions and classes. Returned soldiers, last year the nation's heroes, are now black marketeers. They stand alongside careerist *yakuza* gangsters and other criminals, some important, most petty. "The distinction between professional and amateur is blurred; as it is in society at large, so it is here."[54] All the old accepted patterns and assumptions have broken down. It is a new world. It is still somewhat unreal,[55] a fictional world that Sakaguchi Ango succinctly described, in typical understatement: "Things have changed in the last half year."[56]

The group of women who work as prostitutes and live nearby are consistently portrayed as a pack of animals in a Tokyo that has become jungle. Casting them as animals, as innocent children, seemingly not fully aware of the business they are engaged in, Tamura underscores their displacement from "society," whether that of men or of adults in general, making this, on one plane, a coming-of-age story. Their community is primitive and innocent. Their business of prostitution is purely for the purpose of survival: "Even though she sells her body [*shintai*] she has not yet experienced fleshly joy."[57] The *pan-pan* are too young to know the "pleasures of the flesh." The story's central conflict arises when adult, mature emotion – love – interferes with an emotionless sex-as-trade that is the *pan-pan*'s means of survival. Their naiveté and youth is underscored by the fact that they market pleasures of the flesh but do not themselves experience that pleasure.

Their aboriginal community is bound by ritual and taboos (even so, Tamura's point is that these are *their* taboos). The strictest of commandments in this community demands expulsion should it be transgressed: "If there is one who exchanges her body [*nikutai*] with another without the exchange of proper fees, she becomes an outcast from this community."[58] Sex exchanged for pleasure and not a harder coin is the principal taboo of their community. Transgressing that taboo threatens their economic existence and therefore their survival. This governing principle is not set up out of any moral concern for right and wrong, for such concerns have no place here. Only measures that ensure survival are tolerated. Sex exchanged for pleasure marks adult responses, and the transition to adulthood also threatens the survival of their community by threatening their ability to carry out their trade. It signals the end to their childlike innocence, which also places them outside "society."

The idyllic community is threatened first when one of its members falls in love. Machiko is older than the rest – twenty-three – and a war widow. She had been married and thus, we are told, knows the pleasures of the flesh. She is mature in contrast to the naive youth of the others. When she breaks the commandment – she sleeps with a man whom she loves at no charge – the community deems that she must be punished. To preserve the group's solidarity and identity, a sacrifice is needed, which also underscores the primitive structure of the community. (The flogging Machiko receives as punishment forms one of the two such theatrical scenes that garnered such popularity in Shinjuku theaters.) Tamura goes out of his way to cast the women as natural and primitive, their actions performed not out of any decadent pleasure or desire, but simply as an exchange by which they might survive. Traditional morality, prescribed by the reigning ideology, has no place here because it is meaningless in the struggle for survival in the society wrought by the war.

Into their hidden den (it is also called a "nest," contributing to the imagery of the wild) wanders a virile young man who has been shot while fleeing the police. Ibuki, a returned soldier cast adrift in murky postwar Japan, is active in the black market, twenty-one, and a loner. He disturbs the equilibrium for he has been outside, abroad; he is Other. He quickly tires of the prostitutes' youthful naiveté but plans to stay with them until he recuperates. He falls in love with Machiko, the widow expelled from the community. The relationship between Ibuki and the war widow portends the loss of innocence, for maturity is marked by knowledge of fleshly pleasures. Not only Machiko's former marriage, but now the relationship with Ibuki means she "knows the pleasures of the flesh." Ibuki has also become the center of the universe for this group of women, the object of their desire, an increasingly mature desire, and an axis around which they all begin to turn. The young returned soldier enters into the women's community – a community that is so far removed from that of men, of the world above – and disturbs the balance they have established.

In presenting this Other society, Tamura establishes the community of women as idyllic and natural to exemplify his vision of liberation. He stresses through the imagery that this is atypical, therefore ideal. Japanese society as a whole has become painfully aware of the needs of the physical body, he argues. The world that Tamura presents as a model reflects an idealized primitive innocence of existence where one can live in authentic relationship to one's self. He also insists here that if the old ideologies are not abolished, if this more authentic society is not strenuously emphasized, the old ideology will take over and it will again be like wartime.

At the same time, however, Ibuki, the sole male character to figure for an extended period in the novel, is quickly rendered redundant in the worlds both above and below. He has been driven underground following a confrontation with the police over black market activity and, we assume, thievery. The women have their bodies and can thereby participate in vibrant economies to survive. He, the returned male soldier, has no place in the postwar order and nothing to contribute to this economy. He is little more than a parasite. At the same time he transforms into a centralizing force in their community. The heightened sexual tension he introduces does not translate to exchange value in a commodity economy, as does the erotic energy of the women. The returned soldier is subordinated to the women in this community, even as the momentum of earlier economic and social structures leads to his pivotal role. With the end of the war Ibuki has no role to play in the dominant economy, yet in this countersociety his prewar role as organizing principle is left intact, even as his place in the system of economy exchange is obliterated. This disequalibration and disorientation mark a major organizational trope of this work and all of Tamura's "literature of the body."

Tamura makes clear in his essays that he intended to set up an alternate version of living: a more authentic, less abstracted, manner of existence. He wanted to present a manner of living that would close the chasm between spirit and body that he diagnosed as weakening society. He offers a compelling world with a measure of happiness where basic needs are met and spiritual concerns are superfluous. One finds individual autonomy and authenticity here, and also an admirable fierce courage.[59] The contemporary popularity of his work suggests that he touched a nerve with his postwar readership, with his images of freedom and liberation among the *pan-pan*. These women seem in control of their lives, not subject to the demands and badgerings of "society." They operate outside of a government that commandeers all resources, physical and mineral, for total war or for postwar rebuilding. They live parallel to that society and off that society, without seeming to be constrained by it. (That most of the action is literally underground is no accident.)

Tamura brings a sometimes heavy-handed romanticism to these portrayals. There is no hint of the controlled desperate existence of these prostitutes, of the lack of options so common in survival by means of sex trades. Tamura frequently mentions that the women are unwashed and smell of sweat, living in a basement that is like a cave, to remind us of the animal-like nature of their existence. Their basement is a lion's den and they are cats on the prowl. A closer look, however, reveals moments that work against reading this as a model of living intended as an ideal, natural state. For one, the constricted nature of this world is overlooked, a world without baths or other amenities. The very unreality of its setting, the device that is meant to separate it from greater "society," pushes it closer to utopian fantasy, and the images ultimately work against the goals Tamura intends. Further, Mori Eiichi notices a similar sort of slippage when he quotes from Tamura's essays to show that Tamura was interested primarily in the character of Ibuki, the repatriated soldier, rather than the women. Ibuki was to capture the reader's imagination by representing the despair and bleakness of society, the disenfranchisement of those who have fought for the society. According to his own essays, Tamura intended to paint a picture of a soldier's resourcefulness in the impossible situation he faces when newly released from the oppressive yoke of a military government. It is the women, however, who are painted most vividly and stay with the reader.

I find that the ending of the story also complicates reading it as a model of liberation and agency, for when Borneo Maya, one of the central characters, becomes aware of her body, comes to know sexual pleasure and moves from childlike innocence to adult-like knowledge, she is flogged, as was Machiko. Maya is damned by her move to another realm of existence, the new understanding of society and human relationships that she achieves when she accepts Ibuki as a lover with no money exchanged. "Maya was struck with the idea that even if she were banished to Hell, she would not be separated from the pleasure of the flesh she experienced for the first time [with Ibuki]. She felt that a new life was beginning."[60] A new life is indeed beginning, but this entrance into a fuller knowledge of her body, replete with adult understandings, brings death and banishment. If death is requisite before moving into a new life, then the ideal life does not exist in their community after all. Hers is a rebirth, long awaited, that removes her from the very society Tamura endorses. The salvation he intends is thus not to be found in the society he paints so positively.

Maya's life to this point, like that of her compatriots in this "authentic," primitive community, has been presented as laudable. We have understood the women to be free from society's artificial constraints, living authentic lives of unrestrained naturalness. Yet that life is lost at precisely the moment that Maya achieves a fuller understanding of her body. The self-governing and self-sustaining utopian community is disrupted with the intrusion of adult emotions, signified by pleasure in sex and, here at least, love. The former existence is gladly sacrificed. Maya loses consciousness, perhaps even dies, from the punishment she receives for the transgression of the taboo. (She has been hung by her wrists and beaten by the others, stripped to the waist in the second scene that made for such popular theater. In the theater and film versions this second, and final, flogging is given longer exposure.) She is banished, yet without apparent regret. Nonetheless, death is hardly the freedom initial scenes led us to anticipate: "In the subterranean gloom [of their lair] the body of Borneo Maya, hanging from the ceiling, is enveloped in a faint corona of light and has a solemnity and magnificence like that of the prophet on the cross."[61] This final line of the story casts her as a prophet, a martyr for an impossible cause, a Christ-like savior (with echoes we will find in Noma Hiroshi's "Beatrice of the Flesh"). She embodies the key to liberation (for men), but exercising it destroys her life. Liberation has proven impossible because the movement into an adult realm, which is concurrently the movement to a fuller understanding of the carnal, is damned. Complete understanding of the body in this community leads to her expulsion, and she will never be able to return to that fuller, idealized state. Furthermore, the celebration that Ibuki orchestrates, replete with a sacrificial cow, purifying alcohol, and a dance around the fire, leads to his salvation but her death.

Thus, I find, in the end this story works against the ideology that Tamura expounded in his essays. He has proposed to do away with any ideology, yet his proposal is, after all, an ideology of its own. Its artificiality follows an intellectual, not carnal, logic, seeming to follow the path of those he decries and proves ultimately unhelpful in life's crises. In that sense, the story remains the "truer" by putting the lie to enforced and cerebral ways of living.

"Shunpuden" ("Biography of a Prostitute")

In another early work, "Shunpuden" ("Biography of a Prostitute," 1947), we find many of the same themes, but the portrayal of the women varies considerably from the works discussed above. Set on the Chinese mainland, "Shunpuden" focuses on five "comfort women"[62] as the main characters. They have been conscripted by the Japanese army and are being transported to the front line of battle. The themes and story line foreshadow an important later work from 1964, "Inago" ("The Locusts"), discussed below, where Tamura retains more critical distance from his work. Both stories initiate a more sympathetic understanding of the life that this ideology of the *nikutai* might actually mean for the women he describes. In a repressed preface, Tamura wrote the following about this work:

> I dedicate this story to the tens of thousands of Korean women warriors [*Chōsen joshigun*] who, to comfort ordinary Japanese soldiers deployed to the Asian

mainland during the war, risked their lives on remote battlefields where Japanese women feared and disdained to go, thereby losing their youths and their bodies [*nikutai*].[63]

As "Shunpuden" starts, a convoy of trucks taking supplies to the front makes its way across the Chinese continent. While the contents of the trucks are supposedly secret, the soldiers who are driving know that Harumi and two other "comfort women" are traveling in one of the trucks. In the exchange of voices and banter, a soldier asks the driver of this particular truck when he will "open for business" and they exchange jokes about who will be first in line for the sexual services of the women. We quickly discover that the women are under no illusions either, having in fact volunteered to move from behind the lines in Tientsin to the front, for various complicated reasons. In Tientsin (Tenshin in Japanese), even though the customers were rustic soldiers originally from the Japanese hinterlands, there was still something relatively elegant and refined about them. The front-line soldiers, in contrast, exhibit the stolid dullness of bears, and in their dull eyes one sees the unabashed libidinal desire buried within their bodies (*nikutai*). Front-line existence is brutal, lacking even the niceties of a straitened wartime city.

The unchanging dreariness of the landscape mirrors life in this barren place. The yellow of the mountains and land is unvaried; blue of neither sky nor water is to be seen. Objects and people all take on the yellow hue of the dirt that covers everything. The women are Korean by birth and the racial slurs hurled at them by the Japanese soldiers reveal the assumptions that these women, and probably all such women, are ethnically Korean. Various points of this story, as well as the later "Inago," turn on this fact: the women's language is not native; they are treated as second-class prostitutes because of their national origins (Japanese women being the "first-class" of prostitute, reserved for officers); we read, for example, in a catalogue of stereotypes that their rooms smell of garlic and kimchee.

This establishes, as in many of Tamura's works, a complex set of issues and assumptions concerning ethnicity and state politics. Japanese are thus and so, Koreans and Chinese also embody certain innate qualities, all of which have a vague connection to blood and land. For example, since all of the women have come from different corners of this same continent they should feel a geographic connection of land with the Chinese soldiers under attack, but the Japanese soldiers can sense none. That is, the narration accepts as fact that the individuals' connection to land – being from the same continent – should make all of them more or less of the same ethnicity. Yet since they had gone as very young girls to work among the Japanese, we read that "in their way of thinking and feeling, they may even be like the Japanese in some aspects." Issues of ethnicity are overlooked until their companions, the Japanese soldiers, grow nostalgic for the old country over drink. Then the women are forcefully reminded that they are "different." The narrator also assumes that the Japanese soldiers are little different from the Chinese soldiers in the Occupied territory. Contrary to the official ideology and many of Tamura's assumptions, this suggests that ethnic identity is not fixed and may not even be based on blood. Thus, the women may even at times "get beyond ethnic differences" (*minzoku wo koeru*) and fall in love with their customers. There are other suggestions that even with the ethnic hierarchies built upon assumptions of racial purity, these Japanese soldiers could see these women, ostensibly Korean, as "Japanese" and transgress ethnic and racial divides.[64] At the same time, while acknowledging this possibility, Tamura evidently felt it necessary to have these women be part of Japanese society from a young age, to the point that they are "almost" Japanese. Even their names have been taken from them. They are known by the names used in business, and while they must surely retain their given names in some corner of their minds, we read, those names only exist deep within their bodies. Ethnicity is almost elided, but it remains a powerful marker of identity and personality. Here too, as in "Nikutai no akuma," one set of crises is marked by the potential dissolution of such markers. In moments of crisis, the women "revert" to Korean traits, yet they can also be taken as Japanese. Sexual encounters, especially the relationships of the main character, are therefore ambivalent. The soldier has easy access across all such barriers and his body takes him beyond these artificial borders even as he resists. In short, Tamura belies a willingness to accept that ethnicity is not firm or stable, but the actions of the narrator and other soldiers reveal acceptance of essential distinctions.

This story ran afoul of the censors on the pretext that it would incite the resident Korean population, the issues of miscegenation being but one contested issue. Shortly after Tamura tried to have it published (it had been written at the request of the editor of *Nihon shōsetsu*), Sakaguchi Ango published his "Darakuron." Tamura suggests that it was the publication of Ango's work (which I will discuss in Chapter 4) that made it possible to publish "Shunpuden," which Ginza Shuppansha eventually brought out in book form (*tankōbon*). The censorship prevented Tamura's story from heading an impressive list of works in the inaugural issue of *Nihon shōsetsu*, a distinction that went to Sakaguchi Ango. There were also misunderstandings at the time of publication on the question of his oblique references to the women's Korean ethnicity, since he did not mention "Korea" (*Chōsen*) or other code words (e.g. "the peninsula") in the work. Tamura points to the censorship restrictions in explanation.[65] Conformance to censorship laws may mean that any fluidity of identity the story allows may only be accidental, the result of legal practices and realities rather than the narrator's fluidity of understanding.[66]

The early description of the lifestyles of the "comfort women" reveals some of Tamura's main concerns: we meet the women as individuals who follow their own volition. They refuse any customers who are foul-mouthed towards them, yet will lend money or buy drinks for the customers they fancy: i.e. they have the autonomy to make such decisions. But this is quickly cast into doubt when an officer decides that he wants to claim Harumi, who despises his cursing and racist condescension. His rank ensures that he will gain access to her regardless of her feelings on the matter. Again, the actions of characters cut against the fluidity of views expressed verbally and belie Tamura's romanticized portrayal of these war victims. We learn that when the women are happy they sing and when they are sad they cry loudly and uncontrollably. There is no affectation in their lifestyles. They embody passion that is not "ordinary." Nor do they follow a logic gained from books. The turbulent reasoning that undergirds their lifestyle is fashioned directly from their bodies (*nikutai*). What their bodies desire is enjoyed without limit; what they dislike they hate in the extreme. The violence in their verbal expressions follows from the violent life contained in their bodies. They live according to their passions, with no regrets afterwards. This sounds like wording straight from Tamura's essays, as discussed earlier. However, Tamura here hints at a biological determinism by tying such volatile energy to their diet of garlic and chili peppers; the women express the violence they have ingested. Ethnic difference may not be fixed, yet we find the characterizations rely heavily on ethnic (Korean, essentialized) stereotypes to explain the women's personalities and actions.

The officer who comes to visit Harumi embodies all the worst qualities of officers:

> Among the officers were many who thought quite highly of themselves, but who did not consider the girls to be of the same order of humankind. The time they spent with the girls was in order to satisfy physical desires; they treated the women as so many tools.

Officers behind the lines have many opportunities to spend time with Japanese women in the entertainment quarters away from the front, and for some "real human" contact they visit these "real" Japanese women. They address the Japanese women by their proper names and treat them as the same order as themselves; in contrast, Harumi is known only by a name that is not her birth name. The time they spend with Harumi and her associates, however, "they considered as no different from such physical activities as drinking sake or going to the bathroom," physical needs that needed to be seen to. The rank-and-file soldiers, however, even though they occasionally have the chance to visit the cities, find that the Japanese women there look down with disdain on their lowly stripes and dirty uniforms. The men thus bear great resentment towards them and subsequently all women, and they bring their misogynist anger with them when they visit Harumi and her co-workers.[67] Tamura captures here the simultaneous desire for and hatred of women that underscores the masculine structure of the military, a theme of particular interest to the women writers I discuss in the final chapter.

The soldiers return from their missions hungry for the women. Six women were to be available for the almost 1,000 soldiers in this area, and there were none who did not make their way to the women's quarters, we are told. The women's quarters were

> a shower for the [soldiers'] soul. In the same way that there were showers to wash off the grime and filth that had caked on them, in [the girls' rooms] they cleanse their flesh [*nikutai*] and their souls. No matter how tired they might have been when they came they are returned to health after a visit here. As if reborn the soldiers were able to face the next day's tasks and battles.[68]

Here again sexual intercourse becomes a ritual cleansing, the source for salvation, expiation, and renewal. Connection with a woman allows connection with the subjective and individual, and provides an antidote to the depersonalizing brutality of the front line.

Harumi had left Tenshin because of betrayed love: she had been madly in love with a Japanese soldier and was saving money to become his wife. He had promised to marry her when he returned from a trip to Japan; he returned, however, with a Japanese wife.

Harumi suffered a breakdown, threatening him and his new wife with a knife, displaying all the signs of "hysteria" (although here the cause is clear and sympathetically described). She has since pursued a course of sexual abandon in order to forget him, as though more physical contact could also cleanse her mind of his memory. Thus:

> Harumi was very diligent in her work. It was only by means of crawling inside and being enveloped by the brawny masculine body [*nikutai*] [of the soldiers] that she would be able to forget her Tenshin lover. She seemed to feel this instinctively.[69]

This male vision of release and liberation through sexuality is common in the "flesh writers," and Noma's characters are particularly driven by a desire to crawl inside the bodies of women for salvation. Tamura adds a twist by suggesting that the same freedom through carnality might be pursued by a woman.

When love interest is introduced, the story quickly becomes melodramatic: something within Harumi's body causes her to respond passionately to the physicality of the officer, even after rationally deciding to rebuff him in disgust at his actions and words. Her body betrays her and she cannot resist the attraction of his physicality. Her situation is complicated because she is in love with the assistant who comes to arrange the rendezvous with the officer. Their clandestine affair is a threat to their lives. The assistant, Mikami, is subsequently caught with her and imprisoned. When he asks her to steal a grenade and bring it to him, she is thrilled because she assumes it means he will use it so they can escape together. She takes it to him only to find that his intent is not escape but suicide. In the moment of awareness and utter disappointment, he pulls the pin. She clasps him tightly, and the grenade he holds, and they both die in the explosion, following a flash of happiness that they can at least go together. She is yet another woman, along with Maya of "Nikutai no mon," who dies at the moment she feels the greatest happiness, doomed by the very flesh that is to save her.

"Inago" ("The Locusts")

Tamura published an important work, "Inago" ("The Locusts"), in the literary journal *Bungei* in 1964. Separated by more than fifteen years from the stories discussed above, this work reflects many of his earlier concerns, but its lack of utopian optimism provides an important counterpoint to the earlier stories. The degree of sympathy for and acknowledgment of the brutality inherent in the lives of the forced prostitutes depicted here is striking, especially in contrast to the valorization attached to such women in the earlier stories. It is also better crafted, which is to say less prone to melodramatic themes, more subtle and less polemic. The imaginative landscape contrasts markedly to Tamura's earlier infatuation with the prostitute as embodiment of liberation and freedom. Tamura chronicles with an unflinching eye the slavery and bondage, the physical horror and rape, and the lack of freedom implicit in the lives of women conscripted to sexual service on the front lines. That is, in this story, none of this suggests liberation. In addition, "Inago" serves as a critique of his earlier stories, in part because the narrative records more of the complicity of his subjects in the structures of power. Much of the force of this story comes through its recognition of the violence that Tamura so naively espoused in this early fiction.

"Inago" begins with echoes of both "Nikutai no akuma" and "Shunpuden": Sergeant Harada is a Japanese officer on the Chinese mainland assigned to supervise the rail transport of a group of five "comfort women" destined for the front lines. As the women sing on the train, their songs mix with the rattle and bang of the metal lamps as the train skitters and moans. They share space with a trainload of empty coffins. Sex and death form the parameters of the narrative, here collapsed into the space of a single train car. The sergeant and his squad escort these women, very much alive, to soldiers who have no hope of a living return; the cargo of dead bodies that will leave the women's destination is many times greater than the number of live women that will go in. Even as the women sing and seem full of life in the oppressive heat, the pall of death casts a cold shadow over their story.

Everyone glistens with sweat. In the heat, the women have rolled their blouse sleeves up to their shoulders and hitched their skirts to their waists. When the train grinds to a halt in the middle of the desert, the soldiers posted in this remote area know that on the train are a number of "comfort women," and they brusquely demand that they be handed over. Harada is unwilling even to admit that the women are on board. His sympathy for the women leaves him conflicted, for he finds it difficult to treat them as mere chattel. He resists handling them in the bureaucratic manner his role demands because he knows what use they will be put to, and how often this scene will then be repeated on the way to the front, for there will no longer be any reason to refuse access to the women. The soldiers outside the train become even more agitated in the face of Harada's refusal. Ethnic slurs are exchanged, revealing the assumption again that the women are Korean. Harada can do little in the face of their vulgar, unconcealed lust, especially when backed up by an order from a superior officer on the other side of the door. He will be consistently stymied at this point: motivated by a concern for the welfare of these women, he is prevented by higher administrative demands from acting on their behalf. Harada's powerlessness in the military structure at times puts him on a level closer to that of the women he accompanies than to the officers whose whims he must obey, without question, even as do the women. There are times in postwar fiction where male soldiers are cast as "feminine" by their powerlessness and lack of agency; this is especially evident in Noma Hiroshi's fiction. When portrayed by writers such as Noma and Ōoka Shōhei, the low-ranking soldier's experiences emphasize the powerlessness the soldier feels before his commanding officers.

When the train door is eventually opened to the officer's command, a blast of hot, dry air and needle-sharp yellow sand assails the occupants. The ever-present sand is a dominant motif of the story and underscores the barren harshness of existence here. The cut of sand into flesh, followed later by an assault of locusts, forms a palimpsest of the story's imagery: flesh is assaulted and degraded, impressed with the marks of unrelenting storms, subjected to a never-ending deluge of sand, insects, bullets, and men.

Tamura consistently compares his characters to animals; in his earlier stories the women were compared positively to wild animals, which followed a natural logic that provided freedom. Here, rather than the women, the soldiers are the animals. They are compared to the insects that mix with the arid soil, ravaging everything in their path, scoring and attacking flesh and bodies, denuding anything standing. Shortly after the train doors are opened, the women have disembarked, and the dust has cleared, an attack of another sort begins. Harada and the others on the train feel what seems to be the stinging of pebbles hurled through the air. In fact, it is a swarm of insects, the locusts of the title. This image becomes increasingly horrific as the story develops; there is no end to the crevices and crannies, the physical orifices, which these insects (and like them the soldiers) will swarm into. The men are assaulting, they are also assaulted.[70] The soldiers are starving beasts, rapacious animals. In fact, the animals and insects are better off than the soldiers. "The locusts, being locusts, seem to move in accord with a volition that is unknown to humans; the soldiers, however, being soldiers, move according to orders that follow a volition not their own."[71] Locusts enjoy more freedom than do soldiers. It seems that they, not the soldiers or the women, are living according to the logic of the flesh.

The women are hauled off by the soldiers. Harada and his squad are concerned for them, clearly worried about their safety and quite agitated when they do not come back. Harada worries because he knows that the men in these remote posts are occupied with their tasks, driven by the sterility of the area and lack of holidays – although, as the text comments, a holiday may well be meaningless in a place where there is literally nothing to do. He knows that the soldiers will hungrily attack the women's flesh (*nikutai*). The soldiers need the women for their own survival, for they are never sure when they will be sent into battle, whether or not they will live, whether there will even be a tomorrow. Into this proximity with death and the assault of nature, the constant struggle, the women come as a cleansing force, in the mystic-religious role of purifying priestess ascribing meaning to a meaningless existence. These may be the last relations the soldiers ever share with a woman, which makes them all the more desperate and brutal. The violence done to the women is rendered the more horrific in its understatement:

> They are aware that what they spend during the short time allotted them with the woman, that the exquisite sex they imagine is in actuality a heavy, insufficient, sterile, fevered activity that resembles sex, but is somehow removed from it. They know that this may be the last sexual relations they will ever share in this world. There on the surface of the sand they are like starving arid insects swarming to nest in the central area of a woman whose two white thighs are spread wide.[72]

This is a much darker picture of the life of the flesh than that we found in earlier works. Even "Shunpuden," written shortly after "Nikutai no mon," was an attempt to relay the story of a woman living by a logic of the flesh, although it is now exceedingly difficult to imagine liberation there because of the sheer brutality to which she was exposed. "Inago," written fifteen years later, follows essentially the same story line while making that horror explicit.

The women finally return to the train. They have been sent off on their own, released into the darkness and sand without even the common decency of a single soldier as guide:

Out of the darkness that Harada and his men have been expectantly staring into, a pale something bobs into view. It draws closer, bobbing in the darkness, and gradually reveals with more and more clarity its shape and color. The women had returned. The pale something was the chemise wrapped around each of their naked bodies.

– What happened to you? Are you alright?

Not a single soldier appeared to deliver the women. For the women to get to Harada's side clearly took all of their remaining energy. They walked on unsteady feet, tramping across the sand, seeming about to pitch forward at any step, swimming through the space separating them. Harada and the others found it difficult to look directly at these women who had been returned, sent off as quickly as possible when their use had been exhausted, as if to send them away from this land as quickly as possible, blown by the overheated air mixed with the swarm of locusts and the sand, hopefully never to blow this way again.

When finished, the men cast off the women when they were done with them "just as though they were throwing an unclean object into the trash."[73] They have been used as disposable cleansers, scrubbed raw and thrown onto the rubbish heap.

Harada's character establishes a poignant tension throughout the story. As much as he is attracted to Hiroko, one of the women he has conveyed to this place, and, as we learn from the text, as intimate as their relations have been in the past, he will not allow himself to sleep with her now. Nor does he allow his men to sleep with her or the other women either. This causes no little tension for, as the soldiers routinely note, they can deliver the women to other soldiers but they cannot enjoy them themselves. Harada's hesitancy is not explicated for the reader, although his conflicted feelings towards them as both friends and objects seem the cause. Earlier, Harada went

to her in search of that seemingly bottomless dark region between her legs. He was only too aware of what could be found in that area, of what was there, of just how warm and moist was that area. One found there absolutely nothing. More, the sensation that nothing was there gave one the sense of a something.[74]

Sex with Hiroko leaves him disoriented, not sure if he is dead or alive, with a disquieting sensation remaining in his mouth. But that disorientating uncertainty, seemingly poised between life and death, prepares him for the uncertain future on the battlefield the following day. "In order to push aside the terror of death, to become intimate with death, he worms his way into that dark region, hoping to be enveloped."[75] He hopes for liberation in this chasm, the entryway that promises much while holding, literally, nothing.

Having reached their destination, Harada has the women sleep in the day and move at night because he fears what will happen if the Japanese soldiers find that the women are there with them. It is a surreal landscape where few people move during the day for all are hiding or fighting. When a bomb falls in the midst of the town, Hiroko is seriously hurt. It takes considerable effort, but they finally track down a medic to treat her. He is curt and unwilling to help, concluding that there is no chance left for her. Harada asks that she be taken to the field hospital. The medic refuses: the hospital is open only to soldiers, and she is definitely not a soldier; all the beds are full anyway. If Harada can find someone to carry her on a stretcher maybe he could do something. This too is a death sentence, for try as he might (and he tries mightily), there is no one to be found who can carry her.

By the end of the story only two women remain; the others have been killed as they travel to the front lines. The last scene is unstinting in its portrayal of the regimentation even of sex and the brutality this brings to the women. Harada goes to visit a woman who had traveled on the train with him. He knows her well, and she should know him as well. After waiting in line with the other soldiers, he enters her room, but he cannot quite get used to the level to which things have sunk: the small room is dark and dank, the smell of garlic is in the air, hinting at Korean ethnic origins. The woman is lying on her back with her legs spread: she does not recognize him and he hardly recognizes her. She urges him on with cries of "What's taking so long?" and "Don't just stand there, lots of other boys are waiting."

> Harada loosened his military trousers and pushed them to his knees. Kyoko lay there without moving, like some dead animal, fully extended. He climbed atop her white flesh.
>
> – Ouch!
>
> At that very moment he felt a sharp pain like a knife cut on his inner thigh and he separated from her. Then, in order to ascertain what it was exactly that had just now given that sharp pain like a knife on his inner thigh, he drew his face closer to inspect that part of her anatomy.[76]

He finds there the deep crevice that holds so much and so little. Between that crevice and her thigh was a brown locust that had bitten him as he drew close. Harada surmises that given the line of men that had just left this room she had passed over into another world beyond normal sensation and was completely unaware of this locust astride this most sensitive area.

There is no liberation here, no cleansing. "Inago" ends on the note hinted at throughout the story: that the assaulting men are being assaulted, penetrated as well, by rapacious insects. Attacked and assailed from all sides, these men and their milieu are worlds removed from the naïve idealism of "Nikutai no akuma" and "Nikutai no mon," both in vision and in time. The loss of optimism indicates how far Tamura traveled from the original sense of possibility felt in the immediate postwar period. "Inago" appeared during the ascendance of the next generation of writers. The fiction of the young Ōe Kenzaburō, for example, expresses similar despair in even more poignant imagery, tying the issues of sex and power much tighter, in violent depictions of the loss of postwar possibility, and the dissolution of democracy's promises and freedoms. The spareness of language in "Inago" is much closer to that fiction, which is to say, at quite a distance from Tamura's earlier works and the possibility expressed by a postwar *nikutai*. "Inago" focuses on the individuals and the landscape. Sex work brings degradation and death. Ideologies are distant. The anti-establishment promise of an egalitarian society no longer seems tenable; it is not even mentioned. All action is physical, and locusts display more volition and control over their movements than do men. We feel the disconnection of individuals unable to establish community rather than the oppression of a military society about to crush the individual. Salvation and liberation do not even figure in this tale. Tamura Taijirō has ended at a very different place from where he began.

4   Noma Hiroshi

Noma and the postwar body

Widely credited with having introduced or discovered the style now associated with "postwar writing," Noma Hiroshi's work was grouped with the "flesh school" (*nikutai-ha*) of *nikutai bungaku* in the earliest years of his career, the late 1940s and early 1950s. When one considers his entire oeuvre, his differences from writers such as Tamura and Ango may be more striking than his similarities, for his writing exhibits a committed Marxism, and it never attracted the popular, general readership that Tamura or Ango could claim. In the early years, however, the years immediately following surrender, he was treated as one of the writers related to them because of his focus on the carnal individual who was facing oppressive structures and was also the source of individual liberation and identity.

Noma's early stories, in particular his first work, the 1946 "Kurai e" ("Dark Pictures"),[1] evidence many of the troubling issues and concerns of Japanese literature after the Asia-Pacific War. It was immediately hailed as the important work of a new literary voice. Many found the convoluted style of "Kurai e" appropriately difficult for a difficult time. The style was what first drew the attention of writers and critics, but Noma is also representatively "postwar" for the emblematic concerns and issues that he raised. For example, he is often discussed as one of the "first wave" of postwar writers that also included Shiina Rinzō, Haniya Yutaka, and Umezaki Haruo (whose gritty, often pessimistic rawness pervades mainstream literature as it had not before).[2]

However, the body is insistent in Noma's early stories as well. His characters are soldiers wounded, more spiritually than bodily perhaps, on the battlefield. They have returned home to find the domestic landscape ravaged by battle and the people scarred physically and spiritually. Japan is the country of the walking wounded, the war hanging over and haunting soldier and civilian alike. The men in Noma's fiction are rendered helpless by the war, unable to form relationships, unable to rely on others, unable to get out of the prison of their bodies. Its cruelty and brutality have destroyed the possibility for human interaction. Nonetheless, they pursue a relationship, usually a sexual relationship, in an attempt to restore human contact and thereby their humanity. The lessons of the war continue to structure postwar relationships: in the wartime struggle for survival no one dared trust another and sharing rations meant suicide. After the war, Noma's characters find that they remain cut off from the Other. This becomes very clear in Kitayama Toshio's experience, in another story ("Kao no naka no akai tsuki" ["A Red Moon in her Face"]) where the Self is nothing but alone:

> He had learned in violent battle that a man preserves his life with no power but his own, he eases despair by himself, and must watch his own death. Each man, like the water in each canteen, must hold himself in that canteen.[3]

The radical physical isolation of war continues in the day-to-day struggle for survival in postwar society. The war's end was, in many ways, no end at all. This relationship of physicality and war is consistent across his fiction; as he wrote,

> The war bore deeply into people's sensibilities and it is played out on the surface [of their bodies]. "Hōkai kankaku" ["A Sense of Disintegration"] develops from this idea that if one fails to consider individuals in the postwar from this angle, there is no way to explain contemporary man.[4]

The war is the integral element in postwar existence, he suggests, and it must be accounted for in any fictional representation. The physical is not all of that representation, but it is a significant portion of it. Much of Noma's energy went to capturing the damage and difficulties the war wrought in individual existence. An accurate portrayal of physicality constitutes a key component of Noma's fictional enterprise; it is consistently played out in anxiety about sexual interaction that is frightening and unknowable – a dark country to be explored, to reinvoke Peter Brooks' scheme – reflecting the postwar intellectual concerns that I have been focusing on.

Noma's fiction is structured around impossible relationships doomed from the start because one "body" is cut off from another. The body of another – as a physical relationship – proffers the possibility of liberation from one's isolation. Touch seems the way to get beyond the boundaries of one's own physicality, but liberation always proves impossible because connections between individuals can no longer be made. The feel of skin is an important image as Noma describes the sensations and understandings of his characters;[5] it also constitutes, obviously, the sexuality that structures their interactions. The characters consistently attempt to transgress their radical aloneness through tactile contact that always proves impossible. The consciousness of being "bound in a body" overpowers readers and characters alike who find they are physicality only, a lump of flesh, a material object. Wartime deprivation reduced individuals to a bodiliness they cannot escape. Nor can they transcend their bodies and situation to take the Existential risk of acting and being. The struggle begins when two bodies come together; it ends more as a collision than a sharing. Two fleshly bodies can only bump against one another to find that the physical barriers separating them are impervious. Understanding and transgressing that boundary will lead to a restored humanity, the liberation that his characters seek. We immediately recognize here the carnality of *nikutai bungaku*, where a celebration of the physical and of individual desire is placed in direct opposition to the demands of the nation during the war and the postwar years, and where the body is the site to develop an autonomous identity. We also recognize the masculinist construction of man pursuing woman, searching

for a salvation and release in her compliant body. Yohana Keiko discusses this work as
an example of male desire in a world organized according to masculine desires. When
woman is constructed as womb, the receptacle for and originator of life – as she is in
many societies and especially in wartime Japanese discourse – active desire is the male
role. Such pursuits then reassert a male identity.[6] Noma weaves the fabric tighter than
the other flesh writers, however, by the tautness of his diction and imagery. The organizing concern for Marxism and his status as a self-consciously "literary" figure also set
him apart from writers such as Tamura Taijirō and Sakaguchi Ango.

Ōe Kenzaburo, who often acknowledges his debt to Noma's writings, has divided
those writings into two categories: those that describe humanity through the filter of
military life and those that treat the relations between men and women through the
filter of the body.[7] I will concentrate in this chapter on Noma's early short stories and
novels, the works of the immediate postwar period, which focus on the body because
they seem representative of the themes I have emphasized in the fiction of the late 1940s
and 1950s. The postwar experience is generally described as being very different from
that of wartime with the new regime. As portrayed in the fiction of the "flesh writers,"
however, it proves to be essentially unchanged, with no liberation or freedom in either
time frame. In Noma's work the body engages in a quest for liberation and desires to
connect with another, to be understood, to feel human. Noma's stories of this period
pivot on the material body and its desires: the body draws one into relationships, the
body engages in sex, the body prevents these relationships from continuing. Liberation
equates to connection with others, a freedom from lonely discrete existence. His men
desire to crawl inside the woman to be connected with her, as Other, but the barriers
of the body prevent it. This frustration unites this oeuvre: what promises liberation
also renders it impossible. Sexual desire and its promise of liberation mark the soldier's
body experience, as does the materiality of the body, by its borders of skin, which
prevents two bodies from connecting one with the other: the means to liberation then
prevents that liberation. Noma attempted before and during the war to understand sex
as a philosophical category, attempting to make it one of the terms, along with politics
and ideology, requisite to fully understanding and therefore describing the human.[8]
He does not, however, exhibit the optimism of Tamura's early fiction. On the other
hand, we will find in the next chapter how military experience infuses his work with a
particularly poignant pessimism that distinguishes it from Sakaguchi Ango's treatment
of the same themes.

Communication and liberation

The method of liberation that the flesh writers pursued most relentlessly as a means
to escape wartime and postwar oppression is carnality itself, a contradictory pursuit of
release from the pressures of the body by means of that body, which echoes Tamura's
"salvation from the body by the body." Noma's characters search for liberation from
a body whose needs have been made inescapable by wartime ideologies and postwar
realities. They try to throw off the confines of the body through an exploration of the
body, yet they discover that sex alone is never sufficient to restore the lost continuity.
"Connecting" does nothing to break down the borders of separation that the skin

imposes. Noma's characters want to occupy the same space as another, to crawl in as far as the womb where it is warm and safe. They want to be one with the Woman/Other, no longer to be alone and separate. The desire is to break the barrier, the membrane, that separates people. This quest for connectedness carries with it the potential for body-rending violence, for literal success in this scheme would destroy the woman.

Nishikawa Nagao finds the impossibility of communication between persons, which would release one from individual loneliness and despair, to be the central theme of these early stories:

> In concrete terms, this [impossibility of communication] results from the disruption between men and women, and the difficulties that returned soldiers faced in the adjustment to [civilian] society. The two are closely linked. Noma's initial pursuit in "Kurai e" and the fiction following always begins from the critical issue in postwar freedom, the issue of the *nikutai*. This is testament to just how warped sexuality and the *nikutai* was for Japanese during the war . . . To the individual self [*koga*], the *nikutai* is everything, it is society and it is history; yet the literature of the left wing and the Communist Party seemed to be overlooking this aspect.[9]

The difficulty in communication between men and women is compounded by the impenetrable border between two people, marked by a barrier of skin. Physicality had become "warped" or "strained" (*hizamu*, in a favorite word of Noma's) during the war years. The brutal requirements of both military service and the civilian life had deformed bodies. Two bodies remain separated in these stories even when pulled close in a desperate embrace, an experience all the more harrowing because in getting so close, one must acknowledge the stubborn divider of skin that separates Self from Other. The most elastic of barriers paradoxically proves the strongest, as the protagonist of "Futatsu no nikutai" ("Two Bodies") experiences:

> The train became increasingly crowded and Mitsue's body was pushed firmly against his. While he touched Mitsue's body he sensed between their two bodies, pressed together, something transparent. He sensed that a thin steely membrane stretched between his skin and her skin and firmly separated them.[10]

This "thin, steely membrane" marks the barrier that confounds all these characters; it also marks the boundary between Self and female Other. The man desires the woman, searches for liberation and identity through communion via that body, i.e. sex, but is thwarted. He identifies the Other that will complement his being, but the barrier of skin prevents transgression.

Bodily orifices provide access to the liberating body, a "reality" forcing the students of "Kurai e" back, again and again, to the representations giving the work its title: "Dark Pictures" refers to a collection of Brueghel paintings around which huddle four young, progressive, radical university students. They stare at the holes and openings in Brueghel's surreal landscapes: "[The area] around the mouths of these holes [in the landscape] are luscious like lips filled with the excess of life, they are gaping in the

center of numerous grave mounds."[11] The humanoid figures scampering across this
landscape are reduced to sexual organs and urges: "All of these people seem to have no
organs, other than sexual organs, which function."[12] Sexuality is insistent and sex is
written into the landscape.

In the same vein, Ohara Hajime and Yoko, two lovers in "Nikutai wa nurete"
("Drenched Flesh"), search, with hand upon hand and lips pressed upon lips, for
liberation and find nothing but flesh. Reaching across the chasm to connect, they meet
only another barrier, the physical barrier of the skin: "As if to clarify a deeper meaning in both their beings he felt they were mutually searching with their lips, for the
direction of the other's life."[13] Similarly, Fukami Shinsuke, in "Kurai e," feels "the tension of the skin that exists in self-consciousness and is in the other's consciousness."[14]
The membrane separating individuals comprises the foundational reality for Noma's
characters; they are constantly racked against this divider, the wall rendering any
promise of continuity an illusion. They search for a relationship with other individuals
which would liberate them from their Existential loneliness. They cannot, however,
find it.

Political ideology also threatens them:

> [Yugi Osamu] felt that her body feared his body. But no, that's not it either: What
> Mitsue feared was not this mortal flesh [*shintai*]; he knew that she was fearful of
> the ideology that he embraced. He knew that she feared the ideology that was
> within his physical body [*shintai*]. From this body of hers he could tell that his
> ideology was beginning to weigh heavily on her body.[15]

That is, she fears him and his sexual urges less than his political thoughts. Much is
made of the fear women have of the men in this fiction, and of the radical thoughts
that will likely get the men imprisoned or killed. The women fear these ramifications of
radical thought, but the political situation – fear of imprisonment and death – renders
the men aggressive and blind with desire. National ideology impinges on the physical,
individual body because of the system of thought "embodied" there. The body contains the vital ideals but also prevents the connection outside one's self. That individual
is then damned to the freedom of his thought and choices, damned to know none
other than himself, isolated by the borders of the body.

Ideology threatens like the truck which nearly runs down Yugi Osamu of "Futatsu
no nikutai"; at the same time, it forces him back close to his lover, close to this woman's
body in a movement that replicates the action of the entire story. Two lovers, fearful of
each other's bodies while hoping to find liberation in them, have quarreled and remain
in disagreement; they have ceased speaking to each other. Their carnal desires cast a
dark pall over them, they remain jumpy at the threat posed by their leftist thought.
They cross a street and a truck barrels down upon them, practically running over Yugi
Osamu. His girlfriend saves him by pulling him back to the curb: the force that would
crush them works as the catalyst that pushes them back tight against each other. These
are the struggles that the times present: that is, the ideology of the times, threatening to
crush one underfoot like a squirming frog (in the imagery from "Kurai e").

Body dividers

In Noma's fiction we find that during the postwar years wartime separations solidified into impermeable dividers. Just as, in another of Noma's examples, sharing one's rations on the battlefield meant suicide given the scarcity of food, the frightening inability to share physical space links to the physical and spiritual poverty of the postwar. Lessons learned on the battlefield haunt Noma's characters even with the war ostensibly over, yet the memory of the body as the topos of survival remains. "Life" has been reduced to physical survival. Kitayama Toshio's lesson is again relevant: the body as canteen, required to preserve its boundaries. Such steely tensile limits prevent these characters from finding what they most desire: liberation and a freedom from constraining barriers. The ability to communicate between persons would bring liberation, and such connections seemed possible before the war. [16] Now, skin, steel, and glass prevent it. Near the end of "Kurai e" individuals are described as sausages laid out in a butcher's window: close to one another but irrevocably separated by the casing of skin. The skin proved on the battlefield to be strong as steel, strong enough to keep a man together, to keep him intact, to save him, forming the boundary between totality and dissolution. [17] The horrors and extreme situations of the war forced a thorough awareness of how constraining the body is.

Noma's men confront the steely barrier separating them from all others every time they try to establish a relationship with a woman. In these stories spiritual and physical constraints are located in the body and became focused in the extreme situations of the war; the body marks the only reality, the sole place where action can occur; it represents, therefore, the single location for freedom and agency. Noma's characters face this contradictory situation: the body that promises liberation, which hints at communication between persons, prevents that same liberation, and dooms any hopes of freedom. A connection with another individual is requisite for liberating identity, but that liberation is made impossible by the boundaries of the body. The body becomes the only alternative available in the face of the disastrous idealization, the cerebral intellectualization, of wartime ideologies and their legacies.

At least, so it has been constructed in the imaginings of the flesh writers. One wonders if, in this time of doubt and despair over possibilities and roles, male writers (and perhaps men in general) fall back into traditional conceptualizations of male identity and stability via a sexual relationship with a woman. Of all the male writers I discuss here, Noma's war experience weighs heaviest in his representations. He writes of soldiers abused and exploited. Rather than identifying with the feminine in society, his ideal of liberation relies on the imagery of male-initiated relationships vis-à-vis the protecting, nurturing female Other, even though his imagery often takes him close to a feminine position, particularly when he depicts men made abject by masculinist military hierarchies. (A woman, after all, saved Yugi Osamu from the path of a truck.) Noma does not posit the strong aggressive male of Tamura's writing; instead, he portrays the anxiety of men without a role, men who sense that women are fearful of them, even as they find themselves cut off and powerless.

The characters site this anxiety on their bodies and they struggle to be released from the confines of the body on two fronts. (We have seen how, in Tamura's fiction, this anxiety led to the inscription of bodies, with whips and tattoos.) At the most obvious level, they contend with the physical demands of nutrition, nourishment, and physical companionship. They also struggle to extricate themselves from the wartime ideology, in all its forms. As I have noted, Tamura Taijirō's main complaint is consistent with these points, that the *nikutai* had not been given the attention it deserved. Thus, I find, at precisely the moment when survival, whether on the battlefield or at home, during the war and after, was uppermost in people's minds, ideologies disregarded the material in favor of the abstract and spiritual. This inability to connect is rooted in very real issues facing the returned soldier. The physical desperation of postwar Japan overlaps with remembrances of the battlefield, inevitably recast in physical images, which still haunt him. Escape from the physical body seems impossible. A man wants nothing to do any longer with the militarist government that organized every aspect of his life for wartime goals. Aggressive selflessness has been rejected as an acceptable behavioral mode. The abstract selflessness promoted by the national body pulls the individual in one direction, while the physical body pulls in the opposite direction. The war seems to have strengthened the opposing forces of this dialectic of contradictory forces which now threaten to destroy the unity of the body. The result, as Nishikawa Nagao comments, is the highlighting of the *nikutai* in "Kurai e" and the stories which followed:

> In "Futatsu no nikutai" and the story which followed it, "Nikutai wa nurete," we find expression of the attractive power of the *nikutai* and also the reaction to it, we find the disgust and also the fascination that exists between men and women; that is, we find just how wide is the separation between men and women . . . The *nikutai* in Noma's work bears the stamp of the times and is simultaneously the stamp of Noma Hiroshi. Noma's main characters, virtually without exception, are pulled along by an oppressive *nikutai*.[18]

The body as *nikutai* forms an oppressive image following wartime deprivations and official discourses. Nishikawa continues:

> Noma insists that the *nikutai* of the Japanese has been twisted under the emperor system. Furthermore, true societal liberation is nothing other than physical liberation for Noma. Any revolution that does not accompany a fundamental revolution of the body is meaningless.[19]

Again, liberation begins and ends with the physical but, I am suggesting, it is ultimately impossible because it is contradictory, threatening to destroy any unity the body might enjoy. This duel between the individual and the national is made explicit in "Futatsu no nikutai" when Yugi Osamu feels his body being torn in two. He feels octopus suckers, one on his back, one on his stomach, about to tear him apart, reiterating an image from the opening paragraph where a young man is literally about to be torn in two by sex and by ideology, with sex lashed to one leg and ideology to the other:

> The young people of that time were fearfully tearing their bodies into two, bodies that should have been laid in all their nakedness before their lovers. Half

was offered to their lovers, the other half to justice. It was like the ancient practice of tying a criminal's legs, each to a different wagon, and pulling them apart. Each of these young people, alone, was looking for love and ideals in their developing bodies. Love and ideals were lashed, one to each leg, wrenching them in entirely different directions, to be torn apart at the crotch. The love between Yugi Osamu and Mitsue was going like this.[20]

This division of spheres is not only *about* the body, it is located *in* the body, and the forces will pull it grotesquely in two. The competing forces of the physical and the ideological (i.e. the spiritual) confound the characters.[21] The body offers the only real escape, but that body is then threatened by the ideology from which it is trying to extricate itself. Liberation from this situation begins in the body and is to end in the body. The body will be crushed, torn in two, smashed flat, a casualty of this ideology and of this war. This sense of angst is captured in a graphic scene near the close of "Kurai e":

> Something appears which is stepping over the thing he is working to preserve, which then gets crushed underfoot by that thing appearing overhead. His self is like a frog crushed under the wheels of a truck, forced to flicker out, twitching slightly, in a deep darkness. Fukami Shinsuke thought of the times in this way. He was then gripped by the strange sense that his self, haunted in and by his body, was being twisted somewhere near the middle of his spine.[22]

The men are paralyzed at the point of trying to connect with the Other. In Noma's fiction this Other is always a woman who extends the possibility, through physical fulfillment, of freedom from materiality. The self is the only reality and it looks for salvation outside, in the Other, in a search that only highlights its radical solitude. In "Nikutai wa nurete" Kihara Hajime "wants . . . a body that will correctly lead his body . . . that is, a Beatrice of the flesh."[23] He looks for liberation in a woman as savior, ideal, the ultimate Other. He wants to be led to an external salvation by a female guide. Fukami Shinsuke of "Kurai e" despairs: if he is going to preserve himself, keep himself going, then "eventually something from outside, a great big something shooting out rays of light would have to appear."[24] This "great big shooting something" reminds us, in gendered imagery, of the sexual nature of salvation, directed towards the Other, to Woman, to Beatrice, Dante's guide, even as it also points to the Buddha floating down in rescue. The Savior and guide is Woman, and Woman corresponds to sex. The men's partners embody both fear of and fascination with sex.

Woman will guide Man across the chasm that is no wider than the space between two bodies clasped together; she forms the bridge across the reality that prevents him from connecting with the Other who shares his emotions. (We will see this imaged most poignantly in "Kao no naka no akai tsuki" ["A Red Moon in her Face"]). Yamada Minoru homes in on the recurring phrase in Noma's prose, "to loosen the binding," which he understands as the "desire to 'want the bindings loosened.'"[25] These men desire release from their Existential oppression and loneliness. They want to be liberated from the restraints that prevent them from becoming the connected individuals they can conceive of, can see, but cannot become. Kitayama Hajime ("Nikutai wa nurete") wants to be led by Beatrice; as spiritual guide she would lead him to the perfect land and the perfected body. "Kurai e" ends with Fukami Shinsuke's resolution to forge this path from deep within himself. Like Dante's road through Hell, Fukami's is a winding road, circling upward like Brueghel's tower of Babel. Thus Yamada Minoru asks,

> In what form is this desire for "tranquility" [i.e. salvation] physically expressed [in Noma Hiroshi's stories]? It is expressed entirely in sex; that is, in the connection with a woman's body . . . I think that the obvious interpretation is that this is connected simply to sex. That is because Noma's desire for tranquility is expressed physically. This is not an expression for physical desire. This is, literally, the stealthy, but persistent, desire to get one's existence completely nestled inside a woman's body . . . this is not unlike the desire to return to the womb.[26]

But such liberation never comes. The search begins with the body only to end at the same place. Traveling this eternal circle brings Noma's characters back to the beginning, to start again, having failed to find the object of their quest. Yamada also identifies here an underlying image system expressed by soldiers in Tamura Taijirō's fiction, as I noted in the previous chapter: sexual connection promises not simply a completed identity, but a cleansing and a rebirth. The women partners quickly transpose to transcendent Woman, the fulfillment of the category of Woman, with the maternal ability to make everything right in the world.

Critic Tomioka Kōichirō notes the centrality, in Noma's work, of the *ana*, the hole, the void, the lack – the all-important something that is a nothing – as a substitute for the entire *nikutai*. The students in "Kurai e" look at the body of Brueghel paintings and see the holes and orifices in a sexualized landscape. Described in positive terms as "viscous" and "pulsating with life" they also appear in rather threatening terms as mollusks, as the strange sexually warped creatures scurrying across the Brueghel landscape. The four students look, from below, at Christ on the cross, and this "Christ from below" ("shita kara no kirisuto") forms another layer in the entire scheme. Inhabiting the "below," they feel the societal oppression of medieval Europe represented in this sixteenth-century painting, but there is more, for looking from below reminds all of the importance of that lower region of the flesh and its relationship to the above, the region of the rational. Looking from below parallels the students' sense of oppression bearing down from above while located in the genitals and the lower region, the sexual organs, the lack, the *ana*.[27]

Ideology

In Noma's stories this Self–Other split yields images of the Self being literally pulled apart, whether by buckboards in "the ancient practice of tying a criminal's legs, each to a different wagon, and pulling them apart" or by octopus suckers. Establishing a relationship in the postwar chaos moves beyond the merely impossible to something akin to a cruel cosmic joke. Noma wrote that he wanted to liberate the self-consciousness from the main pressure of the times, the pressure of ideology. Tomioka links the two impulses by asking "Why is a man's body wrenched apart in this way? Because the woman is frightened by his physical desire and frightened by his left-wing ideology."[28] Anxiety about male identity prompts male aggression towards the woman as he obsesses about sex and her body. The violence of the nation (also imaged as male) towards political ideals threatens these characters. Ideology (ideals) and love (sex) mark the two principles threatening to pull them apart at the groin. This imagery reinforces what we read in Tamura Taijirō, where cerebral, abstract ideology has been emphasized at the expense of the material and physical body. As Noma explains it: "[In my early works] I tried to illuminate the individual strained under Japan's militarism [rather than war as such], limiting myself to those beings made helpless under it."[29] He focuses the source of oppression not in war in general, but in the particular war waged by the Japanese government.

That is, Noma's characters struggle under more than the battlefield experience he represents so well, but also under the strain of the country's militarism. This emphasis on militarism in society reflects Noma's experiences from the 1930s, in another reminder that "postwar" literature is firmly rooted in prewar experience and sensibility. "Kurai e," for example, was published shortly after the war but conceived and written during the war, and drew from Noma's student experiences in the French Literature Department of Kyoto University in the 1930s, at the time a political hotbed. Japan was at war with China, and Kyoto University, as one of the centers of radical student anti-war activity, was the object of much government pressure and repression. Many of his fellow students were arrested and jailed for left-wing activity.[30]

Literary critic Togaeri Hajime's war experience showed him that no radical break between the war years and postwar existed. He writes that while many people in the decade after the war no longer believed that the Pacific War had been a holy war (*seisen*) and not one of aggression, there were just as many during the war years who quickly judged the reality of events and predicted Japan's defeat. Few had any intention of giving up their lives for the "holy cause" of the emperor.[31] Likewise, he comments, and Noma Hiroshi's fiction portrays this more dramatically than many, postwar scars and disillusionment came not from losing the war, but rather from the inhumane treatment soldiers received at the hands of the armed forces officers. Togaeri provides a personal anecdote underscoring this: after he was drafted into the army at a rather late age – which convinced him of the truly desperate nature of the war – an officer accosted him to ask: "How about it, your whole view of life and humanity has changed since you entered the army, I bet?" To which he responded: "Just the opposite, everything I thought before has been confirmed by this experience."[32] That is, he had long suspected that the military was mistaken in its policies and brutal in its organization; being drafted and subsequent service confirmed those assumptions.[33]

Yet, like Tamura, Noma trips over his own ideological preconceptions. Noma's fiction first earned him the censure of the Communist Party because his were not the preferred images of workers and the masses, but of individual men and women in a bourgeois romance. Noma's involvement with the Communist Party was important to the initial reception of his work. "Kurai e" received kudos not just from established literary figures such as Hirano Ken but also from ensconced Communist Miyamoto Yuriko, whose praise was an implicit endorsement by the Japanese Communist Party.

Miyamoto praises "Kurai e" for its scientific approach and attempt at representation, and for the way Noma describes Fukami Shinsuke as being:

> always, and at every moment, [sunk in] self-reflection. This is the pure manifestation of his desire for self-completion, and in the space between this and the reflex for self-protection, he constantly discriminates between [the objective/scientific and the subjective]. This is a point worthy of attention. Within the focus on the individual displayed by the *Kindai bungaku* [group] this important poignancy and sensibility is entirely lacking. They do not peer into the internal, rather, it is as though they are aware of nothing and see nothing but the responses engendered from outside themselves.[34]

Later in this same essay, Miyamoto continues,

> What is especially noteworthy of this writer, Noma Hiroshi, is that he does not write either from the subjective viewpoint of a Takami Jun, nor is he stuck in a flat representation in the style of the *Kindai bungaku* group. He has fashioned an objective foundation that serves as the base for his understanding of societal history and he consistently builds upon this understanding. This, of course, is related to the central theme of the work, the anguish of the protagonist Fukami Shinsuke who struggles with the issues of establishing a self and completing individuality. With this work Noma Hiroshi has written with a full understanding of the [Marxist understanding of] historical development that informed leftist student activities.[35]

Leftist orthodoxy is also ideology, of course. The imagery of ideology cuts two ways for Noma Hiroshi; the ideology of the state threatens dissenters and unifies culture and thought, but the ideology of Socialism and Marxism can be equally oppressive. Marxism could be a particularly harsh ideology and Noma was not always spared censure by its adherents. The "ideology" that destroys bodies in "Kurai e" is certainly that of the government, but the ideology of the Party also contributes to the plight of Fukami Shinsuke and his friends. Noma's commitment to portraying the internal, i.e. the discreet individual, as well as the external, led Party members such as Miyamoto to strictly criticize Noma's later works. Noma's concern for the individual put him at odds with the Communist Party and frequently brought him into conflict with its Party apparatus. The antipathy he displays against the wartime regime and ideology leads him to criticize Marxist ideology. That is, he is not critical of the militarist ideology while accepting official Party ideology. Leftist political ideology and state ideology are equally monolithic; both downplay the physical, depriving individuals of half their existence, and instead stress proper ideological commitment and temperance in the service of higher goals. The reaction to such ideological threats sets the stage for Noma's emphasis on the body, just as it did for Tamura Taijirō, and we will find the same in Sakaguchi Ango's energetic disavowal of the established order of things. In Noma's work, when faced with a political agenda and the insistence of the physical, the body wins out over the appeal of a system of thought that he espoused.

"Kurai e" ("Dark Pictures")

Noma's earliest short story, "Kurai e" ("Dark Pictures," 1946), is set within the milieu of university student life in the 1930s and is a poignant record of the pressures and fears in the politicized prewar climate. It also made clear, in retrospect, the existence of radical political activity at Kyoto University at a time when it was thought to have been quashed by the authorities.[36]

"Kurai e" is a challenging work to read, particularly the opening section, a dense, horrific description of the monstrous bodies and sexualized landscape of a Brueghel painting: a landscape portrayed as the mediating body of a woman, filtered through the obsessions and fears of radical male students. The story reproduces part of a single day in the life of a Kyoto University student, Fukami Shinsuke. Money and love haunt him: "He was living in extremely straitened circumstances, and his hapless romantic involvement was nearing disintegration."[37] He carries in his pocket, for example, a letter recently received from his father that outlines his mother's sickness and the need to severely curtail his monthly stipend. Financial woes are the most pressing of Fukami's problems, but romantic engagements are also presenting serious difficulties. His father's letter also bears a message related to the third issue that will circle around Fukami throughout the tale, his ideological and political involvements: "At the end of the letter was the phrase that his father always included: Be cautious with ideological [*shisō*] issues. Be prudent every day and adhere strictly to a policy of not becoming involved with the Party."[38] Plagued by economic worries, troubled by romantic involvement, concerned that arrest may visit him or his friends at any time, Fukami makes his way through the day. He is besieged by dual ideological pressures: the desire to uphold Party ideals while also fearful of the political ramifications. As noted above, these fears also complicate his romantic relationships.

Early in the story, Fukami walks with this letter in his pocket, its contents in his mind, to a restaurant where he will ask for a loan from the proprietor, who specializes in small loans to students. In the back of the shop is a group of Fukami's classmates who interrogate and pester him with off-color taunts. Financial concerns are at the counter, carnal concerns await in the back. The jokes also carry a political edge, but they end with a serious admonition for him to relay to his friend Nagasugi Eisaku:

> – Fukami, you going to Nagasugi's place from here? asked Koizumi Kiyoshi, leaning forward, in a tone that carried a sudden intimacy.
> – Be careful over there. That apartment [where he is now] isn't safe anymore. A damn cop showed up at my place today wanting to know Nagasugi's recent activities. He claimed to be gathering evidence and that the next time Nagasugi isn't going to get away. He left saying he'll back him into a corner with his evidence and then arrest him . . . The political types are out for blood.[39]

This scene reflects the conflicts listed in the letter in his pocket, the three issues that surround and haunt Fukami throughout the day: financial woes brought him to the shop; he walks into taunts about sexuality and romantic involvements; warnings about political oppression follow. He leaves and walks towards Nagasugi Eisaku's apartment.

He now considers the contents of another letter, also in his pocket, received three days previously. This from his girlfriend Kitasumi Yuki, who lives an hour's train ride away in Osaka. She wants to end their relationship because she fears Fukami and what he thinks. Ideology frightens her and she wants to pull away: "I will probably never again draw near the house where the body [*nikutai*] of Kitasumi Yuki resides, never again near that house that holds those hands, those eyes." He remembers her eyes vividly, and the room where she and Fukami last sat in her small six-mat room and "glared at each other."[40] His friend Kiyama Shōgo will later ask about Kitasumi and this relationship, to which Fukami responds.

> – I don't know, it's not going well. We got tripped up on issues of the *nikutai*. I can't figure out what it is with physical relationships [*nikutai*] . . . I mean, before, it was my intent to work on my plan for liberating the *nikutai*. I always thought the *nikutai* of the Japanese was twisted. I thought that our *nikutai* was contorted and rotting and I wanted to set it aright and help move ahead.[41]

Kiyama understands immediately that "liberating the *nikutai*" refers to all these concerns tormenting Fukami: philosophies of romance and politics, demands of the Party, and Fukami's father's admonitions against political activity. His father was only too conscious of the police arrests and the government's lack of patience with left-leaning radicals. Near the end of "Kurai e," Fukami Shinsuke accompanies Kiyama Shōgo on a cold walk home and explains what happened in his relationship with Kitasumi Yuki: "Our bodies [*nikutai*] tripped us up. You know, I know longer have any idea what the 'body' [*nikutai*] means."[42] No one in Noma's stories ever does, but that diminishes neither the body's promise nor its appeal. Kiyama then offers his assessment, theorizing that Kitasumi Yuki has left Fukami not because of any sexual deficiencies or perversions, nor because of issues concerning the nikutai, nor for any reason but ideology: "I don't know what Yuki feels about this, but here's how it seems to me: In the end, it's your ideology [*shisō*] that's frightening. That is, left-wing ideology. Maybe that's too simple, but that's how it seems."[43] Fukami's ideology is criminal and dangerous and it forces a wedge between two bodies. Ideological commitment – i.e. political activities – threatens the physical, not only through the fear of arrest and jail it initiates, but also through the pressure it puts on relationships.

The body represented in "Kurai e" is not a woman's actual body but a body meta-phorized in landscapes exuding mordant sensuality. The four students gather around the book of Brueghel landscapes because the location promises liberation, if for no other reason than that it provides an opportunity for the sharing that defines this liberation. The original promise of liberation is located here: one hopes that the barriers dividing individuals can be broken through because one senses another who shares the same emotions. Fukami Shinsuke realizes in retrospect that the simple act of sharing while huddled around these paintings allowed these four to be as close as disparate individuals will ever become:

> The spiritual atmosphere of that small six-mat room of Nagasugi Eisaku's was such that they did not each melt part by part into a single entity, because

differing perceptions and colorings remained; yet from the point of anguish [that they found in the paintings] an intimate communion, a mutual touch, a mutual circulation, a tumid intimate something filled the room to overflowing.[44]

The shared experience is the promise of liberation. In Noma's later stories that promise will be found in a lover; here, four students who share the pain of existence amongst themselves hold the means to that liberation. The Brueghel landscapes with their sensual orifices represent the female body. These serve as a metaphoric body by which individuals might find connection. The four students in Nagasugi Eisaku's room gather around the exotic abyss represented in these dark landscapes and stare into the vertiginous darkness. But the body as landscape that tempts them with potential liberation also revolts them. Like Yugi Osamu, in the later story "Nikutai wa nurete," who writes in her diary, "My lips felt like two slugs emitting light,"[45] the students in "Kurai e" find that the figures in the landscapes are reduced to sexual organs and that sexual urges are represented in the landscape itself, which is dotted with funnel-shaped holes and,

> the mouths of these holes, lustrous like lips filled with the excess of life, open in the very middle of various grave mounds, these holes, to say it another way, give the sensation of waiting, heavy, filled with licentiousness, entirely like some living thing, like mollusks, opening their mouths across the landscape. And there, without crotches, with sex organs only, again and again, there appear to be buried the strange bodies of women.[46]

Something is promised in this landscape-as-body and the students keep turning back to look, but they also find something here that they find very disturbing. It fascinates, it repels. Humanoid creatures scuttling across the landscape are horrific and unsettling in their pain. Yet the students also see themselves as pained creatures whose sexuality is paramount, promising release while at the same time becoming all-consuming. Sex also equates with death, because orifices in the paintings open directly to graves and the blackness of death. They cannot bear to look very long on these paintings,

> because looking at these reproductions was quite unpleasant. All who looked on these reproductions were ineluctably forced to recall the oppressiveness of their individual positions in society, their relations at home, their interactions with various women, the ideologies they each held . . . [For Fukami Shinsuke] the images in that collection of many people in oppressive darkness, emitting something like a groan, with pain and anguish, caused him to poignantly feel his own sorrow. Even when he thought to himself "tonight I won't look at them," he was drawn by a mysterious power and found himself turning those pages.[47]

The search takes them round and round, doomed to unfulfillment while able only to begin again, like so many of Noma's characters searching for fulfillment in an ideal woman. Wanting to turn away from the body before them, they can only turn back. As events unfold, conversations are remembered, and the future suggested. The work details the loneliness and alienation, the money worries, the concerns about friends and lovers, the fear of and fascination with sex in the prewar world of these college students. The story ends on a note entirely appropriate to my discussion, with Fukami turning over and over in his mind a phrase that has been with him throughout the work: "shikata no nai tadashisa," a correctness about which nothing can be done, expressing that there is no other alternative for him but to continue on his path of righting the wrongs of the world. This is the path, the correctness he is condemned to, for which and about which nothing can be done, from which there is no escape. He comes close to choosing the path of political activity. (These characters all find it impossible to make active choices.) There are things he must do as he walks, dragging his feet like a condemned man, into the future. The choices that lie ahead contain actions he must take, actions which he even desires to undertake, yet which also threaten his body with imprisonment and other diffi-culties. He faces the unavoidable. He is condemned to the freedom of the choices before him.[48]

Criminal ideologies

Ideology, not sex, is criminal in this fiction. In Ōe Kenzaburō's words it was the "monster of 'ideology,' and nothing else, that smashed love to smithereens" in Noma's fiction.[49] National ideologies of the body destroy relationships by their political pres-sure. Fukami's ideology is criminal as well, threatened by that of the state. Biographical elements also underscore this reading, for "Kurai e" chronicles the fears of radical students.[50] "Kurai e" records Noma's frustration with the war and all the restrictions of the government; he carried the ideas for the work within him for a long time, through the war years, and he attributes the prose style to this:

> "Kurai e" is based on the radical student activity at Kyoto University. Its motif came into being around 1939. I carried all of this around within me during the war; it went everywhere I went . . . I wrote the rest . . . after having traveled to Tokyo in 1945. With writing this all the pressure that had been bearing down on me during the war was released. The pent-up feelings within me exploded as I wrote and there are many clumps of words and turbulent phrasings, many areas where the physical "feel" of the work is unpleasant . . . As I wrote this work there was always in my mind the death of my friend Fuse who died in prison [a political prisoner]. I was going every day to my desk . . . [with] the smoldering resentment I bore towards those that killed him. He appears in this work with the name Kiyama Shōgo.[51]

That is, the much commented on difficulty of the work is directly related to the war. More to the point of this discussion, a prime motivation for Noma's writing of "Kurai e" is his anger and resentment towards "those that killed him," i.e. the government that harassed the students, rounded up suspected left-wing radicals, and imprisoned and killed them. Noma wrote that he wanted to liberate self-consciousness from the pres-sure of the times, the pressure of various ideologies. He emphasizes the individual to protest the imprisoning nation and its ideology. The comrades in the noodle shop use ideology to harass Fukami Shinsuke; his father warns him to be on his guard against it; it gets them all arrested and leads to the death of the other three in prison. This is articulated in a reflective passage later in the novel when Fukami thinks back to that time and rehearses what happened to his friends:

> Right after the outbreak of the Pacific War Kiyama Shōgo resolved to avenge Nagasugi Eisaku's death and had become active in handing out leaflets [critical of the government and its actions]. He was eventually rounded up after three days in hiding; his death came in jail shortly thereafter. Nagasugi had been arrested earlier, right before his graduation. He refused to renounce his Communist ideals [*tenkō*] and after a year died in jail. Hayama Jun'ichi was sent to the front immediately following graduation but was rounded up while a soldier. He was repatriated by airplane, but he too then died in a military prison. The war railroaded over the expectations and predictions that Nagasugi and Hayama made concerning the war, continuing on its way. They each expended all their energy and collapsed. It was much later that Fukami learned of their deaths, only after he returned home following three years of military service. He himself was picked up shortly after that. Fukami renounced his political beliefs and went on to work in a munitions plant to get enough money to survive.[52]

The choices seem to be two: either renounce one's beliefs and live as an apostate to them, or remain steadfast and die as a martyr to them. However, Honda Shūgo credits Noma with forging a third way beyond these equally unattractive choices: he finds that the search for a self as exemplified by the protagonist of "Kurai e" pointed the way to new possibilities in relation to Communism, a third way that was neither as martyr nor as apostate (the choices the official ideology allowed).[53] Hirano Ken follows with the comment that this work is an individual synthesis of Symbolist poetry and revolutionary activism. This is to say that Noma Hiroshi forged a new idiom that resolved some of the most troubling issues of the postwar literary scene. As these critics point out, these are not only issues that address the conflict between the individual and ideology (whether that of a fashionable Marxism or the establishment nationalism/fascism), but also ones that describe a creative, individual (independent and non-conformist) self in the new situation of the postwar. The work captures in poignant detail the loneliness and alienation, the money worries, the concerns about friends and lovers, the fear and fascination of sex in the world of these college students. It ends as lonely as it begins: Fukami, having chastised some of his demons, sets out on a lonely road by himself, with the stars shining overhead and the wind blowing through his hair. Its tone – dark and brooding – caught the mood of the time.

This passage also speaks to the political activities that led Noma to the Party: he knew he could not refuse the draft, but he did refuse to be in the officer corps, in keeping with a commitment he made as leader of a student group. This refusal made him a political fugitive, but, ironically, the army which had already sent him to the Philippines, could not locate him. After contracting malaria he was repatriated to a mainland hospital. Now able to send him back to the front, the army released him from service.[54] Noma, like his characters, finds the space for agency only in the cramped area bordered by a criminalized belief system and the threat from a militarist government.

Communist ideology

I have noted the reception of "Kurai e" by his contemporaries. Noma had proved his Communist credentials by displaying a fully developed Marxist ideology. In this sense, Noma's work can be characterized as ideology-laden for some of the most ponderous sections, and the greatest obstacles to the overall success of "Kurai e," are the often-extended discussions of Party ideology and partisan conflicts.

Marxism will remain a central concern in Noma's literary career, and the history of that interaction is reminiscent of Sartre's. I discussed the importance of Sartre's work in the context of postwar fiction in the first chapter; the parallels between Noma's work and Sartre's reveal another instance of Sartre's influence on postwar fiction. Noma's initial response to Sartre was as a contemporary writer of the flesh, but also as a novelist working within a Marxist framework. Later in life, in his book-length study on Marxist ideology in literary practice, Noma would criticize Sartre's writing and its relation to Marxism. Yet Sartre's work provides a way to write the body and also a way to move beyond Symbolism, an issue of style and expression that would concern Noma for many years.[55]

Noma's debt to Sartre and other French writers, and to modernist writers in general, is great and he discusses them extensively. He takes many pointers from their writings; he is also unstinting in his critique. In "Shōsetsuron (I)" ("On fiction," 1948) he finds fault with Proust, Joyce, and Gide, explaining that even with all that he has learned from their method, he finds they lack a sufficient tie to the exterior, to an external reality. Their characters are all internal, with no tie to society or the world around them, he writes.[56] In a subsequent essay, "Shōsetsuron (II)," Noma credits Sartre with unifying the internal and external, thus rectifying this particular problem: "Sartre's project is to see humankind from a place where internal and external are unified. Pursuing the problem from both the internal and external viewpoint is, provisionally at least, the correct approach." Noma is tentative in his response to Sartre's approach because he sees a gap: while Sartre is able to "get beyond" writers like Joyce and Proust who are stuck in their obsession with the internal consciousness, he lacks a proper view of the future. In Noma's view, "It is only the person with a clear vision of the future that is able to fully live in the present."[57]

Noma is even more pointed in an essay written to accompany volume 5 of Sartre's *Complete Works*, as translated into Japanese. In a short essay entitled "Jōkyō" ("Situation") he writes that only Sartre is able to adequately grasp the *nikutai*:

> For example, Gide, in order to extricate himself from the introverted universe of the Symbolist's pursuit of consciousness, was searching for a restitution of the physical [*nikutai*] as the liberation from desires. While he did in fact realize [the extrication] he has no grasp of method or language for handling the *nikutai* . . . Now Sartre, on account of his bringing about the birth of a language by which to grasp the *nikutai,* could go on to make clear the internal description of an

individual where the consciousness and the physical [*nikutai*] are unified. Sartre could accomplish this because he turned inside out the language of the Symbolists and their hold on the internalized consciousness and pushed on to a place where he could grasp the *nikutai* internally.[58]

This essay is written late in the 1960s, long after the guiding ideals and obsessions of "Kurai e" had changed into something else. Some might call it the temperance of age. In the same way that Noma is here quite willing to criticize the Symbolists,[59] he is also willing to praise Sartre for uniting the internal with the external. Symbolism and the physicality of the *nikutai* remain concerns for Noma, but in the "Shōsetsuron" essays he pursues a unification of the spiritual and the physical, whereas in the earlier stories he focused on the physical as an antidote to the overly spiritualized atmosphere of the war years. Noma finds this in Sartre's method as well, for Sartre starts from the body:

> This is how Sartre is able to give form and shape to gratuitous acts that originate within an individual and can then make clear the connection to that person [of that action]. It is Sartre that could place the gratuitous act in the midst of everyday activity, situate it and give it substance, that is give it flesh [*nikutaika suru*] . . . Sartre's new method comes in his pursuit and grasp of freedom without excluding the physical [*ningen no nikutai*].[60]

One of Noma's enduring legacies to the thinking on these issues is his experimentation with capturing a "totality" in literature, the *zentai shōsetsu*, following a Marxist concern for "totality." This "totality" aims for a thorough description of humankind by describing the individual from three different planes, or aspects, of existence – the physiological (*seiri*), the psychological (*shinri*), and the societal (*shakai*) – and rendering a single image that unifies all three. As Suzuki Sadami rephrases it, the *zentai shōsetsu* is a method to describe: (1) the individual consciousness limited by (2) the body (describing it) via (3) society, which constrains all of these elements. In another phrasing, the three impulses that motivated Noma at the early stage of his writing career include: (1) an awareness of the limitlessness of spirit as he faced the "poetic" universe, (2) the sexual universe (which is the desire for women), and (3) the economic universe, i.e. economics in society.[61] Early work such as "Hōkai kankaku," which I discuss in more detail in the following section, conforms to this novelistic method in its attempt to capture "all" of an individual dismembered by the war. To reformulate it, this work serves as a description of (1) the consciousness of the main character and (2) his body which limits it, all of which is circumscribed by (3) society. Noma describes these impulses as bouncing into and striking one another with a force that threatened to rip him apart; the struggle with the forces that complete the individual threatens to tear it asunder on another plane. These three impulses were more than passing youthful passions; they proved to be concerns with which Noma would wrestle for many years. The struggle with ideology, in its various forms, is rooted in the physical. The economic concerns reflected here highlight the Marxist (and underlying Proletarian) sensibility that informs his work.[62]

Reflecting on this only a few years after completing the early stories, Noma records his dissatisfaction with the degree to which he emphasized the *nikutai*. In retrospect, he finds the dichotomy between the spirit and the physical, the *seishin* and the *nikutai*, over-emphasized and wants to work at bridging the gap between the two. My argument is that Noma reflects a sensibility keenly felt at the time, where the spiritual was opposed to the body, and emphasizing the body seemed a necessary antidote. The *nikutai* and the *seishin* remained primary concerns for Noma and many of his contemporaries for years to come. He recalls, for example, the way these early stories affected friends: "Simply put, I now think that developing and expanding a focus only on the *nikutai* was a mistake. However, regarding 'Nikutai wa nurete,' there are the kind words of a friend of mine who claimed that he had been rescued by this work."[63] This friend, like many of Noma's readers, felt the emphasis on the *nikutai* was appropriate and necessary, and was itself a sort of salvation from all that had come before.

"Hōkai kankaku" ("A Sense of Disintegration")

Oikawa Ryūichi, the protagonist of "Hōkai kankaku" ("A Sense of Disintegration"), is, like so many of Noma's protagonists, a young man returned from the battlefield to the ravaged landscape of Japan. The story opens as he steps out of his student room to meet his lover, for whom, however, he has no great depth of feeling. This is a "relationship" only in that there is physical exchange, and even precious little of that, as a result of a war that has left no real possibility for exchange or sharing between individuals. His landlady detains him: another student has hanged himself in a room down the corridor and she wants someone on the premises while she calls the police. She asks Oikawa to stand watch (*rusuban*) for her. This situates the narrative, for from this point on he is suspended between life and death, between sex and a corpse.

He walks into the room down the hall: the dead man hangs from the rafters and children's voices waft through the open window. The happy chirping of life mixes with the death in the air. Where Kihara Hajime and Yuko ("Nikutai wa nurete") feel existence in their lips, eyes, and palms, Oikawa Ryūichi feels it in the scars on his hand, the stubs of two fingers lost in a battlefield suicide attempt, now hard and tingling as he faces this corpse. He feels in these stubs the remains of what once existed. This begins an association with touching battlefield dead, as the body suspended from the rafters reminds him of a soldier's death and his own attempted suicide. The tingling in fingers dead, fingers not there, calls to mind the woman he is about to meet. She has touched him there and asked about them. (He told her they were shot off.) These fingers, stiff and tingling, become phallic; in their lack, and anxiety about their lack, they are sensual and super-sensitive. Oikawa's war experience – like that of so many – refuses to stay in the background even though it is the source of this disillusionment. The bodies of men like Oikawa were dismembered. Wartime and postwar experience is inscribed on their bodies, just as it was for the *pan-pan* of Tamura's stories. They have been placed ("left behind" is more literal) in the postwar situation with its difficulties and disillusionment and they find they cannot live. Neither can they die. They have seen and very nearly experienced death on the battlefield, and it no longer holds the Romantic sense of escape that it once did. Death is no better, but certainly no worse, than their lives as they live them.

In "Hōkai kankaku" the strands of sex and death are tightly woven, The dead man hangs in front of Oikawa while he hears sounds of life, of children playing in the street. Down the hall wives are cooking suppers for their families in the communal kitchen. He is gripped by the raw smell of fish being prepared for family dinners in the boarding house, the living smell of dead and dried fish in an apparent paradox: "He realized this smell was similar to the smell from one part of Shizuko's body. Something in his body was beginning to swell. Desire began to move, openly. Something was filling his body."[64] A dead body and the sounds of live bodies, the live smell of dead fish bodies mixed with the live fish smell, remembered from a woman's body. Death prompts desire, and that desire is described in sensual terms, yet Oikawa is stuck in the space between. Even as he remembers submerging himself in Shizuko's body, he finds the union, which is to be a liberation, to be a sham. The dissolution of sex promises liberation, through orgasm, which parallels the dissolution of death in his failed suicide attempt on the Chinese battlefield. Orgasm and death are both enveloped by the resilience of skin.

Oikawa Ryūichi remembers sitting behind a stable on a Chinese battlefield. A grenade is on his lap and his hand is on the pin. He then finds himself

> lying face down [and] a tepid something covers his face and he senses a moment of stickiness, as though his body has been forced into a liquid like glue, with nothing to grab onto. It seemed his consciousness and the fluids of his body were flowing together.[65]

This white stickiness resembles the nausea Sartre described; it is the stickiness of existence so prevalent in Noma's fiction, a clamminess many have found in his prose. It replicates the condensed milk heated up and passed around the small room as four students peer into the abyss of a Brueghel painting in "Kurai e," and is echoed as Fukami awaits that "something from outside, a great big something shooting out rays of light [that] would have to appear."[66] The sense of disintegration, the dissolution and dismemberment, introduced by these associations is both recoiled from and desired, like sex, like death, with both fascination and repulsion. Sex's orgasm provides a temporary release and respite, and its liberation is lost in a sticky glue, as white fluids are released in an orgasmic, hallucinogenic grenade explosion. Barriers break down and borders are obliterated in a vision of liberation suggesting that two individuals may connect with one another, but one also loses one's bearings. Such connected liberation is ultimately impossible and barren:

> Eyes respond to eyes, lips respond to lips, hands respond to hands and he felt himself sinking into her skin. His cheek submerged into her cheek, his face entered the center of her body, he buried himself in the pliability [of her skin]. At these times his consciousness was freed from all objects . . . and existence erases itself from its surroundings. [. . .] He is being submerged in a dark seething, a flash of light [. . .] His brain matter dissolves, disperses, loosens, and emits a dark hue, a yellow color. An expansive, wide skin rises in resilience to cover him. He sinks into that resilience and stretches his body to full length. There is not even the possibility of

the slightest obstruction here. He moves from the everyday world to an entirely different realm. He is being separated from this world. That resilience stretches [as a barrier] between him and this realm. It protects him. He moves from the everyday world to a separate world. With that he is free, he is liberated . . . But of course, it is a counterfeit freedom, a counterfeit liberation . . . He rebounds off that tensile strength, he finds himself being returned to life. But it is a false life . . . Yet the woman's skin envelopes him lightly. Her body, over a short span, provides to him a guarantee of his existence.[67]

The liberation he desires seems possible, yet it proves false, a sham. Like so many of Noma's characters, he gets so close he can taste it, but it is elusive and out of reach, ultimately prevented by the body which promised it and brought it into reach.

"Kao no naka no akai tsuki" ("A Red Moon in her Face")

Kitayama Toshio's experience in "Kao no naka no akai tsuki" ("A Red Moon in her Face," 1947) replicates the experiences of the characters discussed above. Kitayama finds himself attracted to the beauty of a widow named Horikawa but even more so to the ache and the pain he finds in her face, which are mirrored in his own soul. Shared pains consistently offer the possibility that two people may connect with each other, that two people may be some release from their own loneliness.

Kurako Horikawa, a widow, had a kind of painful expression on her face . . . [H]er face gave an impression of a slight distortion, for something had robbed it of the full and natural growth of life . . . Toshio Kitayama had to admit that the expression of that face gradually stole into the depths of his heart the more he saw her . . . He knew that her form, which seemed drenched in sadness, resurrected and drew out painful memories from his past. To be sure, her face had a beauty that resonated with the pain within him, yet he could not understand why her face nestled into his heart in this way. In any case, that face of hers touched him deeply.[68]

The loneliness he feels is reflected in the face of another and suggests a commonality and the possibility of freedom from the oppression he feels.

They ride the train together in another situation that offers the possibility of connection. They had been waiting and waiting but their train did not come. They board a train (Tokyo's Yamanote line) going the long way, the opposite way, around to their destination. The Yamanote line is appropriate, being the train that travels in a circle in central Tokyo: all Yamanote trains go to the same place, even when running in opposite directions. Since the Yamanote train line is circular, it is always going where it has already been, while going "nowhere." Around and around, this movement replicates the action of Noma's early stories, the futility of all action, and the circles of life and death; we also recall the circular holes and orifices in the landscape that open "Kurai e." On this train Kitayama looks at the widow's face and body in which reside pain and suffering like his own, suggesting the possibility of communication.

Kitayama Toshio saw Horikawa Kurako raise her head and look in his direction. Her pale face floated in the dimly lit space in front of him. He was staring directly into her face . . . he was sure that it was agony brought on by the war that he saw on her face. He thought how he would like, somehow, to enter into that agony. If, in a person like himself, there remained any truth or sincerity, he would like it to touch her agony . . . If, in that way, two people's hearts could face each other and exchange agonies, or, if in that way, two people could exchange secrets of existence, or, if a man and a woman could, in that way, show each other truth . . . then life would hold new meaning . . . But he realized that for him that sort of thing was impossible.[69]

It is impossible because in the end he cannot take the step off the train with the woman for whom he feels this attraction and affinity. He stays on the train to travel back/forward to familiar terrain, and the door closes between them, she on the platform and he still on the train. On the other side of the pane of glass in the door, the red moon that represents the past war spreads across her face, splitting it apart in the reflection in the glass and in his imagination. A pane of glass, a hard steely membrane, the experiences of the war, physicality, the taut barrier of skin, all ensure that two beings remain irrevocably separated. The past battlefield has made the self's aloneness and individuality only too clear and now obstructs the salvation that is in sight.

This is the original promise of contact and the original illusion: that feelings can be shared and that a relationship can be made based on those feelings. A promise is offered, but it cannot be fulfilled. One is left alone and the chasm cannot be crossed. As Watanabe Hiroshi has written of Noma's fiction, "Pain draws two people together but pain also prevents two people from connecting."[70] That original point of contact is the body, which seems to offer the salvation for which these men search. The desire for liberation prompts the desire to crawl bodily inside the body of the woman/Other, but her very body prevents it; her body's borders are firm, the skin that stretches between two people seals them in their individuality, in their loneliness. The body is all there is. Seeming to offer salvation, it imprisons them.

The returned soldier shuffles home from a dead-end job. He encounters the widow who is employed and has lived through the war at home, which brings their separate wartime experiences face to face. Kitayama's fear and timidity are the legacy of soldiering, but they also reflect the anxiety in the changed landscape of relations between a man and a woman. She was married, while he lost a lover in the war; she is not the virginal young woman he had fantasized about on the battlefield, and he is not the confident young man he was before. The ideals he searches for have disappeared on the battlefield, as have hers, on the domestic battleground. The symptoms of what we now call posttraumatic stress disorder manifest themselves as the battlefield past intrudes on his walks through the city and his postwar life. His flashbacks are always physical – people eating, struggling, loving – yet all connect to a horror of bloody dissolution. The freedom he can envision via a relationship with a woman is always thwarted by his body and the experiential baggage which forces itself into the present.

Noma Hiroshi's prose style

Nishikawa Nagao traces this inability to communicate to the war experience and its horrors. He explores how a writer like Noma feels compelled to write of those experiences but finds that the reality often lies beyond representation:

> Many of the writers of the postwar group [*sengoha*] felt that they had been assigned the fate of passing on their horrific experience in the name of those who had died, or in place of those who had died. But because their experiences during and after the war went beyond anything imaginable, it seemed practically impossible to relate that experience to those who did not share them.[71]

The attempt to capture and convey an unimaginable, and even inexpressible, reality via conventional methods led to Noma's convoluted prose and style. Miyamoto Yuriko follows her initially positive assessment of "Kurai e" with the criticism that it "still carries too much excess baggage. The surface of the prose is thick and clammy. It is unpleasant, like sweating in one's sleep."[72] It is as though Noma wishes to explore the "thick and clammy" quality of existence Sartre was attempting to articulate in such works as Sartre's seminal novel *Nausea*; Miyamoto's essay reads more like Roquentin's visceral response, in *Nausea*, to the "existence" he finds in a chestnut tree,[73] than a critic reacting to a fictional representation. Many of Noma's contemporaries found possibilities in this literary difficulty. Its "thick and clammy" quality, its very opacity and obscurity, seemed to permit articulation of the heretofore unutterable, the means to express the complicated feelings of the postwar experience. This quality was precisely the point, was exactly what was required for the difficult times, was precisely the expressive method needed that had not yet been hit upon. An oppressive sensation comes from paragraphs that seem to stretch the limits of the Japanese language. It is not only the description, but the rhythm and density of the prose itself that assails reason: clauses embedded in embedded clauses work with extended modifiers to stretch the reader's cognitive limits, making it almost physically impossible to form a coherent image. The descriptions are so abundant and the sentences and paragraphs so long that they present more information than the human brain can physically process. Perhaps this was the goal, to embody in the prose the irrationality of the times, to assail the reason, to underscore the difficulties posed to human understanding, to push physical limits. If so, the prose conveys, along with the descriptions, the complexity of the scenes described. Representative of initial reactions to Noma's "thick" style is the following reminiscence by Iwasaki Kunieda:

> I read this early collection of short stories in my high school library and was startled by the writing style that allowed for no intimacy, so different from the works I had been reading passionately every day. At that time I did not think about, nor use the word "style," but I do remember thinking how this work read like a thickly painted canvas.[74]

Even Honda Shūgo, whose praise of this work I have already noted, describes the style as one that "drags one to the depths of a muddy quagmire, that at places is thin and unclear, that at places bogs one down with its weight."[75] Nishikawa Nagao writes that it "shows [that] he thinks [*shikō*] through his body [*nikutai*] and internal organs."[76] This latter is exactly the sort of visceral response felt by many other readers as well, and it is a comment that practically repeats Sakaguchi Ango's comments on Sartre. "Kurai e" exhibits a visceral quality that reaches to the physical construction of the piece, right into the placement of the words on the page. It is the work most representative of this stylistic approach, yet only the initial paragraphs exhibit this obtuse thickness. Noma's later stories also differ in structure.

Noma's experimentation with phrasing and with European literary influences such as stream-of-consciousness was also understood as a technical breakthrough, a way out of the impasse many writers felt following the oppression and deprivation of the war. His often-convoluted prose and use of internal monologue show his debt to such writers as James Joyce and Marcel Proust. The Symbolism of Noma's literary apprenticeship under the poet Takeuchi Katsutarō is also visible in the prose of his descriptive passages. Noma used Symbolist techniques to very different ends, however: "There were various experiments after the war by writers attempting to describe sex from a new angle. Noma Hiroshi struggled very hard to bring together an ideology of the body [*nikutai no shisō*] via symbolism and realism," wrote Okuno Takeo.[77] From Joyce he borrowed a stream-of-consciousness narrative to forge a new literary idiom to represent the intellectual crises of this generation. From Proust he borrowed a method to describe and capture the inner workings of character. I have noted how the move from Symbolism to Marxism replicates the trajectory of Sartre's experience. Noma explained it this way:

> As to why I felt I had to take on the methods of Joyce and Proust as my own, it is because the manner in which they pursued the minute [details of their characters'] internal consciousness struck me as a method to liberate the contents of my own consciousness, bound within me by the oppression of the times and the suppression of the *nikutai*.[78]

Thus, "Kurai e" is often discussed as a work bringing together Symbolism and Realism, or uniting egoism and humanism, two conflicting forces in the work. "However you explain it, it is a work short on a sense of Japanese mentality, a work that has been obviously and heavily influenced by translated fiction,"[79] notes critic Furubayashi Takashi. Central to that experiment is an articulation of the individual body, the self constricted and oppressed within society, and the convoluted language contributes to that sensation.

While "Kurai e" is unusual in Noma's oeuvre for the extent of its Symbolist phrasing and convoluted style, such stylistic considerations would be of central concern for the rest of Noma's career. The first paragraph of "Kurai e" is rich with the repetition of adjectives, such as "heavy," "dark," and "sterile." As important as these are in determining the mood, the repetition of phrases signifying lack, however, contributes even more. We read, "There were no grasses, there were no trees, there were no buds." In each four- or five-syllable phrase, three are this "there were no . . ." repeated in a rhythmic cadence. The barrenness that characterizes the story is forcefully imaged in the first sentence and emanates from the repetition of this phrase. The sentence continues as *Fukisusabu kumokaze ga koryo toshite fukisugiru*, which is, in literal English, "The violently blowing cloud-wind blows desolately across [the land]." (And this is preceded by "There were no grasses, there were no trees, there were no buds.") This intertwined sentence is comprised of multiple modifiers. "Blowing" is the main activity of the sentence, and the modifiers work to ensure that it is a cold, barren blowing. Together they render an image of exceeding sterility. Further, the modifying "blowing" reflects the modified "blows" to form a circle of barrenness that sends the entire descriptive sentence rolling along like a tumbleweed. When this same sort of strategy is extended over longer expanses of prose, the sense of a difficult jumble is only heightened. In this way, the manner in which the landscape is described becomes itself a descriptive technique, and this characterizes Noma's much-discussed style. The initial chapters read like this, and these are the best known of the work. Exasperated readers have commented that these initial chapters are "absurdly overwritten" and "obscurely worded. . . it is hard to understand his sentences unless one rereads them." The sensation that seems written right into the prose gave a palpable Existentialist feel: the "thick" quality, the "sticky" quality of his prose.[80]

For all that, this work is not, technically speaking, a Symbolist work, but the influence is clear, and is integral to Noma's entire production. The reader is faced with a preponderance of images with no apparent referent repeated in mantra-like repetition. Thus, we get a sentence like the following, which Noma wrote as one complete sentence, early in "Kurai e" (Donald Keene's translation):

> When this art book with its photographic reproductions was exposed to sparks from an oil bomb, page after page of the pictures bound together caught fire in the bomb, charring and peeling in flames that were like some flowing black liquid, and the starfish-like people in the picture, the dog-faced people, the naked people with tails, the people who grasped the dark festering holes between their thighs as if they were something precious, were surrounded by the hot glow of a conflagration that no force, regardless of its size or nature, could hold back, and one after another they were burned to death by the little flames that had already spread under the paper; their flesh, so foul and hateful one could not contemplate it directly, was scorched, and their ugly bodies, convulsed into even uglier shapes by the fire contorting them, for a moment revealed themselves plainly in the flames of the burning paper, their lines standing out blackly like words written in invisible ink that have been brought out on charred paper; and when, moments afterward, these bodies too had turned to fire and disappeared, the whole city of Osaka, from the sky in the south to the sky in the north, was bright with the flush of burning flames, and a storm of engines swept across the sky, spreading heavy, minatory echoes that transmitted the imminent danger of death, and layer upon layer of thousands of giant heavy overlapping wings emitted a dull luster as they passed over the densely billowing fires towering over the streets which threw the whole vast city of Osaka into even more brilliant relief in their brightness; perhaps the groans of the people with those weird holes could then be heard somewhere

among the flames, as they faded away, crushed under the weight of the innumerable motors and the great engines sweeping across the sky.[81]

Noma writes as he does in order to describe a horrific scene. He pushes grammar and the limits of cognition (but does not transgress them). By forcing the reader to process the phrasing of a passage like that above, he achieves a replication, more than a description, of the oppression of the experience. The reader receives more than the situation that is described. If sense was not destroyed in the war, it very nearly was. Noma's style reproduces the attenuation of sensibility and relays it to the reader. He catches the sense of being pushed to the breaking point, not simply by the adjectives he uses in description but in the manner of description, as the sentences comprise an element of the description. His contemporaries felt they had encountered a style of writing that could replicate the assault on reason, a descriptive technique that recreated the sense of a humanity pushed to the breaking point. Noma is not trying to destroy grammar or sense (that had already been done by the war) but to duplicate the "sense of disintegration" he points to so clearly in that title.[82]

The original Japanese of these paragraphs, while exceedingly complex, is "grammatical," although at first it does not seem so. Noma has taken full advantage of particularly Japanese styles of modification and diction. In describing a collection of horrific pictures consumed by fire he communicated something much larger than the conflagration. Short sentences could have described that scene, but the long complex sentences provide much, much more. The stream-of-consciousness jumble that this yields can be related directly to his war experience. He writes as though expelling the phrasing in catharsis, pouring forth strong emotions that had been welling up inside him for a long time.

These experiments with phrasing and description come from a desire to overturn the literature of the past, repeating a novelistic impulse found in writers of the previous generation. Thus, while he concedes that writers such as Yokomitsu Riichi and Kawabata Yasunari had dealt with many of the same themes and issues, it was only in writers like Tolstoy and Dostoevsky that he could find methods and models he could use. That is, he had to go outside of the Japanese tradition to find models of expression appropriate to the task. He had long felt that Japanese literature lacked the methods for expressing his concerns. Nor does Noma stop with this, for when he discusses the motivations behind his work, and "Kurai e" in particular, he expresses his disgust with the literature that preceded him because it was unsupportive during the darkest hours of Japanese history. This is another way of saying it had no substance, that it was ethereal and ephemeral, echoing, thereby, the sentiments of other writers in this study. In a literary sense, Noma is always working against the tradition that he feels binds him, a tradition which precludes adequate description in novelistic form, and which crimps the sort of architecture he would like to construct for his novels, as he was to write:

As a high school student I read Natsume Sōseki, Shiga Naoya, Tanizaki Jun'ichirō, Yokomitsu Riichi, and Kawabata Yasunari. After that, I read foreign literature almost exclusively, then I read writers such as Kobayashi Takiji, Nakano Shigeharu,

Miyamoto Yuriko, Sata Ineko . . . However, as the War grew gradually increasingly intense, I began to feel very strongly that there was nothing in contemporary Japanese literature that could support the heaviness of war. There was not a single element in contemporary Japanese literature that could wipe away the anxiety, pain, and darkness wrought by the War. There was not a single thing that could well up from below in support and correct the contortions, defilements, and ugliness within myself . . . [My prose style] was a method to liberate the contents of a self-consciousness hemmed in by the self, by the pressure of the times, and by the oppression of the body.[83]

This is a powerful indictment of the literary past. This locution, "oppression of the times, the oppression of the body," reflects, among other things, a Proletarian/Marxist sensibility and concern for both the oppressed body of the exploited worker, and the oppressed body of left-wing writers jailed before the war. To speak of a "self-consciousness hemmed in by the self" also recalls the image of a soldier holding himself and his body fluids in by his skin. Further still, invoking phrases such as the "contents of a self-consciousness hemmed in by the self" also links back to the *watakushi shōsetsu* tradition, criticized by Marxists and Proletarians alike for its lack of totalizing vision, yet the phrase captures the sense of a self that has been forced back to a very small defensible area, as I noted earlier. The modern self was to have been liberating, yet again we find it marking its own seemingly unassailable final stronghold. Noma is searching for a way out of this claustrophobic structure, where the self finds itself restricted to the smallest possible area.

Noma claimed to have written "Kurai e" immediately after the war with no consideration as to who would read it. It is hard to imagine writing without an audience in mind, but he claims that the issue of readership never came to him: "I wrote this work trying to get in a single grasp all of those things that had piled up within me during the passage of the war years."[84] He describes the times as claustrophobic, a time when people and friends were separated and jumbled, when one was unable to share one's thoughts with others, when individuals felt under siege. He writes that he carried on internal discussions for years, honed and sharpened by the psychotic schizoid nature of post-Surrender Japan. These discussions became part of "Kurai e." The words (*kotoba*) of those internal debates are not single words but expressions and phrases, a private language almost (again, with resonances of Symbolist poetry) that strike a reader as difficult but, at the same time, carrying a singular descriptive power. The emotional force of the early paragraphs of "Kurai e" captured his early readers, and they credited him with being the first to get the feel of that disjointed age onto paper.

Wartime and war glorified the athletic healthy body while urging its suppression and control. Precisely because it was wartime, however, the body demanded a central focus:

In that idealistic age of the [Pacific] War, in that age when in the name of idealism the body was galloped off towards death, terms we find in Noma's stories – "incomplete," "anguish," "darkness," "twisted," "dirty," "ugly" – were forced onto the body. The body is foundational to individual existence, but in an age when it was forbidden, in any sense, to focus on the individual the body cries even more urgently, "I want to live."[85]

Like the other flesh writers of postwar Japan, Noma explores possible avenues for liberation through the flesh and carnality. He was unique among them for the centrality that Marxism held in his imagination, and the way he brought this ideology, together with his style, to bear on the questions of agency and human connectivity. The anti-government position of Marxism provided much structure to his fictional enterprise even as it often turned into another constricting ideology. His "thick and clammy" style gave his writing a physicality that was matched in the descriptions. The degradation of the body is portrayed in the fiction while the assaults on thinking are matched by the complex sentences. These explorations of the technical possibilities in fiction are brought up short by the barriers of skin that prevent liberating communication. Ideological barriers are proved insurmountable by both the ideologies and the bodies that promised a means to reach them.

5   Sakaguchi Ango

Introduction

Sakaguchi Ango made his mark in postwar literature with a series of explosive stories and essays. He wrote largely unhindered by concerns of rational consistency – or so it may first appear given his sometimes contradictory, often extreme, pronouncements. His apparently off-hand statements seem designed more for shock value than for reasoned discussion and can obscure his piercing intelligence. He enjoys an enduring reputation as an iconoclast, only too happy to tear down all structures, praising dry ice factories and penitentiaries more highly than ancient temples, and blithely suggesting that replacing Kyoto's ancient Hōryūji temple with a parking lot would be no great loss to the "Japanese." The electric power exuding from much of his writing energized the myth that came to be associated with his life of highs and lows, of troughs and crests, of irrepressible energy and obsessions. His confident disregard for existing structures and niceties of discourse, his frankness and forthrightness, blew fresh air into the confusing and stifling postwar years. His powerful prose and confrontational style exerted a profound influence on generations of writers.[1] His thematic focus on individuals who live according to physical and carnal demands unifies these works. His (male) characters protest – usually by ignoring – proper and sanctioned actions as they search for their own complete individual identity.

Ango's literary debut came in such prewar works as "Kaze hakase" ("Professor Sneeze," 1931) and "Kurodanimura"("Kurodani Village," 1931). His essay "Bungaku no furusato" ("The Birthplace of Literature") was published in 1941 and "Nihon bunka shikan" ("An Eccentric's View of Japanese Culture"[2]) appeared the following year. These are precursors to "Darakuron" ("On Decadence"), the 1946 essay most closely associated with his name and reputation. Never losing its power, "Darakuron" served as something of a manifesto for generations of readers. "Darakuron" and "Hakuchi" ("The Idiot") appeared in the same year, and these works were complementary and, even though the term "explosive" has been attached to most of the other work discussed in this volume, and much else after the war, these complementary works carried an explosive charge. Ango's writings were carried by protesting students onto the barricades of the 1960s protests and a recent "boom" marks another cycle in the Ango industry, with the publication of one more, new *Complete Works* (*Zenshū*).[3]

Ango's images and descriptions of postwar decadence became iconographic of the postwar cultural landscape and experience. His *daraku*, as "decadence," calls for a return to carnality and the body, and almost all of his work of the late 1940s makes the body a central theme. Ango's antidote to the war and wartime's propagandistic, essentialist, national culture is a return to the individual by a recovery of individual desires and needs, which he found necessary after decades of state oppression and control. Like Tamura Taijirō and Noma Hiroshi, he conceives of that individual in physical relationships which requires, in its structure, a sexualized woman as Other. In this situation especially, but in the human experience more generally, liberation of the individual is manifested by means of a "fall" from artificial strictures, a return to "decadence"; this is his famous *daraku*, and *daraku* comprises the representatively postwar, carnal imagery of *nikutai bungaku*. It is also "masculine" in many of the ways discussed in previous chapters, given how he locates liberation and identity in the body of a woman. (Because of the difficulty in given a satisfying translation – although I will discuss the term at length below – I will leave it in its original Japanese.) He advocates a return to the elemental in existence that can, for example, admit to finding beauty even in falling bombs. And, as I will further suggest, this body is the place from which one forges an individual identity.

His concern for the individual yields the most sustained articulation of the self found in the flesh writers. Like the others, however, his denial of ideology leads him, paradoxically, to construct one of his own. And, like the others, his characters effectively work to deconstruct his statements, for they become equally embroiled in a "liberating" ideology that produces ideological strictures similar to those they decry.[4] Basic to this return is a masculinist understanding of the individual that harkens back to a male imagined as active and assertive, even while this aligns to now-discredited militarist ideals. Ango records the anxieties of the age more powerfully than most, but the journey takes him to a place only slightly different from those he would dismantle.

The physical body in Ango focuses the elemental and provides the means for liberation; it maintains the means for *daraku*. The irony of his imagery is that the liberation and community of humanity promised by *daraku* leads to a place of solitude and dissolution of that individual, physical body.[5] The *daraku* he imaged in his writing style and characters is conceived of spatially, as the location of a radical loneliness and individuality. In contrast to Tamura Taijirō, Ango does not present a restored community. Individuals search for a geographical space that proves to be as lonely as any in which Noma's characters find themselves. One does not progress forward to the place of *daraku*, but must travel back and down, in a carnivalesque topsy-turvy approach to an ideal state. Individuals are required, indeed forced, to rely only on themselves and their bodies in this place. Nothing else exists and no assistance will come from outside. Further, in Ango's logic of the individual, a woman is requisite for the Other of identity. These issues combine to organize my analysis of Ango's writings: the individual within culture (the community); the location of the decadence that promises a fully developed individuality; the woman that forms the Other for identification within, and through, decadence; and a conception of the individual that follows from assumptions about the relationship between individual and national culture.

Philosophical considerations

At the heart of Ango's thinking is the meaning of the individual in culture. Following Karatani Kōjin's lead, I note first that the intellectual rigor that suffuses Ango's writing evidences his refusal to accept at face value the self-serving and essentialist definitions in vogue during the war.[6] Ango's ideal individual lives a day-to-day existence and responds, *should* respond, to immediate physical needs, rather than rational ideals. Individual identity, nonetheless, proves dependent on the group, even though he can be nearly anarchic – refusing to accept any outside organizational principles – in his conceptualization of the individual. Ango portrays individuals following their desires so that he can provide an antidote to both the ideology of the time and to essentialists. Individual desires are responses to the "necessary," and the desires congeal into cultural practices as individuals encountering the demands of everyday survival. This valorization of "necessity" develops from the wartime experience. Tired of battles and struggles, Ango wants unadorned simplicity. He offers the same response as Tamura and Noma: the proper and effective response (antidote) to wartime (totalitarian) society is to ignore a prescriptive ideal of culture and to follow the body's dictates, coded as "necessary" and "real." *Daraku*, in particular, with its nuances of physical carnality and depravity, emphasizes natural activity replete with sensual and carnal overtones.

As Ango describes the war and postwar experiences of deprivation, he posits an individual-focused everyday life as the best way to live. That is, the day-to-day instinctual struggle for survival that does not rely on "thought" is ideal. For example, he recounts surveying the bleak expanse of a bombed and destroyed Tokyo and finding no need to think; in this situation the most elemental "human" response was to absorb the beauty that existed, even in a time of great destruction and want. It is beautiful simply because it is *there*: "Wartime Japan seemed an ideal place, as though made-up, with a simple beauty opening into full bloom."[7] Tamura Taijirō began from a similar disgust with fabrication and a fascination with the vitality in survival as highlighted by his war and postwar experiences. Ango advocates a return to the "really" real following the disruption of the war and disillusion with the postwar, the years when one found that all the "truth" of the previous fifteen years had become lies, and vice versa, according to some "rational" fiat.[8]

These apparent contradictions – fulfillment in lack, splendor in destruction – allowed Ango to find beauty in the charred expanse of Tokyo neighborhoods that had been desolated by firebombings. He looks out over the destruction, trembling with fear, yet finds real beauty in the rubble. He peers across the Tokyo skyline as the bombs are falling and finds: "There was no need to think. There was only beauty; there were no people."[9] This also describes that place under the cherry blossoms as found, for example, in his important story "Sakura no mori no mankai no shita" ("Under a Forest of Cherries, in Full Bloom"), where a frightening and sinister beauty can be apprehended without any abstract rational thought. It makes no rational sense: if understood, it will be visceral; if complete, it is only in being empty.

No structures exist for processing or organizing this scene and this beauty; only the cold sterile wind blows (as it did in the opening phrases of Noma's "Kurai e").

No people live here and this contributes to the sinister lonely beauty. No people: there were, he writes, therefore, no thieves. He notes the incredible safety of wartime Tokyo where one could sleep without fastening doors or shutters. "It seemed almost a joke the way that wartime Tokyo was an ideal city, [where] a vacant beauty had bloomed."[10] Life was easy under the bombings, provided one did not think; that is, provided one proceeded on instinct and "natural" responses, following a logic of the body, and resembling a "Hakuchi," the woman of his tales who is incapable of rational thought.

Ango's characters respond naturally, i.e. physically, to their postwar surroundings, thereby denying the efficacy of the state and any group-based identity and highlighting the constructed and false nature of societies in general and the national project in particular. Ango insists in his writings that the postwar decadence – the often-lamented collapse of values many found in soldiers, who became illegal black marketeers and women who worked the street as *pan-pan* – reflects the truest and most basic of human drives for survival. In fact, he believes, the decadence was not something new, but a return to primacy, an enduring "fact" of humanity. The iconoclasm of such imagery, together with the call to action contained there, reiterates the destabilizing power of the individual body in the face of national agendas that Peter Brooks, for one, has identified (and I have previously discussed). Thus, for example, after writing in "Zoku darakuron" how the Japanese love of gardens and flowers represents Japanese culture's tendency to overlook the individual, Ango focuses on that overlooked individual as the source for a complete existence. "Decadence" provides the means to a complete liberated existence, yet it is not its goal. Rather, his interest lies in a life without self-deception, one aware of bodily needs and not constricted by manmade rules and false structures, especially, he writes, in our (Japanese) case where those structures were used by politicians and others for "grander" (i.e. wartime, authoritarian) agendas. Thus, Ango the voyeur peers across the cityscape as bombs fall and can record the excitement, even while acknowledging the "decadence" – the bad taste – of taking delight in such destructive fireworks. Perhaps there is indeed something beautiful about this incendiary display in the night sky, even if we do not usually admit it. He records the sight of fireworks, but with an edge, for this is no outing in the park of an evening; this experience at the border of life and death differs only slightly from the struggle for life and death taking place during the light of day; the charred bodies he sees in the park highlight the transgressive nature of living. Individual bodies are on the front lines of this war waged by nations; his imagery is intended to remind us that physical responses are primary and "natural." Such "facts," as "actual" bodily responses to stimuli, are presented as the "true."

The lack of concern that Ango extends to genre differences between essay and fiction derives from his interest in the "sense" of things, a reality that exists wherein one senses "something" that defies, and may even be destroyed by, rational description. "Sense" enters his lexicon at this point as he moves from an understanding based on rational systems to one of a physical logic relying upon the body's sensate capabilities. This helps explain his narrative style in which characters are not fully realized, but remain simply "people" – a man, a woman – in a practice reminiscent of premodern narrative, myth, fable, and *monogatari*. Characters develop as image rather than ideological or rational constructs, and they exist in their bodies, without need of the cerebral. They rarely have names, only attributes; attention is not given to their "personalities," i.e. *seishin*, but to the physical (*nikutai*). Ango's characters are not made wooden thereby, but the character development does suggest the less-defined characters found in folk tales. This use of, and affinity with, older traditions ties his work to "Japanese culture," a national identity, as one important basis for identity formation.[11] However, this predilection for a "premodern" style of narration suggests another paradox, because it shares much with narrative styles preferred by essentialists, Romantics, and others who wish to recover the (so-called) fundamental and unadulterated aspects of Japanese culture.[12] Ango gets caught in a chicken-and-egg dilemma because those older traditions and narrative styles, being so closely associated with essentialist "Japanese culture" theorizing, invoke the imagery of a preexisting national identity even as he insists that culture should be, can only be, created by individuals in their own particular historical situation. There seems more than representational equivalence here, for Ango apparently endorses these assumptions about individuals. Ango's use of lone individual characters leads to a heavy representational burden that must be borne by the men and women in his writing. While the particular imagery of his tales is rooted in postwar realities, style and setting suggest the past that those of nationalistic predilections configured as unique, which includes unstated, implicitly understood cultural forms of communication, taken as "commonsensical" to members of the (ethnic) group. These shared cultural norms are then mobilized into a basis for identity formation which cultural essentialists within Japan have often relied on: e.g. meanings and actions that only the Japanese can understand, thereby registering the boundaries of Japaneseness.[13] Such affinity carries risks, and though Ango may not have been entirely successful, he explored more completely than his contemporaries the prospect of using this sort of anti-rationality to escape the prefabricated structure of Western rationalism. In Alan Wolfe's words: "Ango's discussion of politics and history manages to do something that leftists found difficult to do: to rationalize or humanize Japan's past history, with its emperor and Bushidō, *without*, however, glorifying or romanticizing it."[14] The traditional past represented in the tea ceremony, Zen, dilettante painting, and samurai comes in for a degree of iconoclastic ridicule equal to that he levels at the militarists. Even so, I find that Ango reflects the idea of a substantive core of cultural identity integral to an essentialist understanding of culture.

Daraku: the decadence of the *furusato*

Occupying a central place in Ango's imaginary is the nostalgic home – the *furusato*. The *furusato* provides the setting for *daraku* and describes the topoi of the individual. The decadence and change bemoaned by many in the postwar only reflect the times, writes Ango, and not a fundamental change in people; those "changes" are only superficial. Nothing has changed at a more substantial level. Contemporary actions should come as no surprise because individuals have always responded in this "natural" way to adversity and new situations. Noble wartime ideals are quickly forsaken, not because people are shallow and debased, but because people must get on with life and the business of survival. Therefore, this "decadence" (*daraku*) is positive because it registers the human, virile response to the contemporary situation; it highlights the individual actor in society, claims Ango.

What exactly is *daraku*, the concept so central to Ango's work and writing? Kenkyūsha's *New Japan–English Dictionary* defines it as "depravity; (moral) corruption; degradation; fall." According to the encyclopedic *Kōjien*, *daraku* is "to fall, to not govern [oneself] morally, to be debauched." It is, in this way, usually defined in negative moral terms: retrograde, depraved, fallen, immoral, and so forth. Ango, however, wants to make it a positive concept, a return (by means of a falling) to the basics of existence, the most elemental and therefore "true" experiences. In "Darakuron," he argued that the "decadence" of postwar society represented the "truest" society, for example, suggesting that it was most closely aligned with "sense." Perhaps his inversion of directions makes it so striking: we are not being exhorted to strive upwards or forwards to discover the self or culture, but rather to descend and tumble back to that which is basic and necessary, to where we were before (and the opposite direction of most modernizing projects). Much of the power of "Darakuron" comes from Ango's assertions that the "decadence" he espouses is not something new to humanity, but is basic, and therefore to be celebrated as foundational. Ango makes much of this word "daraku" that suggests a falling, a slide from grace, a descent into the nether regions, from the high and mighty, a defection from reigning morals and societal strictures. What prevents us from being fully human is ideology, he claims: the various, capricious, and self-serving societal structures arbitrarily put into place by politicians and other authorities, the ethical systems enforced by tradition and society, urging people upward and forward to some "ideal." These systems distort and twist people by preventing them from being themselves; furthermore, he adds, they have been established for pernicious goals – a conformist culture to benefit armies and capitalists.

The most basic of desires were, for Ango as for Tamura, physical, but the wartime structuring of society directed attention away from their physical selves. Ango's images proceed from this understanding: the wartime structures of propaganda exhorted people to ethereal, spiritual values, and seemingly succeeded, at exactly the time when the physical was paramount, i.e. when daily existence was pared ever closer to the physical limits of sustenance by the unavailability of goods. The physicality of that experience led to a heightened awareness of one's individuality.

Daraku is the means to reestablish the individual. Ango offers clues to his concept of *daraku* in two essays that include the word in their titles: "Darakuron" and "Zoku darakuron" ("On Daraku" and "On Daraku, Continued," both 1946). The primary meaning is that offered above: a return to an "authentic" humanity by means of an exploration of the physical, especially the carnal, and achieved by awareness of and obedience to physical logic. *Daraku* gives one access to a complete humanity, a return to basic realities and conditions. It is an attempt to achieve authenticity by casting off pretension and false systems. One of the most succinct statements of this is found in "Zoku darakuron" (in phrasing that echoes writers discussed earlier):

I ask, what precisely is humanity and mankind? It is to desire unabashedly what one desires, it is forthrightly to declare unpleasant that which is unpleasant. In essence, that is the all of it: to proclaim forthrightly that which one finds desirable, to proclaim one's affections for the woman one is drawn to. It is to cast off the sham garments and the [wartime] slogans we wrap around ourselves: "doing all to preserve proper relations between subject and superior," "to forswear illicit relations," "to uphold the proper balance of duty and emotions." We must strip off these robes and bare our souls. The first condition to restoring our humanity is to look hard and close at humanity in its naked defenseless state. This marks the first step towards the true birth of individuals and of humanity.[15]

Daraku is a return to the elemental and Ango is, in Okuno Takeo's phrasing, "searching for the extreme, the limit." For Ango the individual self is that extreme object, the place where the contradictions between rationality and non-/anti-rationality, between ideal and physical worlds, between physical and spiritual, can be resolved. This is the search for *satori*, i.e. enlightenment, a place to unify all things, to assimilate all contradictions, a concept that Ango would have encountered in his college study of Indian philosophy. It is a form of enlightenment where one achieves awareness of the illusion of the reality we "see." (We also will find that this resonates with Ango's concept of the *furusato*, the place that is no place, where one finds the salvation that is no salvation.)

After the war, Ango suggests, humanity remained what it was fundamentally, only the surface of things changed; in order to return to that originary place, the surface now needs to be stripped away. In his subsequent essay, "Zoku darakuron," Ango invokes the imagery of clothing being cast off, to insist that the first condition for returning to a true humanity is to shed the false garments of constructed morality:

> We must become naked [as babes] and cast off the taboos that entwine us and search for our own true voices. The widows need to fall in love again and descend into Hell. The returning soldiers need to become black marketeers . . . If we don't rid ourselves of these false robes we will return to the sham country of wartime. This happens by betting [our entire holdings, i.e.] our bodies: searching for a surface prettiness will prevent us from reaching the inner reality. There will be nothing pretty and proper about this. It will take an existential gamble, betting with one's blood, with one's flesh, with the most basic of screams. When *daraku* is called for it must be complete and entire, thorough with no holding back. Only by approaching the gates of Hell will we be able to approach Heaven. Only when the nails of all ten toes and all ten fingers are smeared with blood, have been pulled out in the struggle, can we approach heaven. There is no other way.[16]

That struggle is the return to something natural, it is to break the artificial strictures and cast off artifice in order to become "true." It is also a lonely business, for we will be rebuked by family and friends. One has only one's self, one's body.

This *daraku* also contains Ango's hope for a new world: history begins when the soldiers return from loyal duty to the emperor and nation and engage in illegal activity as black marketeers; when widows who had pledged to remain faithful to their husbands, as a mark of loyalty to nation and family, actively search for new lovers after their husbands' deaths on the battlefields; when the emperor is deemed a mere human being.[17] The location of *daraku* resembles the nurturing womb, a place from which will be birthed, for the first time, a true and authentic humanity. The womb is also imaged in the Ango story/essay "Koi wo shi ni iku" ("Going to Make Love," 1947), where we get an eroticism that echoes the prewar writings of Tanizaki Jun'ichirō, in the figure of the desirable woman who is beautiful yet cold, teasing and inaccessible. She never tells the truth, never reveals anything of herself, and this seems only to add to the whiteness of her skin, her beauty, and perfection. This story, and the one to which it is a sequel, "Nyōtai" ("A Woman's Body," 1946), expresses a disgust with the body that is only flesh, *nikutai* only. The narrator of "Nyōtai" has gone to Nobuko to confess his love. (Her name, Nobuko, is a parody of herself: 信子, where the first character of the pair signifies belief and faith, for there is nothing trustworthy about her. She is a flirtatious tease.) Nobuko is nothing but physicality and she prompts him to the discovery that "What we call woman is a thinking body (and nothing else)" ("Onna to wa, shikō suru nikutai de ari").[18] He wants to form a sack to contain all of her and then incinerate the entire thing, suggesting the atavistic return to the womb. She is the *genjitsu* or "actual" as opposed to the *nikuyoku* (the "desires of the flesh"). Her physicality is "real." This set of images conflicts with the liberating power of the body that Tamura and Noma portray. It captures some of the contradiction that one senses in Ango, for this woman's body is the object of both reverent awe and morbid fear. Violence to the women with such bodies will be suggested again in other works.

Without *daraku*'s journey down and back, goes the argument, we usher in the situation that initially invited the militarists. Only in *daraku* can humankind discover the means to authenticate humanity and prevent such a relapse. It is in service to this thinking that Ango developed some of his most powerful and controversial images. As has been noted already, Ango intends these images to be positive, even though the situations he describes were often taken as evidence of the immorality and spiritual decay of postwar society: soldiers become black marketeers; war widows find new loves; and old generals who had spouted patriotic platitudes in war about the nobility of death and the fearlessness with which one should meet the enemy, urging suicide rather than the humiliation of being led in chains before the enemy in service to emperor and nation, now wet their pants when led into war crimes trials. For Ango, these generals are at last revealing their "humanity" and fear of death – in addition to which, the emperor himself has now declared that he is human.

Thus, we find that individuals revert to the basic and elemental (*daraku*) and reveal their intrinsic humanity – they are people who do not wish to die, who will do what is necessary to survive, and only want peace, affection, and simple pleasures. Ango shows how people love people, men are attracted to women, and individuals follow their own desires, all without regard for the complex structures and taboos that are established by national ideologies. All return to the elemental and become, or at least reveal, their true humanity. That is, the war and postwar experiences made people "decadent" by revealing their "true" elemental natures.

Ango is not suggesting, however, a simple wallow in carnality, as much of the aura surrounding his work might suggest. The psychological power and astounding contemporary appeal of this writing is that it helps make sense of the self-loathing that accompanied the postwar years, a time when people were forced to transgress the morals and ideals they had taken to be sacred and upright. Karatani posits that the opposite of *bungaku* (literature) for Ango is not politics but reality (*genjitsu*). Ango tries to capture the war experience, and does so in a very powerful manner, but not by faithfully, or "realistically," describing what took place. This is part of his power and his accomplishment. All the writers I am considering are searching, in some way, for descriptions of war and postwar realities, but go about the task differently. A duality of the authentic and inauthentic, paralleling the dialectic of spiritual and physical, runs through Ango's writings. He pursues the "real," in the sense discussed above, but not necessarily "realistically."

The spiritual values of official rhetoric contrasted with the lived reality of wartime and postwar Japan. At that time, buying foodstuffs meant evading the police, because basic items were available only on the black market. Obeying the law was to invite starvation.[19] Law-abiding citizens who had dutifully followed the dictates of the government in wartime found they must become criminals in order to survive. "The sense that we were doing something we shouldn't welled up inside us," writes Okuno.[20] That is, Ango's call to decadence reflects the postwar experience wherein survival is an act of transgression or, as I noted in previous chapters, as explained by Kuno Osamu and Tsurumi Shunsuke, survival forces one to be a traitor and a heretic – *tenkōsha* – suggesting that all postwar Japanese are *tenkōsha* and, by extension, Existentialists, because of these facts of existence.[21]

Transgression marked the reality of postwar life. Its physicality was not only inscribed on the treks to the black market for everyday food supplies – packed trains, body searches – but with the renewed interest in sexuality as well. Tormented by the sense that they were, already, depraved and decadent, despite all good intentions and noble aspirations during the war, many Japanese found they were now outlaws and transgressors. "Darakuron" reflects such realities, but insists that this "decadence," and the activities that foster such guilty feelings, are only natural. It legitimizes the responses to postwar realities. As Ango wrote, it was not the war making people decadent, for people were "decadent" prior to this. We are decadent because we live; in order to live we must be "decadent" for this decadence is simply another definition of humanity. Such "decadence" is simply living according to the needs of the individual. Ango's statements thus afforded a sense of salvation, a sense of desperate freedom: we needed this affirmation of our decadent lives, insists Okuno. Ango's hearty affirmation of this lifestyle was itself a comfort and an endorsement.[22]

Essay: "Darakuron"

The first essay to discuss these issues in depth, "Darakuron" ("On Decadence"), is likely Ango's best-known work. The themes articulated in this essay reflect those consistent throughout these and subsequent writings. The opening paragraphs set the tone with their valorization of the individual and the body of carnal desires and continue by developing the relation of this individual to the state and national culture:

Six months pass and nothing seems the same.

"We, the humble shields of our Sovereign Lord, march forth." "We are resigned to die at his Majesty's side and never look back." These young men, the kamikaze, did die, scattering like the cherry blossoms. Those who escaped with their lives, though, now peddle goods on the black market.

"We dare not hope for long lives together. And yet we pledge ourselves to you who will one day sally forth as his Majesty's humble shields." It was with admirable commitment that these young women sent their men off to war. Six months later, though, they're only going through the motions as they kneel before their husbands' mortuary tablets – and it won't be long before they've got their eye on somebody new. It's not people that have changed; they've been like this from the very start. What has changed is just the surface of things, the world's outer skin.[23]

Soldiers conforming to the most elevated of wartime admonitions have now "sunk" to illegal, black market activities, complain the commentators; these are the activities of individuals committed to getting on with life, Ango responds. People have always done what was needed to continue. Ango's ironic quotation of the lofty phrases of the *Man'yōshū*, the eighth-century poetry collection regularly invoked in militarist admonitions, underscores the parodic pointedness of his rhetoric. Nothing has changed: the misguided years, when people followed lofty platitudes rather than the natural dictates of life, constitute the source of the problem. The war years were not some ideal situation from which they have now fallen. Postwar decadence merely reflects the natural response. This ability to follow natural desires in the everyday struggle for existence and survival, Ango stresses repeatedly, is what had been lost in wartime emphasis on idealized responses. Wartime ideology stressed humility and service to the sovereign. Soldiers' postwar involvement in illegal marketing and trade is hypocrisy in terms of this ideology, but a practical necessity for survival, and entirely in keeping with the human response to natural needs. The women who publicly pledged to remain faithful to their patriotic husbands even if they become war widows have quickly become perfunctory in their mourning. They have even taken to thinking of other partners. Ango's point is that this is how it *should* be, because this is how people *are*. There is nothing "immoral" – or even unexpected – in this. The state has been wrong in imposing such "noble" but essentially artificial and ethereal, insubstantial, ideals. We find here the concerns underlying the "literature of the body": disgust and impatience with the artificial trappings of society, in particular the manipulative state that has seduced and made a mockery of the individual by its abstractions, ideologies, and propaganda. In Ango as well, the response is a celebration of the concrete and the physical as the individual responds to the needs of a carnal body.

Ango's power and importance come not just from this call for decadence: that is an old theme that has been written of throughout history. What is unique to Ango's writing is the vibrancy of his splendid descriptions of the postwar situation and people's actions during these years. The soldiers turned black marketeers, the bravery of war widows, the response of the common people who had been burned out of their homes, gave his writing an immediacy for his readers, for he described postwar life as it was being lived. For example, in the story "Hakuchi," a man and his daughter sit on a packing trunk in the park looking for all the world to be having a summer picnic, yet the scene is jarring when our gaze is turned to the corpses lying on the ground nearby. Off to the side, a group of young girls are laughing in the midst of charred ruins. During wartime it had been forbidden to treat such situations realistically, even as many were experiencing them. Ango's descriptions, at odds with the official versions, accorded with the lived experience of his readers.

These postwar themes were not, however, new to this age, nor, for that matter, to Ango. As Karatani Kōjin notes, the only difference between the postwar "Darakuron" and Ango's wartime "Nihon bunka shikan" ("An Eccentric's View of Japanese Culture") is the former's attack on postwar "ideological fabrications" and illusions. "Nihon bunka shikan" reads like a postwar document – which Karatani long thought it was. The spirit and intent are consistent across these too easily separated periods. Here, too, Karatani notes that "*daraku*" does not simply mean working the black market or surviving as a *pan-pan*, but getting to that which is elementally individual and physical. Thus, of the flesh writers, Ango feels, after close readings, the most "philosophical," meaning in this case the most closely argued and consistent, even though initial readings give the opposite impression. *Daraku* corresponds to the primal place, the *furusato*; it is not simply an excuse for carnal debauchery or for a pandering eroticism, but marks a thorough exploration of identity wherein one has been brought up against one's physical limits, pushed to that place where one has only oneself and one's most basic – therefore most "real" – desires. In fact, Karatani finds that Ango's use of *daraku* places him at odds with the "decadent writers" (the *buraiha*), with whom he is often grouped. His tales of relations with women are not to celebrate a decadent lifestyle as such, nor are they the cerebral, elegant eroticism of Tanizaki Jun'ichirō and Nagai Kafū; rather, they "put flesh on his intellectual coup d'état" of subverting the official order.[24]

At home in the *furusato* of decadence

In "Bungaku no furusato," Ango singles out for discussion the "sense of cruel beauty" of the oldest Red Riding Hood tales; not those that offer a final resolution where good wins out and grandmother and filial granddaughter are reunited, but where the little girl is eaten by the wolf. At the moment she is snapped up, claims Ango, one senses a contract being broken: we feel left out in the cold, left behind and forsaken. The shock of these tales – he conducts a similar analysis with a Kyōgen tale and with one from the *Ise Monogatari* – forces our eyes open to see ourselves as we really are: alive, vulnerable, and alone. This wide-eyed realization marks a *daraku* (which could also be read as a tale of Buddhist *satori*: one receives a smack on the head from the preceptor monk and is shocked into enlightenment). Enlightenment means many things in Ango's writings: arriving at the *furusato*, the place of basic truth, the cold lonely expanse of the self, that one reaches by *daraku*, a return to what we always were. The *furusato* is the place of *daraku* and returning to it follows the directional logic of *daraku* of "back to" and "down to" the location of authenticity.

The *furusato* proves to be a place of extreme loneliness, for nothing exists there but one's own body. There we find individuals working out their existence through action that is not based on rational thought. The *furusato* is the location of the radical loneliness of existence, represented in Ango's work as the barren moors and plains one wanders in search of liberation, hoping for liberation without any basis for that hope, even while aware that the place of salvation is not to be found. One is condemned to search for it nonetheless. This geographical sense of place, rather than a state of mind, marks the location of Ango's liberation and enlightenment. Only in the realization that no salvation (*sukui*) exists is a salvation possible. (Here again, we find the overlap of Existentialist themes in this work.) This realization takes place at the birthplace (*furusato*) of literature, which is the birthplace of individual persons as well, being the place where one finds oneself.[25] One finds oneself in this lonely place after being reduced to the most elemental state, often following a search for liberation; yet having arrived in this place of extreme solitude, salvation and relief are nowhere to be found. The space represented by this *furusato* appears throughout Ango's writings and is a key tying them all together. Yet "salvation" proceeds from apprehending the truth (aloneness) of this situation. It also describes the situation of literature (in a passage I quoted earlier):

> Literature is always a revolt against the system, and against politics, a revenge [waged against] human systems. Even so, it is via this revolt and this revenge that it cooperates with politics. Revolt is, itself, a form of cooperation. It is affection. This is literature's role [*unmei*], it is the unchanging relationship between literature and politics.[26]

Ango thus acknowledges the need for the excluded element of an ideological Other, even as the revolt against it is structurally necessary. This strikes me as one of Ango's prescient statements. He seems to acknowledge that the state has need of him in his role as iconoclast, and the established system is dependent on protest to the same degree that protest writers need to make such statements. He expresses an irony absent in Tamura, who used his fiction to protest the hold that state powers have on the body, yet did not construct a position external to the system of power. Ango addresses both sides of the circularity that has plagued these writers, where the attempt to undermine ideology only results in the constructing of one's own. Tamura's resistance, for example, was found to be firmly enmeshed in the existing power structures and, indeed, reproduced them. The protest reconfigured the source of protest in a manner that Foucault leads us to expect, as I suggested in the introduction. Foucault articulated the circularity that results when one structure is demolished and another raised, writing how the body is "directly involved in a political field; power relations have an immediate hold upon it; they invest it, mark it, train it, torture it, force it to carry out tasks, to perform ceremonies," continuing, "Where there is power, there is resistance, and yet, or rather consequently, this resistance is never in a position of exteriority in relation to power."[27]

Ango's women inhabit the *furusato* that, even as it seems to offer the primal community for his characters and to serve as the location for *daraku*, invariably proves exceedingly barren and lonely at the same time. In Ango, too, we find this place of self-construction is always a place where the individual is threatened with destruction and dispersion. At the moment when the self is constructed, it disintegrates, in a form of Buddhist enlightenment (*satori*). Loneliness that one must endure, the angst that results from the realization that there is a morality in amorality, salvation in the knowledge that there is no salvation, are repeated themes in Ango's writings. The moral is that there is no moral: we have seen this in the jarring scenes in the old Red Riding Hood tales in which the wolf snaps up Little Red Riding Hood, and in old Kyōgen tales. There is also the incident found among Akutagawa's posthumous papers – an old farmer comes to Akutagawa with a manuscript telling a dark tale about a poor family torn between raising another child and struggling against starvation, or killing the child so all could live fuller lives, with enough to eat. "Could such a thing take place?" asks a stunned Akutagawa; "Hell, I did it," replies the farmer and disappears. This disturbing resolution deposits one at the elemental originary place that is the *furusato*, the cold slap in the face that follows a broken contract, even as the chilling wind of realization whips past.

> At that point I can't help but think that "there is no morality" or "we are left on our own" is not [alone] the stuff from which literature is made. Yet it seems that in this path of life we come across impediments just like this that seem meaningless. And there it is: there is no morality; this fact itself becomes the moral.[28]

This is a truth that we come up against in life; it follows, then, that it is not antithetical to literature. Indeed, Ango suggests, this is the place from which literature must be constructed. Without some sense of this truth, literature is not possible.

And yet, Ango's works often turn on the point of a man's powerlessness to care for the women (and children) in his charge. Most of the men in Ango's work are ineffectual, rendered powerless in the postwar crises. In "Hakuchi" for example, a young man confronted by the constrictions and meaninglessness of society is saved by a woman who knows and understands only the physical. The woman who saved Izawa is less equipped, in most senses, given her handicaps, to deal with the everyday world than he is; nonetheless, she opens another plane of existence to him via her sexuality. Likewise, the bandit of "Sakura no mori no mankai no shita" ("Under a Forest of Cherries, in Full Bloom") is presented as a "reasonable" fellow (albeit a burglar) with a stable family group until a beautiful woman from the capital usurps his role as strong controlling male: one of the first acts of the new wife is to have him kill off his former wives. Whether starting from strength or weakness, the crises of action mark the central crises of the stories.

Referring to such places as the *furusato* introduces another level of irony that helps dilute the essentialist associations. The Japanese *furusato* usually represents "home" and is associated with a warm inviting place, one's family birthplace, the seat of the familial unit Ango castigates, the nexus of family–state ideology (*kazoku kokka*). Ango's is precisely the opposite: a frigid place of extreme loneliness and isolation, of howling wind and snow, of madness and dissolution, where the moral is only that there is none. The place where one can find oneself is "extreme loneliness pregnant with life itself" as Ango phrases it in "Bungaku no furusato,"[29] the space under the cherry trees described in his important story, "Sakura no mori no mankai no shita," or a quiet marshy place encircled by forest deep in the mountains.[30] While the traditional Japanese *furusato* promises the nurturing place where one is surrounded by family, the home one returns to for the holidays, Ango's proves devoid of people, particularly the very family and friends that usually bestow on a *furusato* its meaning. One can rely on no one for enlightenment but oneself; one often finds no one else there. The path of *daraku* is solitary and lonely; the end of this path, the *furusato*, is equally lonely. One of the most basic aspects of *daraku* is solitude, as Ango writes elsewhere: "One will be overlooked by others, will be ignored even by mother and father, it is a fate that demands one rely on the skills of none but oneself."[31] (He notes, however, that although this loneliness is the cradle of our existence, the *furusato*, it is not necessarily the only topic worth writing about, for we start from there and grow beyond it. Nonetheless, writing which does not reflect this awareness is not trustworthy.[32])

In these "amoral" (Ango's word) endings is a moral: nothing is certain. Being left behind, cast off, at a loss because what had been promised is undelivered, leaves us duped, and the unexpectedness of this hits the reader (hearer) with great force. A painful heart-rending *furusato* remains, with a sense of great quietness, frigidity, and transparency. This *furusato*, this goal, has the unearthly spirit of Buddhist enlightenment, where all contradictions dissolve. This is also Ango's parry to the essentialists: he deflates premodern values as equally bankrupt and artificially constructed as any current ones, as any that took Japan into war, by his language of reversal. Within the realization of amorality and abandonment arises a calm beauty. In being lost, we are found. The central question arises when faced with these situations: what am I to do when I should flee but I cannot? At this moment in "Sakura no mori no mankai no shita" the main character disperses, literally to the four winds, soon after being aided – it seems – by the woman who is his traveling companion, in a Buddhist sort of absurdity that underscores Ango's amalgam of East and West. Buddhist metaphors follow close on the heels of a Kierkegaardian Christianity.

Liberation in the body of a woman

> Recently I have found something that gives me some respite from the horrors of existence and Hell: I am no longer kicked around by the gods nor by the demons, I am no longer stripped of my robes, having my hair pulled, and I can even think about the possibility of an existence without great trials and accidents. What has given me this peace of mind is a single woman. There is not much to recommend her: she is vain and none too bright, and lacking any concept of reliability or fidelity . . . there is nothing external about her that I like. It is simply her body [*nikutai*] that attracts me.[33]

Such is the power of the *nikutai* and the promise in the body of a woman. No surprise then that in "Sakura no mori no mankai no shita" the woman leads the burglar to the quiet *furusato* under the blossoms, for Ango "discovers his *furusato* in the body [*nikutai*] of a woman."[34] (Such could be said of all the flesh writers. Women represent an idealized existence, a life that responds to the physical, unencumbered by rationality and thought.) She exhibits neither hope nor even any thought for tomorrow; she embodies unencumbered life under the bombs. Many of Ango's women appear bearing the promise of liberation, like Noma's Beatrice, who will guide us to the place (*furusato*) of liberation. Ango's women disappear, at times turn into hags, or lead us to dissolution ("Sakura no mori no mankai no shita"). As he describes her in "Watashi wa umi wo dakishimetai," he embraces the woman only to find he is embracing a some-thing, a nothing, that is simply cold, beautiful, empty, heart-wrenchingly sad in a way separate from the sexual disappointment of her frigidity (to use a word consistent with Ango's imagery). Again, we encounter a woman who, by the lack signified in a dark space, embodies the promise of release and fulfillment. This woman's vacant body, even when dissatisfying, feels and embodies purity. There are times, we read, when "I am overcome by the ability of this purity to release my indecent soul."[35] Her emptiness and purity purge his filth, save him. "I discover, in the body [*nikutai*] of a woman who cannot feel sexual fulfillment, my own *furusato*. In that emptiness where exists no hint of fulfillment, my heart is cleansed."[36] Woman as spiritual and physical cleanser has been described by all of these writers. Yet the woman to lead him is an illusion, and she always disappears:

> The more carnal desire I feel, the more it seems that the woman's body becomes transparent. This is because her body does not feel any sexual pleasure. This desire has me very excited, at times makes me giddy, at times causes me to despise this woman, at times I love her more than anything. But since the only one who is stimulated is me, there is no response [from her]; what I find myself loving is that solitude, that desolate shadow [*kage*] which I am embracing.[37]

She is associated with that space, the lack, a mere shadow (*kage*). She represents the *furusato*, the place that is *no* place, for to embrace this woman is to embrace a vacancy. Embracing the chilling, beautiful, empty body fills him with the deep sadness associated with the space beneath the cherry trees. While the space marked by the cherry blossoms should leave one comforted and "at home," that *furusato* is empty and void, just like the woman's body. Yet in embracing this body of lack he finds a refreshing cleanliness. Paradox becomes conundrum. This woman finds no physical pleasure in sex. Living as an entertainer, a prostitute, she survives by providing physical pleasure with her body. Yet, like the woman from "Hakuchi," she lacks the intelligence for the emotional/mental pleasure that follows from love and affection. She lives by treating her body as a commodity, a mechanical toy. Yet, for him, her body is the location, the motivator, and the goal of existence. The narrator has come to feel great affection for this woman's body that is deformed because he finds there an unusual responsiveness. This makes it a body that has been abandoned by reality. "[Thus,] I have the sense that it is not a woman's body that I am embracing but water that is in the form of a woman's body that I am embracing."[38] He embraces "her" but she seems not to be there in any "real" way.

Yajima Michihiro notes in his comments on Ango's essay, "Watashi wa umi wo dakishimetai" ("I Want to Embrace the Ocean"), that the only thing that Ango desired after the war was the body (*nikutai*): "That body was without volition, emotionless, a mannequin. At the same time that body had to be isolated and lonely, anguished [*setsunai*]. This isolated anguish comprised Ango's foundation [*furusato*] of litera-ture."[39] That is, the woman that he desired could only give; she received nothing from him, rendering her oddly like a god (*kami*). She needs nothing and she gets nothing

emotional from him. She barely "knows" he is there, yet she gives him the salvation and
rest he desires. She gives what he prays for and takes nothing in return.

Fiction: "Hakuchi" ("The Idiot")

Ango's short story "Hakuchi" forms a fictional complement to "Darakuron" by
expressing equivalent ideas in the language of fiction.[40] Appearing almost simultaneously, the two works were taken as part of a single package, the story providing a
complementary fictional treatment to the essay's themes.[41] The anguished, lonely, and
unresponsive female body was necessary for his characters to feel connected to the
world. This is the woman of "Hakuchi" who lacks even a name, who is quite literally
nikutai only, without a cerebral component, being, as the title indicates, mentally
handicapped and without speech. As such, she represents the individual distilled to the
most elemental of components, the most human, the carnal, as revealed in crises such
as falling bombs. Only basic desires, instincts, and natural human responses remain in
this bleak Tokyo. Indeed, the only "sensible" reaction is one that does not incorporate
rational sense at all but follows fleshly physical demands. This description characterizes
the chaotic postwar years and also describes an integral part of his plan to reconstitute
humanity. The fact that this sensibility is shared with so many of his contemporaries,
that so many who have come through the war expect to find liberation and release in an
emphasis on the carnal and the physical, underscores how important and central this
conceptualization was to his readers. The first paragraph of "Hakuchi" describes the
location where this crisis and liberation are realized:

> Various species lived in the house; human beings, a pig, a dog, a hen, a duck. But
> actually there was hardly any difference between their style of lodging or in the
> food they ate. It was a crooked building like a storehouse. The owner and his wife
> lived on the ground floor, while a mother and her pregnant daughter rented the
> attic. The daughter was pregnant, but no one knew who was responsible.[42]

Humans are of a species not unlike pigs, dogs, and ducks. This story explores and
pushes at that fine line between man and beast. Like Ōe Kenzaburō, Ango proposes
that there is no substantial tenable distinction between animal and human, or between
sense and body.[43] The central character, Izawa, has recently come to this neighborhood
to live. Shortly thereafter,

> Among the ruins of the great air raid of March 10, Izawa had also wandered aim-
> lessly through the still rising smoke. On all sides people lay dead like so many roast
> fowl. They were neither gruesome nor dirty. Some of the corpses lay next to the
> bodies of dogs and were burned in exactly the same manner, as if to emphasize
> how utterly useless their deaths had been.[44]

One day he returns from work to find a woman cowering in a closet in his apartment.
She is an "idiot." She cannot speak but can show physical desire.

From that day the feeble-minded woman had been no more than a waiting body with no other life, with not so much as a scrap of thought. She was always waiting. Merely from the fact that Izawa's hands had touched a part of her body, the woman's entire consciousness was absorbed by the sexual act; her body, her face, were simply waiting for it . . . When it came to the question of what the woman was thinking about when awake, Izawa realized that her mind was void. A coma of the mind combined with a vitality of the flesh – that was the sum and total of this woman.[45]

She is more than animal, but it is not clear to what degree she (or anyone else) is different. The "human" aspect of physical needs and desires is nearly indistinguishable from the "animal." She is a person, yet her desires are entirely physical, and her humanity is evidenced in her physicality. Her consciousness is hard to locate, so she is a supreme example of the individual as *nikutai*. We know from her desires that she is closer to something fundamental in the human experience. The narrator is moved from his ennui to action by the physical relationship she initiates. Words are of no account to her, the physicality of sex is sufficient: "There was no alternative but to come down to her level," thereby repeating the downward movement of *daraku*. It is parallel to the desire expressed in "Watashi wa umi wo dakishimetai," in which the narrator finds himself wishing for a doll that does not speak, a woman in whom he can submerge himself and be liberated, and thereby be fully constituted.[46] Another paradox: this is all he needs to feel complete even though her mental handicap suggests incompleteness. At the same time this state is like a permanent *furusato*: "Izawa began solemnly, 'The *nikutai* is not the only way to express feelings. The ultimate abode for us human beings is the *furusato*, and in a strange way you seem to be living permanently in such a *furusato*.'"[47]

The inhabitants of this postwar neighborhood are all decidedly carnal; all of them live lives immoral by any prewar or wartime criteria, but fully "logical" in the postwar situation. This contrast would not have been lost on Ango's audience: the wartime setting of this story describes the postwar situation where none of the old rules hold any longer and the noble ideals of the spirit have been proven a sham. The "logical" action contains nothing of the cerebral. Daily life is one where the concerns of the flesh are foremost, the only ones of any importance, the only ones worthy of concern. One of the women in the neighborhood is now pregnant, but the father is not known. She had been given lodging in the neighborhood association's office, and all the "morally upright" officials have slept with her. The result of the carnal act – her pregnancy – is visible to all in the way all things are now known, in "the flesh," i.e. her expanding belly. Ango never fails to highlight the ironic contradictions, pointing out the hypocrisy of a wartime ethos in which the neighborhood association – charged with overseeing all activities in the neighborhood from food rationing to air raid drills, a de facto government surveillance post – is complicit, literally to a man, in these carnal transgressions.[48] Again, the office from which these policies were handed down is the place where she was impregnated by men who transgressed the moral order they were to uphold.

Many of the tenements in the neighborhood are rented out to prostitutes and, "Since these women had no children and since they were all inclined to keep their rooms neat, the caretakers did not mind about the disorderliness and immorality of their private lives." There was also here a "soldier of fortune from Manchuria, who proudly boasted that his profession used to be murder."[49] All of these images underscore a favorite theme for Ango, that below the surface of an orderly bourgeois society, especially during the war, thrived this sort of decadence of lives lived according to the demands of the flesh and the need to survive. The outward orderliness preferred by the state, a proper *seishin* to support the war effort, merely whitewashed a carnal reality. When the state's order had been shown to be false, the carnal reality reasserted itself.

The woman who saves Izawa, awakening him from his slumber to the meaning of his humanity, is entirely in keeping with the masculine vision of the saving woman we have seen thus far. The woman is nameless, characterized as *nikutai* and sex object only. As Okuno reads the story, "Hakuchi" may be the first work of its kind in Japanese history to be so liberated in its descriptions of sex; it definitely set the tone for all subsequent postwar literature. This is the first work to show sex not as dalliance (*asobi*), as emotion or lewdness, but as a way of thought (*shisō*). Ango revealed the extent to which the quiddity of humanity (*ningen no jishitsu*), the natural beauty, could be taken up as a theme in this context. This story offered the possibility of a method for treating, in fiction, the physical body that had been torn to pieces during the war.[50]

Even so, the characterizations are revealed to be as misogynistic as those in another brilliant Ango short story, "Sakura no mori no mankai no shita." We find again the structure that attracted him: a man alone – here among cherry blossoms (a seeming evocation of the traditional and sedate) – meets a beautiful and bewitching woman. He is a mountain bandit who attacks travelers who wander too close to his lair, appropriating their possessions and, if it suits his fancy, the women traveling with them. He has amassed a sizeable collection of both. He is ruthless, yet only the cherry blossoms provoke fear in him – until, that is, he collects an especially beautiful woman during one of his forays. He finds himself helpless before the sensual flirtatious woman, who drives him to murder and near madness; she is later revealed to be a witch, a harpy, and a whore. When she leads him to the lonely place under the blossoms where he might conquer his fear, she seems to be leading him to the *furusato*, the place of liberation. But she transforms into a demon and then, in the disorienting swirl of cherry blossoms and frigid howling wind, vanishes. He reaches after her, towards the woman who knows only her own flesh and its desires, and she follows them without restraint, and watches himself dissolve right behind her. The woman takes him to a place where nothing exists, and disappears into emptiness. He reaches out to follow her, and finds he is disappearing as well. Again, she is the woman familiar in this fiction, the illusory guide who will lead the man to liberation. The nirvana of physical liberation that her physicality promises does not exist either; it evaporates, here, in a mirage. The alluring woman destroys the man who follows her, even as he thinks she leads him to salvation and reconstitution.

To paraphrase what Ango had written in "Watashi wa umi wo dakishimetai": So I ask myself, what is true joy? And then it came to me. True joy for me would be to fly through the sky like a bird perhaps, or to become a fish and make my way along the bottom of a pond, perhaps to become some wild animal and run through the open fields. True joy is not found in love, but in solitude: "The woman's body becomes transparent, while my solitude's carnal desire is about to be fulfilled."[51] The man expects this place to exist, only to find that both the place and the guide are illusions. In the end his vision aligns with the others we have looked at so far: when the promised liberation is within grasp, something emerges, a wall, a chasm, or death, to prevent it. When the wide-open space of the *furusato* is discovered, it transforms into a clogged white space of static, and the protagonist is scattered with the woman and the blossoms. The woman takes charge and the man dissolves. What is a man in the face of these women? Such questions are subtexts in all the writers discussed here.

The individual identity in culture

There is so much about the individual in Ango's essays that Karatani Kōjin can state that the articles on culture – "A Personal View of Culture," in particular – are not about "culture" at all, but explorations of individuals. I find this slightly overstated, although it is a valid corrective given the trend of much Ango scholarship. Culture is, in the end, of great importance to Ango, and this is, somewhat paradoxically, ultimately Karatani's point. Ango suggests that "culture" and "Japanese culture" are so integral to the process of constructing an individual identity that without first searching out and understanding the culture, there is no foundation on which to build an identity. Ango's sophistication lies (especially in contrast to the German architect Bruno Taut against whom he writes in that essay) in the pairing of "national culture" and the formation of an individual identity in order to interact with and critique that culture.[52] In exploring what it means to be an individual, Ango must first determine the culture in which that individual is formed. An assumption throughout his writing is that individual identity proceeds in important ways from a national culture, yet at the same time, there can be no culture without the individuals who live in it. The two ideas are interdependent. The constricting, essentialized culture of wartime Japan lurks in the background of this formulation. In this articulation, Ango distrusts the rational and abstract and emphasizes the concrete and physical, leading him to make proposals resonant with others we have seen.

Ango turns this discussion, of individuals forming culture while culture also forms individuals, to Japan. He never doubts that he is Japanese, for example, nor that such a designation is meaningful and self-evident. He seems to take for granted that a national culture exists even though he finds it difficult to discuss it in absolute quantifying terms. He furnishes examples but never definitions. An essay on the "Japanese Spirit" ("Nihon seishin"), for example, expresses doubts about the possibility of identifying such a thing as a "European spirit" which might parallel "European culture." The results of a questionnaire conducted by the journal *Les Nouvelles Littéraires* posit that the idea of an essentialized culture is in doubt even in Europe. The Europeans know better than to talk about a "European spirit," so, if European culture resists such essentialism, why are so many justified in essentializing Japanese culture, he implicitly asks his readers. That the individual exists, and that culture exists, does not require definition, it seems. He does not doubt that a quantifiable and identifiable national culture exists even while he reacts to the ludicrous assumptions that underscore much essentialist writing on culture. He seems almost equally essentialist in the end, but to different ends. That is, even while professing a distrust of essentialized culture, he comes close to delineating one himself. In this we find a trajectory parallel to the other flesh writers, who also focused on a radical individual in order to reject one ideological system only to erect another.

Ango notes that Japanese literature (i.e. the literary and aesthetic traditions) has long valued the beauty of landscape. To humans, of course, nothing equals the beauty of the human in the resplendence of the flesh, not even the beauty of clothes and accessories we drape over the body.

> The spirit [*seishin*] resides in the body, as do instincts, and the individual pattern woven from the body and the spirit into a single damask is not something that can be understood by your everyday sort of explanation. We are in a unique world in which everyone discovers these things in their own manner. [53]

We refer to this as individuality (*kosei*), he claims. The "everyday (run-of-the-mill)" life does not exist because society is always in flux as individuals make particular discoveries and live according to them.[54] With phrasing such as this, he tries to describe the individuals that comprise culture, the individuals that result from every-day choices. These are the things and persons that comprise culture. He also expresses a frustration with the ends to which discussions of culture had been put, with culture used as a club by wartime essentialists and militarists to compel citizens to conform to a common ideal. Thus, while distrustful of "Culture," of elitist cultural production and valorization, the essentialist discourse that has no room for the diverse voices of "individuals," he is tempted by it and cuts a path as close to its borders as possible.

Essays on identity and culture

Early in "Nihon bunka shikan" Ango raises the salient questions in reference to national characteristics: What is tradition? What is nationality? These lead him to ask: Do we assume that there was something essential in the Japanese personality that predetermined that they would first discover, and then wear, kimono? Maybe, maybe not: the important thing for Ango is that there are Japanese people, and from these individuals arose the traditions now associated with them. That is, Ango insists that the culture of the Japanese is not located in the objects they have created but within the individuals who made those objects. These individuals constitute society. Mow down the temples and put up a parking lot; throw out the Noh masks and enjoy the flicker of neon: Ango insists that this would diminish nothing of the Japanese because Japanese *people* continue to live their lives, pushed on and adapting to necessity – a quality that Ango appreciates above all else – not living according to ossified forms of culture.[55] As he has it, a culture proceeds from the ways in which people get on with their lives, adapting to changing historical necessities. This is, again, *daraku*, to live in accord with elemental desires. People continue to dream even if their dreams are unattainable. It is when "thought" and ideas proceed from daily life, when concessions are made in order to live as close to one's dreams as possible, that for the first time a substantive flesh (*nikutai*) will come to reside in thought (this in opposition to the entirely idealized, non-physical existence of the war years). That is, if one begins with this everyday life, abstractions and ideals will no longer be sterile and removed from our daily lives and needs.[56] Kimono and temples result not from prescriptive abstractions but from the needs of daily existence. Culture is performative, for the particulars come first – whether the style of clothing or the system of belief – and the culture comes later – a kimono tradition and Buddhist temples. The kimono did not precede a culture of silk and the temples did not spawn monks. Individuals discovered all these things in the process of living and culture spread from the particulars. Such artifacts are the result.

This pairing of the political and the physical gets to the heart of an important Ango project, a sophisticated exploration of the physical as a base for a philosophy of identity in contrast to the wartime political system, which co-opted national culture and daily life to hold the individual hostage by extending its own "grander" project into every facet of the individual's existence. The political system represents the rational and the abstract, divorcing individuals from everyday existence. Ango works with a national vocabulary, which is a cultural vocabulary, to destroy the heretofore-accepted state-sanctioned system. He thus begins the essay ostensibly about "Culture" –"Nihon bunka shikan" – by claiming to know nothing of the great masters of the traditional arts, but rather extolling the pleasure of drunken revelry in neon-lit back alleys. Here, Ango emphasizes *daraku*, individuality and the quotidian, to valorize the everyday people and "culture" he knows from bars and back streets in contrast to the essentialized and ideologized Japanese found (but which he has never seen) in essentialist cultural theorizing. Okuno calls this move from the cerebral and rational to the physical and (in this conceptualization) concrete, a Copernican revolution in morals. In Karatani's language, this represents a coup d'état of the mental state (*chiteki*).[57] Ango has changed the parameters.

In a similar vein, as he expands the idea in "Darakuron," the "sense" exhibited in samurai codes and wartime censorship follows the same logic, revealing a deep knowledge of humankind, but it is ultimately inhumane because it is constricting and artificial in its proscriptions for individuals. (This "sense" also incorporates Kamiya Tadataka's *jikkan*, as I explored in Chapter 2.) Politicians therefore desire to turn war widows into nuns by decrying their desire to take on new lovers, denying desire, individual will, and volition. The bureaucrats and cultural pundits call for abstinence, denying the needs of the body, thereby squashing the individual and with it the people. Culture should develop naturally, from "below," and not be imposed from "above." Thus, Ango is confounded by the tendency of his fellow Japanese to conform to rules and laws. This has been consistent throughout Japanese history and is therefore not a recent, wartime development, he explains. Think of the whole *bushidō* code, he suggests, which goes against the natural tendencies of the Japanese, by valorizing revenge and vendettas. The fact that the samurai code is such an elaborate system to ensure honor and to avenge wrongs only goes to show, contrary to the usual explanations, that the Japanese are not warlike, but must be prodded and legislated into it. Such a system must be codified and enforced because it is unnatural. That is, from the earliest times these societal rules and organizations, these systems of power and control, were devised for other means, namely to control the populace, to prod individuals to certain modes of conduct, to guarantee a minority's access to power and wealth.

When ideology extends into everyday life individuals are divorced from their own desires.

Ango finds equally pernicious the degree to which many Japanese draw individual identity from these systems and organizations. Note, he cites by way of example, the foolishness with which Japanese bow their heads even in passing by Tokyo's Yasukuni shrine, that monument to fallen soldiers. Where lies the sense of identification that causes so many Japanese, almost unconsciously, even while riding by on a bus, to bow in reverence to this institution established for the purpose of ultimate sacrifice to the nation? Here again, he cites historical precedent to underscore that these are not recent tendencies, for even the famous eccentric Miyamoto Musashi, who claimed to need no one and nothing but himself, found himself stopping to pay homage at a shrine as he rushed from one place to another. What is the power of these places, Ango asks, the weakness of these people, that even the strongest cannot escape its grasp? How did these processes and identifications come to be so ingrained as to be unconscious? How did individual identity become so rooted in this national, cultural identity?[58] For Ango, performing these acts is a sign of Japaneseness, suggesting that culture is performative, but the Japanese people will continue simply by living, whether in keeping with these "traditional" practices or not. The solution to this conundrum is a *daraku*, getting back to the elemental. The first task is to live according to individual needs, and culture will follow when the group of people respond in similar ways to their historical context.

Ango insists that culture must be free of constraints in order to follow necessity and move forward of its own accord. This exhibits a now hard-to-accept faith in progress, where advancement forward necessarily takes us towards something better. Even so, we find, at the close of "Zoku darakuron," that society will construct mechanisms only to tear them down. That is, for all his anarchism, there is the assumption, concession perhaps, that structures of some sort are necessary. This is where the individual can act. There is more than simple anarchism in this. Ango is aware that individuals must work within groups and structures, which he admits will be confining and stultifying in the end, but are somehow necessary. His call for *daraku* is for a return to the individual, even though it is only an ideal, impossible to reach. This is also why he must insist on the lonely nature of *daraku*, which can only be individual.

Ango's *daraku* proceeds from Japan's lived trauma in the war and postwar experience. It is a call to return to an authentic existence by forgoing cerebral ratiocination and to act by means of the body in order to be "real," authentic, and essential. Thus, he expresses frustration, in the initial scattered and somewhat frantic paragraphs of "Dekadan bungakuron" ("On Decadent Literature" 1946), with literary precursors – such critics and writers as Hirano Ken (1907–78), Yokomitsu Riichi (1898–1947), and ultimately Shimazaki Tōson (1872–1943). His impatience with the earlier canonical writers resembles Tamura's, and he holds them responsible along with the wartime regime for distracting attention from the physical by writing of the spiritual (*seishin*) and the cerebral. Even though these writers ostensibly treat the themes of physicality that he espouses, and were scandalous in their own time with their erotic decadence, they all hide behind the trappings of rationality, professionalism, and technique, refusing to get involved with the actual living of life. Ango is especially pointed in his frustration with novelist Shimazaki Tōson for using skillful writing, i.e. technique, to make light of the distance that separated his life from his fiction instead of engaging in a "desperate struggle with his soul." Tōson's scandalous public relationship with his niece (to which Ango refers, albeit obliquely) results from physical sexual desire; such desires are "real" because they are natural and should not be repressed or denied. Given the historical context of Ango's writing, a "desperate struggle" echoes the physical battle and strain this wartime generation experienced. Similarly, he describes Yokomitsu Riichi's writing as the agonized, rational, mental anguish of one trying to deny physical distress by concentrating only on the spiritual. Yokomitsu is, in Ango's view, trying to describe the lonely chasm between bodily pain and cerebral interaction. He criticizes Yokomitsu for ultimately favoring the rational at the expense of the physical.

After these opening salvos, Ango proceeds to cast the history of Japanese literature and thought as one that establishes a distance between what "really" happens and beautified words. I find that Ango's imagery of this distance, the "space between," powerfully ties together much of Ango's writing. In its negative manifestations it separates individuals from concrete realities and renders the "real" as ghostly and otherworldly, the subject of awe and even fear. Ango explicates Edo writing as being framed in concepts such as *giri* and *ninjō*, while the "real" remains closeted behind doors of secrecy and is given names like *sabi* and *yūgen* and *mono no aware*. He rails against the family structure for its conservatism as well: "The weird perversions of family feeling become a monster developed according to the most traditional of concepts of *giri* and *ninjō*" in the Edo period, he writes.[59] In the Japanese family (he refers to Natsume Sōseki's novels as an example) there are no people, he claims, only rules and logic. The "Japanese home" is based on instinctual desires to procreate and build nests. Nostalgia about these homes pervades Japanese "culture." The everyday is wrapped in abstract bonds of rules and codes while what might be considered (what Ango seems to consider) the most basic bedrock issues are buried even further in layers of secrecy and indecipherability. Thus, the highest aesthetics become wrapped in layers of nebulous obscurity, as words without referents, i.e. *sabi* and *yūgen* and *mono no aware*. Even though Tokugawa culture is now generally understood as commodified, bawdy, and physical, Ango argues that the truly valorized concepts of that time were the most cerebral, and reveal the chasm yawning between physical life and abstract idealized life. This characterization of history also traces the ideological underpinnings of the militarism of the 1940s, when the family unit was established as the image of the nation. Ango's historical sketch becomes, then, a critique of wider tendencies within Japanese society.[60]

The sharpest imaging of this critique occurs in the first lines of "Sakura no mori no mankai no shita," which mocks the "traditional" practice of *hanami*, of a party under the cherry blossoms: "Nowadays, when the cherries bloom, people think it's time for a party . . . [But] in the old days – the *really* old days . . . they were *scared* to go under the blossoms." The space where one views cherry blossoms, now assumed to be a party and a time to be drunkenly uninhibited under the beautiful blossoms, was originally a place in which one feared insanity and the dissolution of mind and body, as the narrator reminds us by referencing a Noh play. Under the swirling blossoms the physical dissolves; a woman goes mad as her baby disappears. This opening scene is echoed in the final scene where, in the space under the cherry blossoms, at the moment the main character thinks he has discovered the truth of the woman to whom he has submitted, she disappears. He reaches for her, and he too disappears, his arm swallowed in the void, then all of him:

> He reached out to pluck the petals from the woman's cheek. But just as his hand reached her face, something strange happened. Beneath his hand lay only drifted petals. The woman had vanished, leaving petals in her place. And as he reached out to part the mound of petals, his hand, his arm, his body vanished. The space filled with petals and frigid emptiness, nothing more.[61]

Cherry blossom ("*sakura*") has comprised an integral element and motif in Japanese literature from the beginning of the written tradition, often correlating to what the eighteenth-century scholar Motoori Norinaga referred to as "mono no aware" and an extraordinary, enlightened (in the Buddhist sense) appreciation of beauty. Matsuda Yumi suggests, thereby, that in this story Ango has again combined the classic and traditional with a contemporary sensibility. So ingrained is this image of the blossoms that the mention of "flower" (*hana*) refers to *sakura* in the Imperial *Shin kokinshū* poetry collection (and, at the same time, recalls the Ango's imagery, noted earlier, of wartime Tokyo as an ideal city, "[where] a vacant beauty had bloomed"[62]). Further,

> *Sakura* as a motif that is associated with visions [*gensō*] of death and madness is exceedingly common . . . Thus, mature fullness and putrefaction, unsurpassing beauty and extreme coldness, bright flowering and decline, the prostitute and the virginal saint, or in another vocabulary, comedy and tragedy, emptiness and the essential, reality and anti-reality – these mark the essential nature of things. Ango is trying to capture the polarities at the same time, and that project causes chaos and contradiction. Without affirming all these aspects one cannot capture it. This is Ango's point.[63]

The desire to unify traditions is, in Ango's imagery, rooted to a place that is claustrophobic and frightening, yet with borders marked by nothing more restraining than flower petals and air. Indeed, the mountain bandit of this tale sets for himself the challenge of sitting quietly in the midst of a cherry grove in full bloom, partly because attempts to dash through the swirling blossoms always end in disaster. It should be easy to run a straight line through a mass of flowers, but he finds himself going in circles, banging into trees, falling headlong into the soft pink mass. It should be even easier to sit quietly in the midst of their tranquil space. He is unsuccessful in all of these attempts.

"Darakuron" begins by tracing a similar historical progression. Ango quotes eighth-century poetry, and then moves to classical scholars of the seventeenth and eighteenth centuries. "Dekadan bungakuron" continues this progression into the present with an extended discussion of Yokomitsu Riichi and Shimazaki Tōson, writers who have been traditionally cast as serious, diligent and fully engaged with controversial contemporary issues, not trivial or trifling, not at all at play:

Socially, and in attitude, they are not playing at all, but in these writings they are entirely at play. To say they are playing at literature means that, to these men, ethics do not come about on their own but are subject to rational devices. That is, they are thinking by means of a pre-existing structure, they are not thinking through a physical logic.[64]

Because they are at the mercy of societally produced laws, they are unable to follow the demands of the individual body. Ango finds here the damning dichotomy that separates the cerebral from the visceral, so compelling that even for writers apparently engaged with physical issues, the organizing logic proves to be a cerebral one.

Ango insists that this split is immediately obvious if one has any understanding of Western scientific and positivistic method. What is lacking throughout these earlier writers, he believes, is a commitment to knowing the individual self. This is the problem with the work of Tōson and Yokomitsu: they try to collapse by skill and technique, by cerebral organizing logic, the "space between" themselves and the issues they present in their works. Rather than make a personal commitment as they apprehend it, they distance themselves from what they write:

> By distance I mean the white space that clogs up the area between the person and the work. It refers to the fact that they cannot talk about the flesh and blood realities that follow a logic of the flesh because they cannot pin them down.[65]

He faults them for not pursuing the crucial questions of how one should live, for not asking if, and how, fundamental realities exist. (This is another of the nuances of *daraku*, getting the individual in the text. For Ango, these writers represent one more instance of the abstractions and cerebral approaches that plague Japanese culture.) This lack of commitment creates the spaces and gaps in their work, where the authors dance around the hard parts rather than jump in and stake even the most personal. This space is found in Tōson, in Ango's examples, in difficult passages where Tōson tries to make light of, by explaining away (*gomakasu*), this distance. Tōson fights "tooth and nail" only with fictional technique; there is no bloody difficult struggle with the soul, with the essential, with the physical. The physical is denied and covered up by technique and reason. In the end, Ango accuses Tōson of playing around with literature, and toying with issues in his life – like the relationship with his niece – without really confronting them. And so, in Ango's reading, the issue at the heart of Tōson's *Shinsei* – the unhealthy sexual relationship between an uncle and his niece – is presented in a ridiculously healthy novel. *Shinsei* is healthy, almost antiseptic, in its rationality, yet lacks the fear of self-destruction proceeding from a carnal physical body subsumed in the narrative. The antiseptic sense of "health" that dissatisfies Ango proceeds, he suggests, from a skillful manipulation of narrative structures. For all the scandal surrounding this work and the confession it contains, *Shinsei* does not really interrogate the greater issues of literature or society. For all its "immorality," Ango finds it absurdly chaste.

Tōson's greatest concern in *Shinsei* becomes, then, according to Ango, the honor of his name and of the family name. He is caught up in a pose (Ango uses the English word) that he is unable or unwilling to subvert, and is left unwilling to confront the issue, being bound by societal rules. "He is bound by the present world and constricted current ethics, he is unable to be *daraku* in present circumstances." Contemporary society and its ethics constrain him, preventing *daraku*, and he cannot pursue his own physical individual ethics and desires. This denies the basic power of literature: "Literature that is, at its most basic meaning, self-destruction [*jikohakai*] and stands opposed to the common ethics, was in Tōson's thinking decadence [*daraku*]."[66] If literature is a "decadence" and a "self-destruction" in Tōson's own words, how did such a scandalous narrative result in this chaste tale, Ango asks his readers. Thus, he continues, Akutagawa was correct in calling Tōson's writing "crafty," for it is really a self-deception, as is any literature that covers up and avoids the hard issues concerning constitution of self; it hides behind craft. Tōson does not deal with the personal issues that this novel is ostensibly about – the immoral relations between an uncle and his niece. Ango admits that lifestyles and personal concerns vary, and he is not interested in critiquing Tōson's factual, incestuous relationship. Rather, Ango finds that Tōson seemed unable to deal with that issue in his life and chose to "twist" it into a massive fictionalized comment, and this can only point to a self-deception. Literature is the place to explore these most basic human desires, and should stake everything on the outcome by presenting the rawest of the human. This is decadence and this, insists Ango, is the motivating force behind literature.

Ango continues that even the great writers of the last generation proved unable to bring about this unabashed interrogation into the "decadent" and the human, even while they seemed to be fully engaged in physical issues. A cerebral logic and ethics held them firmly in its grasp. This cerebral tendency, even in an ostensibly scandalous confession of sexual improprieties like Tōson's, participates in the greater tendency to divert individual attention from physical desires. The results, as we have seen it explained by all the flesh writers, were discourses that lead to self-denying wartime society. Thus, Ango proposes a decadence, a radical highlighting of the individual body divorced from the apparent physical eroticism of earlier generations of writers such as Tōson, Kafū, and Tanizaki. Ango demands a break from this tradition, demands – offers – a manner of living for a new future, one based on a *daraku* which is found in the oft-invoked *furusato* (birthplace), the same space that clogs the area between the present and the goal.

Writing (in) the postwar period

Three aspects of Ango's prose have garnered special attention: the power of his essays to call for a reassessment of life and the war years; the attempts of his fictional characters to live out those ideals; and his descriptions of the postwar situation. His intense depictions of war and postwar life captivated many but were also scandalous in their highlighting of physicality. This scandal derives as much from the images themselves as from the unrestrained style of presentation. Thus Karatani Kōjin takes "Darakuron" as the quintessential description of the postwar, recording his surprise at realizing that Ango's earlier "Nihon bunka shikan" was not also a postwar essay, but a wartime one because it reads so like a postwar work.[67] Donald Keene ties the appeal of "Darakuron" to its descriptions: "["Darakuron"] makes absorbing reading not only because of its creed of *daraku* but because of the vivid glimpses of the bombing of Tokyo."[68] Ango did not need the end of the war to find this voice, but it seems to have provided an important edge to his writing. At the same time, his wartime attention to what became major postwar themes is a perfect example of the danger in establishing overly neat divisions between war and postwar.

The earlier "Nihon bunka shikan" (1942) has the feel of a postwar work because the ideas and iconoclasm expressed therein pushed against wartime restraints and legal limits while capturing the hope and despair later associated with the postwar. Many have remarked on the "bravery" required to publish such ideas during the war years. Essays such as "Nihon Dunka shikan" and "Darakuron" display an unabashedness of theme and style at a time overshadowed by wartime censorship and government oppression. Descriptions of sex and sexuality were censored during the war as expressions of self-centered concern that were potentially "injurious to public morals,"[69] but they proved of little interest to the Occupation censors (who were much more concerned with ideological transgressions such as latent militarism, Marxism, and Communism). I have noted in earlier chapters the great postwar interest in the erotic and pornographic that contributed to the sense that we were (to paraphrase Okuno again) already engaged in shameful acts, and we hated ourselves for what we had to do. As Okuno has it, "Nihon bunka shikan" (and with it, "Bungaku no furusato" and "Seishunron" ("An Essay on Youth," 1942)) appeared when no one had yet voiced such opinions: it was impossible to do so under wartime censorship. (One need only recall the threat of official retributions experienced by Noma's characters for a sense of this fear.) Then, in the postwar years, only Ango insisted "we must be decadent" when most people found themselves living as though it was still wartime, as though life continued to be fragile, as though everyone was still under the gun, frightened and on the edge of survival. People were happy not to have died. Wartime fears structured the everyday life of postwar Japan even as new freedoms seemed possible. Ango's writing was unprecedented, reflecting what everyone knew but was still afraid to voice publicly: war was not noble, none wanted death, but rather, in contrast to the official valorization of death and sacrifice, "in war it is death that is the most feared." Okuno suggests that this most basic of commonsense truths was deemed taboo. One could not mention these dreads in wartime, for to do so was traitorous,[70] even while experienced viscerally, bodily, by all.

Nishikawa Nagao, who convincingly shows that "Nihon bunka shikan" refutes, point by point, the early 1930s writings of the German architect and exile Bruno Taut, asks rhetorically why Ango waited six years, i.e. a full four years after Taut's death, to publish his response. One reason, he proposes, is that Ango was living a particularly transient lifestyle in those years, but more importantly, while his views on humanity and the arts may have been tolerated under the increasing militarization and patriotic fervor of the 1930s, many of his pronouncements on culture would not have been, whereas Taut's writings were very useful to the regime.[71] Ango caustically points out the hypocrisy of an age when people mouth the slogans of sacrifice and faithfulness to national ideals even while living according to a private logic. In vocabulary and tone his writing suggests the salacious and prurient, even though these essays are much more substantial and sophisticated than this suggests.

Ango dealt with these issues, and sexuality in particular, in a markedly different way, which became representatively "postwar." Okuno explains that, after the war, sex was discussed in the same theoretical register as democracy, humanism, and equal rights, i.e. as a "big" issue. He suggests that this was the first time in Japanese history that sex had been discussed in so open a manner. Ango incorporated sexual liberation as an aspect of personal expression, and a critique of the reigning national ideologies. That is, it was liberation from the Imperial system and a restoration of humanity to individuals. Whether or not Ango was the very first in Japanese literary history to take up sex in this fashion, as Okuno would have it, is debatable, but few would deny the historical importance of these essays. Following Okuno, up to this point sex had always been treated as transgression, as a cause for embarrassment and consternation, as something related to the pleasure quarters, aestheticized, or as part of a Naturalistic attempt at a particular type of realism. Even Tanizaki, who made sex and sensuality central to his work, aestheticized it, taking it out of the realm of the physical, Okuno suggests. During the war, sex was banished from fiction and distorted under official pressure to be stashed in the shadows. Ango's call to "fall back to the human" attacked, with intent to smash, the officially sanctioned ethics established during wartime. Thus, argues Okuno, this is not "decadence" but an attempt to restore the individual, not descriptions of the depraved, but of the normal and orthodox.[72] This valorization of the physical, read by most as sex with a woman, marks one source of the great initial appeal of Ango's writing.

The Ango style

Ango became something of a media star as the scandal promised in his writing was matched by his obsessive-compulsive lifestyle. Taking the amphetamine known as *hiropon* (Philopon[73]) to stay awake, he would write frantically and then drink heavily in order to sleep; press reports of his drunken escapades abounded. He embodied the obsessive Romantic hero, but the lifestyle of frantic production that his newfound fame thrust upon him triggered drug addiction and bouts of mental illness and institutionalization. This biographical element is worth noting because of its role in supporting the Ango myth, in which "his life itself seemed to be a series of acts of rebellion against the established morality and intellectual assumptions of his age."[74] This resulting energy and apparent lack of focus present something of a dilemma for many critics:

> One is struck by the surprising number of styles in which he wrote, all with great talent, on a wide range of subjects: farce, adult fairy tales that read like prose poems, autobiographical fiction, essays on a wide range of subjects, historical fiction, tales of strategy involving games of gō and shōgi, from ephemeral pieces and historical fiction to travel writings, all with different groups of appreciative fans, so that it is exceedingly difficult to determine which was his forte and which were simply extras.[75]

When contending with Ango's work, one immediately runs into these "contradictions": modes of thought that go in different directions and contend with each other, perhaps preternaturally postmodern (although just as likely premodern in the Edo spirit of play and pastiche). This may simply point out the uselessness of standard genre distinctions in analyzing his work. As Karatani would have it, Ango would destroy such divisions.[76] Okuno expresses these as a conflict between the rational and realist (*genjitsu shugi*) and the spiritual (*seishin shugi*) – which is to say anti-rational or idealistic – tendencies, reflecting the dualism discussed in earlier chapters.

Hyōdo Masanosuke did not experience the sort of "attack" (Okuno's word) so common to initial readings of Ango's work. He is taken more by the prose-poetry quality of the essays, which are not to be understood linearly, a source of frustration for the reader because Ango tends toward the prolix and unclear, presenting ideas to be apprehended at a visceral level. In Hyōdo's experience, the prose and the ideas burrow into his head and refuse to depart, establishing a compelling presence where the ideas keep coming back to burn at a slow, steady flame within him. He finds in Ango the need for an instinctive apprehension that relies on the body, not a cerebral logic. As he states it, the profusion of styles and statements throughout Ango's oeuvre is the source of the energy that drives him to explicate Ango's power. (What he writes is a *sakkaron*, an attempt to reconstruct a total image of Sakaguchi Ango based largely upon his writings, considered in chronological time.[77]) He acknowledges the difficulty of his book-length study: he wants to analyze Ango in the forum of rational discourse, via a critical essay, whereas there is something decidedly irrational in Ango's work that resists categorization.[78]

The competing worldviews in Ango's work are one source of this "irrational." While Ango's writing reveals a great confidence in progress (an assumption we also noted in Tamura's writings) and an unquestioning faith in a scientific method built on rationality, he is also very distrustful of the Christian underpinnings of "civilization" that were constructed as "rational" and, more pointedly, has a stronger sympathy for the abstract, ideal, and vague that are tolerated in Buddhist thought.[79] The result is an attempt to navigate between the scientific/rational (i.e. rational and foreign) and the circular and oblique (or Asian and Buddhist), which parallels an antipodal discourse on "culture" throughout the Meiji, Taishō, and early Shōwa periods. Ango is, then, participating in much older discussions about culture within Japan.[80] Karatani further suggests that Ango's deep knowledge of Western traditions, as well as his submersion in Japanese/Asian thought (particularly through his study of Sanskrit and Buddhism), produced a unique perspective on both strains of thought, augmented by his study of Japan's hidden Christians. These all gave him a feel for the irrational characteristics undergirding Western "rationalism." Karatani credits the simultaneous navigation of both streams – Western rationalism and Eastern anti-rationalism – as one of Ango's important contributions to postwar thinking.

That being said, it is hard now to recreate the shock that "Darakuron" evinced. Like much of the work I am considering here, when read at the beginning of the twenty-first century the cause for scandal is not at all obvious. "Darakuron" signaled a new way of thinking and the beginning of a new era. In Okuno's words, this essay marked the beginning of the postwar by signaling a break with the previous ways of thought. Reading this convinced him that the war was truly over:

> I imagine I will never again receive the same sort of explosive blast from something
> I read as I did from "Darakuron." I – nineteen at the time – was freed in one fell

swoop from wartime ethics, ideals [*kannen*], and taboos. It was a thunderclap that revealed a new way of living. Politically speaking, the war ended on August 15 with the Imperial edict, but for me, spiritually speaking, Sakaguchi Ango's "Darakuron" announced the end of the war. With "Darakuron," individually [*shūtaiteki*] and humanly, the postwar began.[81]

Ango and Sartre

I have noted earlier the overlap of Existentialism to that time when "the postwar began." Ango's writings on Sartre's short fiction were integral to this development. One finds in much of Ango's writing a substantial overlap with European Existentialist sensibility, in which true freedom and the fullest humanity are achieved only individually and in isolation. The parallels of imagery in Sartre and Ango become even stronger when the representations of liberation are considered, particularly in the imagery of *daraku* as it overlaps with the imagery of the place, the *furusato*. In Ango, in contrast to Sartre, the body and the individual disappear at precisely the moment this individuality comes within grasp. Ango's *furusato*, which provides a place for *daraku* and presumably an understanding of the self, is also the place where that self disappears into a flurry of cherry blossoms. Ugliness and nausea are integral to the "salvation" that follows a realization that there is to be no external liberation, and this awareness is located spatially in the *furusato*, which serves as the locus for the real, the place where existence is situated, and therefore all else in the world. Karatani Kōjin finds in the "ugliness" of "Hakuchi" much in common with Sartre's nausea. All things here, even the characters, are objects lacking subjectivity. "Nausea" pervades this world of matter to which essence must be added.[82]

Ango's interest in the anti-rational and the individual is also iterated in an important short essay in which he praises an early work of Sartre for its evidences of "thinking through the physical." Ango found much in Sartre to praise, and his comments on Sartre's work introduced many of the terms of Existentialist discourse and Sartrean discussion, at least at a popular level, to postwar Japan. There are parallels of image and theme in the work of both writers. For one, the individual in an antagonistic stance against the "ethics" of society, its rules and regulations, is central to Ango's writing and *nikutai bungaku* in general. The *nikutai* Ango found in Sartre's earliest fiction also parallels the imagery in his own writings. Okuno Takeo writes of Ango as one who "fired away [*uchidasu*] with the motif of the *nikutai*'s thinking" in his early works,[83] namely "Darakuron" and the subsequent publication, "Hakuchi." This connection has become so concretely established that a standard dictionary of contemporary (Japanese) literature summarizes Ango's "Hakuchi" as the Existentialist fiction that ushered in postwar literature:

> In "Hakuchi" the characters are placed in an aboriginal setting where there is no distinction made among humans and animals, and the carnal, instinctual pain and sadness of this mute woman with whom the protagonist tries to flee [the fire-bombing of the neighborhood] *was expressed as existentialist fiction*, and this marks the first toehold for postwar writers extending from the first postwar group [*daiichi sengo ha*; i.e. Noma Hiroshi *et al.*], including the third group of new

writers [*daisan no shinjin*; i.e. Kojima Nobuo *et al.*], to contemporary work by Kaiko [Ken] and Ōe [Kenzaburō].[84]

Ango is here credited with discovering the method for Existentialist description in Japan, a method to express a basic humanity based on the carnal. His writing described, that is, a pervasive postwar sensibility, one that is decidedly physical and that establishes a direct relationship between this style of fiction and the existentialist fiction of the subsequent generation of writers as well.[85]

Ango's writings also resonate with Existentialism in that he presents liberation as the place where one discovers that the moral is that there are no morals. Tsuge Teruhiko develops this connection in comparison to Noma Hiroshi:

> In the world of Noma Hiroshi's first novel ["Kurai e"], the self and other appear with an extreme sense of physicality to reveal a very clear convergence with existentialism. However, in Sakaguchi Ango, it is freedom that he has written about the most. The freedom that Ango speaks of is the sort of extreme freedom that gives rise to loneliness and angst.[86]

I find plenty of loneliness and angst in Noma's fiction as well. Ango's correlation of these images from Sartre's fiction is, however, largely responsible for the introduction of "Existentialism" to Japanese postwar writers and readers in general.[87]

Ango and Tamura

Tamura Taijirō and Sakaguchi Ango share a similar sense of urgency when looking at the postwar: that if we do not forswear the false robes of wartime ideology, we will return to the wartime deceptions and situation. Rediscovering an authentic humanity serves as an antidote to the war and can prevent its recurrence. Ango suggests that wartime lessons remind us that we were always physical beings and in order to get back to a more "real" humanity we must return to that physical existence. Women incarnate this ideal life, but that "ideal" existence prevents their continued existence. We have read of Tamura's claim that it was Ango's "Darakuron" that made the publication of his work possible; Hyōdo Masanosuke suggests that Ango's "Nikutai ga shikō suru" proceeds directly from, because it follows so closely on, Tamura's "Nikutai no mon."[88] Their postwar work relates symbiotically after the war, each influencing the other, each, in certain ways, making the other possible.

It may be this overlap, and the resulting sense of competition, that leads Tamura, however, to insist on differences between his and Ango's work. One finds no affection between them; Tamura wrote, for example, "Even though the phrase is *nikutai bungaku*, there is quite a difference in meaning between what people like Sakaguchi Ango mean by this and what I am referring to." He misreads Ango's intent, however, defining Ango's *nikutai* as entirely separate from the spiritual and signifying a flesh that is base and decadent. Tamura reads Ango's *nikutai* negatively, as a dichotomy that posits that the spirit is to be upright while the body is tainted. Tamura does not want to deny the spiritual (in this essay, "Nikutai bungaku to ningen no jiyū") while raising the *nikutai* to a place equal with it; he insists, rather, that one is unable to separate the physical from the flesh, nor would one want to, for the flesh has the power, essentially, to lead and direct individuals. He interprets Ango as praising the spiritual while castigating the physical (*nikutai*) as dirty and tainted. Tamura can agree that pursuing the body does lead one to a fuller understanding of humanity; he seems to take issue with what he sees as Ango's characterization of the body as depraved and therefore negative. Tamura wishes to reverse the usual understanding by turning this all into carnival, where the lower becomes the means to attain proper balance. Yet, as I have noted, this is also Ango's position, and Tamura is grinding a different ax, which leads him to misread Ango in this way.[89] Tamura reads Ango's *nikutai* as negative and close to a medieval Catholic worldview where people are plagued by original sin.

Tamura claims that, in contrast, his *nikutai bungaku* is based on the Japanese experience of living through the long war that, when finally over, left them without self-confidence. The foreigners found Japanese dazed and despondent. Their lack of confidence followed the realization that all previously held "truth" was baseless and unsupportive. All the preexisting viewpoints had been stamped "unreliable." So, asks Tamura, what can we trust in now? Only physical desires or instincts, only that which is experienced via the flesh (*nikutai*):

> One wants to eat because one is hungry, wants to sleep because tired, or wishes to embrace [one of] the opposite sex, one is hot, or perhaps cold – It is only these fleshly desires and experiences that are human and in which one can place any trust. Phrased another way, it is only the flesh that is filled with the desire to live that one can believe to be real.[90]

This body is the base from which one can grow, and it forms the truly human (*ningenteki*). Again, it is a curious discussion because, as I have noted, Tamura and Ango insist on the same points here. Tamura and Ango have a shared history in literary circles, although Ango never seems to have mentioned Tamura's work. Tamura had invited Ango to join the editorial board of a journal called *Sakura*. One wonders what role Ango may have had in the naming, given the importance of cherry trees in his work, especially as a subversion of traditional culture. It seems possible, while purely speculative, that Tamura is remembering Ango's first billing in the inaugural issue of *Nihon shōsetsu*, in lieu of Tamura's own "Shunpuden" that had been suppressed by the censors. Tamura exhibits a vehemence in this reading of Ango's *nikutai* that I cannot account for.

While Ango displays a very subtle understanding of the interplay of national and individual identity, based throughout on this idea of *daraku*, he, like Tamura (and Noma), is snared in the same web of ideology and structure that bind the works I have discussed earlier. The conceptual framework is at fault. The male flesh writers seem to write with a larger project in mind, as in Ango's case, that gives shape, and ultimate constraint, to their concerns. The self, the identity, developed here is male, and is also the individual trying to live through postwar degradation and chaos. The vision put forth by the men was exceedingly compelling, but fraught with danger. More substantive countervisions are provided by women writers, as I discuss next.

6 When women write postwar Japan

Introduction

Women writing in the years after the war share few of the anxieties concerning gender and societal roles found in the flesh writers. The liberating desire reflected in men's writing is largely absent in writers such as Sono Ayako (1931–), Hiroike Akiko (1919–), Nakamoto Takako (1903–91), Shibaki Yoshiko (1914–91), and Saegusa Kazuko (1929–2003). I have chosen to focus on postwar fiction written by these writers because they portray women in a close relationship to sex work. Their works offer a counterreading to the masculine fiction of the flesh writers examined in the previous chapters, who rarely interrogated the gender and identity structures they describe or propose, even in fiction registering the anxiety of unstable social roles during the postwar years. While these writers ostensibly proposed a means of liberation for all Japanese subjects, their solutions, extremely convincing at the time, failed to open possibilities of agency for women. Women writers are not uniformly critical of these power structures, of course; nonetheless, they are much more in evidence in women's writings.

Much of the women's fiction appears somewhat later chronologically than that of the flesh writers, near the end of the Occupation and the beginning of the Korean War. Lack of publishing opportunities immediately after the surrender may be one cause of the under-representation by women writing fiction.[1] Their fiction reflects the changing history in that the men in this fiction, who are still the customers of sex workers and still soldiers, are no longer Japanese soldiers nor necessarily occupying forces. Readers of Tamura's fiction, I have noted, have questioned the historical accuracy of his portrayals of customers as being either returned Japanese soldiers or American GIs. These narratives by women reflect the changed economic relations and different sets of soldiers/customers, for even though the war had ended, many American soldiers remained in Japan as occupation troops or, later, were stationed there for the Korean conflict. In the fiction by these women, one war fades into the other, yet the sources of income and structure of female labor change little. Thus, the emotional content of relationships between women and soldiers, whether Imperial soldiers, occupying soldiers, or US soldiers stationed in Japan for the Korean conflict, proves nearly identical. In all of these situations, a woman must rely on a soldier who may or may not return, who may disappear without warning, in death or for another relationship, and leave her destitute, both emotionally and financially. Thus, the fiction by these women more clearly shows what is unchanged, than optimism about postwar possibilities.

The "masculine" biases of the flesh writers' fiction have come to be representative of postwar literature, while women authors writing on similarly sexually charged themes have been largely overlooked. Their treatment of the body comprises another perspective on the *nikutai* central to this study. The canonical (*bundan*) forces that have posited male writers as "representatively" postwar are traceable to a tradition largely determined by male critics. Ueno Chizuko, among others, has outlined what a contrasting "feminist" reading of literature might look like, identifying two potential lines of inquiry: one, to recover and reevaluate the women's writing that has been relegated to obscurity, and, second, to reevaluate men's fiction that has been overly praised. I will examine the writing of contemporary women in order to understand more fully the issues at stake in men's writing after the war and, by providing an alternative perspective, to better assess the male discourse. The result of that inquiry will, I hope, contribute to the "feminist" project that Ueno identifies.[2] My goal, however, is less to produce "feminist" readings and more to fully understand the imaginative constructs of the writers, both male and female, and thus to assess the changing nature of Japanese society as represented in this postwar fiction.[3]

Women in service to the state

The details of the various narrative conflicts situate the women in ethical webs that question national loyalties as they provide sexual service to the soldiers of other, and formerly enemy, nations. The female characters register irony, sometimes chagrin and resignation, at the unchanging nature and expectations of their service even as soldiers change across these changing political alignments. This fiction records the history of sex work: women served first as "comfort women" on the Japanese battle front, then as escorts for the victorious and occupying army, and later supported the same army as it left to wage war on another Asian country. For example, two characters in Shibaki Yoshiko's "Yakō no onna" ("Women of the Night Lights," 1955) discuss these complicated responses. Sally (as she is known) suggests that Yōko should take US GIs as patrons for they have money and they spend it freely. Yōko responds that to look at a Westerner makes her nauseous. She points to a plane flying overhead: "See that plane? It has your boyfriend aboard. Those same planes dropped bombs on Japan too, and turned it upside down. They are the enemy." Sally's response is pragmatic: "What an idiot you are. Just because war is evil does not make evildoers of Jack and Joe."[4] Yōko does not find this logic persuasive, but neither does she have the economic freedom to refute it. "Soldiers are soldiers," insists another character; "we have lives to live. Money from one soldier is the same color as from the next." In similar fashion, Nakamoto Takako explores this potential for identification with those being bombed, while "serving" those engaged in dropping the bombs. She ties the Korean conflict, during which Japan served as an important staging area for US forces, to the context of the Pacific War, in which Japan was the enemy. Thus, the particulars of each war are not overlooked even though the everyday relations with the soldiers is similarly structured. We meet characters at the moment they must decide whether or not to work as prostitutes; pressing financial concerns often determine the outcome. In the constrained postwar years, money (and, similarly, the gifts of food from the GIs) prove too critical for survival to be rejected on ethical grounds, especially for the large numbers of families without men, or with men unable to work. Jobs are few, yet sex work seems always viable, and in this women have an "advantage." The choice to become a *pan-pan* promises the financial security requisite for survival. (Many stories chronicle how these hopes prove false.) For one, many stories recount a common narrative development: the decision to live from the earnings of sex work follows a history of sexual exploitation. Prostitution follows rape by GIs, for example; "defiled" and therefore rejected by family, the characters see sex work as the only choice for livelihood and income. (In many cases this connection seems automatic, even stereotypical.) Further, when the customers are GIs, we find they have more money, they are well fed, and they are in a position of power. The women associated with the GIs have access to black market goods, to the stockings and chocolate of popular imagery, but also to canned meat and other foodstuffs in a time of near starvation. In the face of such necessities, ethical refusals prove moot.

For example, these dynamics figure large in Ariyoshi Sawako's (1931–84) 1967 novel *Hishoku* (*Colorless*), set in occupied Japan. The novel progresses as a history of the changing facets of "love" (*ren'ai*) before and after marriage. The protagonist, Emiko, falls in love with and later marries a black GI of the occupying US army. He spends all his money on her and her family, treating her as a queen (as Emiko expresses it), providing boxes of foodstuffs for her and her now fatherless family. More important than the value of these gifts as additions to the family diet, however, is the hard currency they provide when circulated on the black market. Even after the GI returns to the US, Emiko's clothes reveal access to the PX store (reserved for military personnel and their families) and make her an object of awe, because such styles and quality are unavailable to her acquaintances. Wearing them is a mark of her proximity to power and carries a cachet of fashionableness. Her mixed-race child and the fact that she is temporarily "separated" from her husband lead many to suspect that she was a *pan-pan*: an "only" supported by this black GI. This is a stinging accusation, for Emiko insists, and the novel suggests, that their relationship is built on respect and mutual attraction rather than commercial concerns. That the awe turns to disgust and suspicion when the other women discover the race of the partner is but one of the issues explored in this novel that, as the title suggests, looks closely at racial nuances.

The "past" plays another different role in these narratives. Especially notable are the lengths many of the characters go to escape it, recreating histories, or forgetting (repressing) them entirely. Yōko, of Shibaki Yoshiko's "Yakō no onna," introduced above, makes up stories on the spot, if they seem likely to satisfy current customers. She hides the truth of her past from her lover and confidant. The past has disappeared and is gone, meaningless because useless in current crises of survival (an echo of Ango's views of tradition). Past family conflicts have often propelled the women into their current situations; such histories are therefore best forgotten. When Sumiko, of Nakamoto Takako's "Kichi no Onna," becomes a prostitute, she is also, thereby, cut off from her past and her community. The loss affects her profoundly and she experiences it viscerally, as a knife working away inside her. Such lack of connectedness may be the source of the women's fierce individualism, but it is also the source of their loneliness. It prevents the foundation of community and the liberations described in the men's writings. Past experiences do not provide clues to negotiating current difficulties; rather, they are the source from which their situations grew. Try as they might, they cannot escape the past: rape and betrayal led them to service as comfort women to the Japanese soldiers; following the war the Japanese government again recruited them to provide similar services to the occupying American soldiers. The transition to serving American soldiers prompts hesitation. Resistance to servicing the former enemies yields a common response: "Soldiers are soldiers. Think of the money." The narrative continues, here in a story by Saegusa Kazuko:

> Hanamaru-san, the recruiter, asked slyly, with a self-satisfied look, as though she knew exactly how this exchange would turn out: "You want money, don't you?"
> – Well, as if there is anyone who doesn't want money, [Someyo] thought to herself.
> Hanamaru-san pushed further: "American soldiers or Japanese soldiers: they're all soldiers, so what's the difference?"
> With that, she made her choice.[5]

In the women's fiction, proximity to the GIs means proximity to powerful social forces. Being a *pan-pan* on the arm of a GI draws disparaging stares and comments from fellow Japanese, but it also yields the necessities for survival and supports families, as in Ariyoshi's novel above. Saegusa, writing from a historical remove in the 1980s, will emphasize in her novels how this proximity cuts both ways, as she describes the volatility of the GIs, ready to draw their guns at any provocation. Their power is backed up by (phallic) pistols, ensuring that their demands be met. As has been noted in earlier chapters, the special status of the US troops also undercuts the (masculine) authority of Japanese men. The Japanese women cannot be protected by their countrymen in this arrangement, for even the police are rendered powerless before the gun-waving occupiers. In Saegusa's trilogy, for example, society cannot prevent, protect, or even pursue the perpetrator of the rape of a young Japanese woman by GIs. The young woman has been defiled and abandoned, and feels she must now forsake all of the dreams that she had welcomed with democracy and the US soldiers – gender equality and the possibilities for post-secondary education. Saegusa thus highlights historical ironies, such as the Japanese government's providing prostitutes to the occupying army, especially as they recruited first from among the "comfort women" they had earlier organized to serve the Japanese troops: they are now actively pimping to provide women for the occupiers. At the same time, such works from the 1950s as Kojima Nobuo's (1915–) masterful "Amerikan Sukuuru" ("American School," 1954) reflects the gifts and attention the occupying GIs showered on a Japanese woman, *any* Japanese woman – in that narrative a school teacher who is also a war widow walking along the side of a road with her male colleagues and not even tangentially involved in sex trades. The Americans' virile energy and ability to provide protection and food contrast dramatically with the inability of Japanese men to fulfill such traditional roles. Male writers have written much of this powerlessness. Nosaka Akiyuki's (1930–) "Amerika Hijiki" ("American Hijiki," 1967) also sharply captures the impotence, literal as well as figurative, as a Japanese male recalls his boyhood experience pimping for the occupation soldiers. These works capture such ironies and issues with particular clarity as narrators look back after some decades have passed. The men have focused on the emasculation wrought by this situation; the women note that the basic oppressive and demeaning structures have not changed.

Soldiers were expected to sacrifice their lives for the nation on the battlefront. Women served on the "homefront" in supporting and secondary roles, meaning they remained at one remove from active roles in state projects. A woman's relationship to the state reflects this two-tiered structure. Nakagawa Shigemi's important readings of wartime women writers, especially the fiction of Hayashi Fumiko, point out parallels between the Anglo-American experience of war and that of the Japanese women writers. He quotes Jean Bethke Elshtain on the ramifications of British women viewing themselves through the construction of "[the] rough and ready division between male life takers and women life givers." Men, Elshtain continues,

> see edifying tales of courage, duty, honor, glory as they engage in acts of protection and defense and daring: heroic deed doing. Women see edifying stories of nobility, sacrifice, duty, quiet immortality as they engage in defensive acts of protection, the non-heroics of taking-care-of.[6]

This, as Elshtain readily admits, oversimplifies, even as it captures the construction of the difference. Nonetheless, Nakagawa continues, this is relevant in the Japanese context as well, for "women, in a war that has been waged entirely by men (regardless of the fact that they may not have desired it in the least), have been left behind by the society that continually makes victims of women."[7] As a result, of course, this means that the body serves in an entirely different mode, if one gender contributes physical strength while another is expected to render emotional support. As Michael Molasky relates:

> For men, the simultaneous loss of Japan's empire and the commencement of foreign occupation signified a loss of control over both national and bodily boundaries. But women in wartime Japan were from the outset denied recognition as full-fledged Imperial subjects. They were not permitted to die for the emperor . . . Consequently, for most women the defeat . . . did not signify a threat to their identity as women or as Japanese . . . women tended to associate their loss with the war and rarely attributed it to the Occupation per se.[8]

The ambivalence of a young unmarried woman's relationship to the state[9] and the more fluid identity roles that resulted are reflected in Hayashi Fumiko's colonial and postwar novel, *Ukigumo* (*The Floating Clouds*, 1951).[10] The protagonist Yukiko has fled Japan to be a typist in Japanese-occupied Indochina. She had been staying with a relative's family in Tokyo where her uncle raped her repeatedly.[11] Fleeing to the colonies to escape an oppressive sexual situation repeats a common theme in women's fiction; they could not flee domestic situations, as could men, to be soldiers. Even when women were conscripted after 1944, they were drafted into factory work and not sent to the battle lines. Traveling to the colonies to be an employed civilian seemed a third possibility beyond factory work or marriage and motherhood. At a layover stop en route to the city where she will be stationed, Yukiko has second thoughts, given the isolation and loneliness she anticipates there. She watches the Japanese soldiers who stream through the streets – a pitiful dirty lot with ill-fitting clothes, with none of the appearance of the commanding colonizer. This strain of "we pathetic Japanese; what are we doing here?" runs through this and many other contemporary novels. One of the older veteran engineers traveling with her turns and, seeing her surveying the Japanese soldiers, says:

> Cheer up; you needn't look so glum. No matter where you go, there's gonna be Japanese soldiers, you know. Moreover, as the sole Japanese woman out here your responsibility is great. You're going to have to be able to work with these guys, you know.[12]

This reflects the double bind of her position: she will be working with these men, very closely, and yet she will not be one of them; she will be separate, not only as a *woman* (vis-à-vis the Japanese men with whom she works) but as a *Japanese* woman (as colonizer vis-à-vis the indigenous population). Her identity and roles are gendered on both counts, which positions her somewhere between the "native" women and the Japanese men. As a typist in the colonies, she will be able, more than most women of this time, to "serve her country" and partake in the larger project in a way denied most women, able to occupy a third space that is neither wife nor whore. This does not circumvent the ambivalence attendant upon being female, which she clearly feels, and which is reflected in the wartime slogan "men give their lives, women give their aid."[13] Postwar advertisements continued such ambiguity (at times deceit), by recruiting women with the claim for an "urgent need to reconstruct national [*kokka*] institutions: seeking new Japanese women." In reality, these "new women" were being recruited to serve in ancient roles as hostesses and prostitutes with the occupying GIs, and to serve as a human "floodwall," a defense, that is, built with their bodies to contain the flood of masculine desire anticipated with the advancing occupation GIs.[14] Here again, women's bodies were offered, before and after surrender, as a secondary line of defense. They were called on to make great sacrifices, while much of this fiction hints at the irony that they were not deemed appropriate for the "ultimate sacrifice" (i.e. death on the battlefield) which only reinscribed their subordinate status.

Sono Ayako's "Enrai no kyaku-tachi" ("Guests from Afar," 1954) is another of many works capturing the ambiguity of gender and a woman's relationship to the state. The "guests" in the hotel where she works are occupation troops who have requisitioned the facilities of a grand old hotel in Hakone, a famous resort area. Namiko works as a receptionist at the information desk of the hotel, a perky young woman able to circulate among Japanese and Americans, regardless of rank, in a manner that replicates many other stories of the postwar era: the ability of these women to access different levels within the hierarchical structures may be an "advantage" of their second-tier status. In a similar vein, all Japanese are subordinate in the requisitioned hotel where the Americans clearly retain power. This service role marks a third space for this young woman – neither factory work nor marriage and motherhood. It is, however, a subordinate position for the men, reflecting the shuffling of roles under the occupation. For many men this replicates their lack of agency as soldiers in the Imperial army, represented in the fiction of Noma Hiroshi, for example, as feminized and in subordinate positions. Some of the tension of male disconnect is found here: even while uniformed in the power of the empire, their own volition was severely constricted within and by that system; and the end of the war has not eliminated it.

The choices available for women writing of such experiences, and thus of their characters, seem to be two: i.e. in Joan Ericson's words, "the Manichean contrast of collaboration or resistance" choices that women like Hayashi Fumiko (1904–51), Sata Ineko (1904–), and Hirabayashi Taiko (1905–72) "cast a cold eye on" for the manner in which they misrepresented women's experience.[15] I have noted in the first chapter Mizuta Noriko's suggestion regarding the binary pull of public and private for men; the structure can pull in two directions: escape from the public towards the private and the woman, or escape from the home, which can be a little "society," towards the woman of the pleasure quarters, the sensual woman. Men may anticipate that they will be made whole in the privacy of their home and via the woman that that home represents; the woman, however, has no such choices, no place to seek refuge, for the home is her "public" space of sanctioned roles. The public is where the man acts, the home is the refuge to which he escapes. As a result – and this suggestion is exceedingly provocative in the terms of this study – the woman's body becomes a reference point for men because the woman leads the man to this area of refuge. At the same time she symbolizes – embodies – that space. The home marks the place opposing the public, which is the realm of politics and the company, and occupies the place of the private and of refuge. To escape from the demands of the public, the workplace, the man desires this private place, the place of the woman. Desire for privacy, escape – and, in the work I review, liberation – is imagined as the desire for this woman and her space. He desires her space; she also is the one to lead him.

Women writers such as Kōno Taeko (1926–), Enchi Fumiko (1905–86), and Tomioka Taiko (1935–) have also explored a woman's "power" to attract and inspire fear in men, power located in the body;[16] the flesh writers revealed an assumption (fear) of this power as well. For women writers, however, the body can serve as a means to subvert systems of societal and psychological organization. Explorations of the body's possibilities seem, for many women writers, an attempt to understand their experience. They envision a different societal order that allows little optimism regarding its actualization. The result is very different from that of the men, who are exploring the woman's body to understand only themselves (and not the woman), while the women explore individuals in order to describe society.[17] The men seem to focus on their own situation, in search of liberating possibility; the women find no liberation in such description as they look outward and describe the reality they inhabit.

Perhaps the differing narratives of the experiences of men and women relate to the striking number of women-authored works that were nominated for the Akutagawa Prize but not awarded it. A significant amount of (male) critical energy has been expended in explaining why such work did not obtain this prestigious prize: the characters were not fully drawn is a frequent explanation. Recipients after the war tend to be stories with a more "traditional" (I am tempted to write "male") story line that follows crisis, climax, dénouement, or, rephrased, follows the trajectory from stability to disruption to a reworked stability. The prizewinners often exhibit linear development, while the writing by women tends to be episodic slice-of-life narratives or group portraitures, for example. The tradition of treating "men's literature" as separate from "women's literature" certainly undergirds, and may have arisen from, this equation.[18] In another context, Komashaku Kimi has written of this same tendency:

> Men, when they write about the anguish and resistance to the family and society, are highly praised within contemporary literature. The anguish of the woman's self [being configured differently] has not been highly praised, however. Women [who write of] anguish in the face of state power have been highly valued but when that anguish is vis-à-vis fathers and husbands – i.e. masculine authority – they have not been properly valued. Or more precisely, it may fall outside of [the men's] understanding.[19]

If such concerns fall outside the ken of the men with whom the women are contemporaries, the fiction will be less well understood, and overlooked, by men who do not share this experience.

To be more precise, women writing in the postwar rarely even try to portray non-power-stratified utopias; they are seemingly aware they cannot be rid of the oppressive structure by exchanging it for a utopian, "freeing" one. Perhaps their experiences revealed the impossibility of a society without sexualized power structures. Conceptualizing an entire structure, even one designed to be freeing, condemns one to erecting borders, and these can only be, by definition, constraining, as one ideology is substituted for another. Perhaps this is so obvious that the women writers are not compelled to think in terms of an alternate structure. (Perhaps it is a masculine proclivity to construct such systems.)

Which is to say, one lesson learned from reading these women is the uniformity of the masculine vision and voice in contrast to the disparate women's voices: the men all write more or less the same woman. Women in their works freely formed a society based on physicality independent of official mores. Because they survived on the proceeds of selling sex, readers were to understand that they are living by their bodies.

The women characterized by female writers are drawn as individuals with very different motivations and responses, however. Their fiction portrays the worlds of sex workers and domestic help as one of limited, coerced choices and constricted freedoms, of violence, and formidable, costly boundaries. No "woman's voice" proceeds from the women's writing that would correlate to the consistency that is evident in the writings of very different men. For example, few women were as taken with descriptions of the underworld and prostitutes as the men, raising the "obvious" question: why were these men so obsessed with such women?

I find that all these writers, both women and men, are trying to establish a ground for identity and agency. The body suggests locations where subjectivity might be formed. That foundation is so different, however, that I intend this section on women writers to help excavate the assumptions and methods supporting the fictional imaginaries. While the negotiation of subjectivity also seems possible in the women-authored fiction, the area in which to maneuver that subjectivity is very constrained and, in contrast to men who envisioned freedom from their constricting situations, women can offer no reason to anticipate that those borders can be crossed. Rather, they admit the possibilities of freedom and agency while drawing attention to the boundaries. Liberation and volition exist in all the fiction, but are hemmed in much more closely when portrayed by women, whose fiction casts doubts on the masculinist assumptions that the individual is a discrete unit with control over their own life.[20] In the fiction of the flesh writers, women act as free agents largely in control of their options; women writers display no such confidence in the individual's ability to change society, much less to determine everyday realities or their own futures. Postwar realities were more likely to curtail women's choices than provide the freedom and liberation the men desired.

Saegusa Kazuko has also suggested that because men and women experience their selves (*jiga*) differently in society, men will not find the women's descriptions of those experiences satisfying. Men writing of reactions and struggles with the state, for example, produce images that look very different from those produced by women. Women must contend not only with the state, but also with husbands and fathers in a patriarchal society. This, Saegusa suggests, accounts for many of the reasons writings by women have been undervalued.[21]

While connecting twentieth-century writing by women to the classic Heian traditions is tenuous,[22] I find recent suggestions proffered by Mara Miller on the reading of women's writing pertinent to this discussion. Miller refers to the classical tradition in Japanese writing where a woman – as subject – addresses her audience not as Other (in the Western paradigm which is also reflected in much of this male writing) but as another equal subject. In this conception, reader and writer interact as equals before the same text, in a conversation of sorts. The gendered gaze of either author or reader is thereby less likely to be explicit, leaving the gender of reader and writer unclear and, indeed, immaterial:

> Masculinity is understood [in classical literature] as a choice and a social construction; moreover, it is accomplished through a variety of avenues, among which are choices of Japanese or Chinese modes of writing. Second, it is impossible for women to be assigned the role of the "other" to the male.[23]

If reading practices among men and women retain even traces of such classic reading strategies, then male readers and critics will come away from women's fiction dissatisfied, experiencing a lack. Expecting a completed Other, rather than a co-creator, in fully realized "mature" work, fiction that retains traces of a community of readers will seem immature. While this does not explain all, and certainly does not explain the paucity of literary prizes awarded women writers, it seems to me that the momentum of tradition could easily be sufficient to direct these works to styles at variance with (unwritten, masculinist) criteria for these prizes. But, more to the point, Miller continues by noting how the "traditional" Japanese modes of writing have been configured as female – *monogatari* and *nikki*, writing in *kana*: that is, works written in first-person narration or in diary format, in the syllabary marked as feminine. Such practices also mark literature as "feminine."[24] Ambivalence about writing literature in Japan, for males particularly, may also be tied to practicing in forms and styles marked as feminine. If such anxieties were heightened in the postwar years – and Nishikawa Nagao suggests that male writers were haunted by a literature that seemed to many to be feminine, with the interest in the marginal figure of the *pan-pan* reflecting the men's own sense of societal marginalization, as I noted in the initial chapter – it adds one more layer to the congeries of issues affecting masculine fears. Perhaps at some level men must connect and identify with the woman, appropriate her body and form (both literary and performative) to feel fully constituted as a writer. Since literature had long been marked as individual and private, practitioners of this literature experience role-anxiety – men are plagued by anxiety about practicing a "female" art. And this, as Elise Tipton suggests, is the source of *ressentiment*: "the terrible humiliation of being dependent in a world where self-worth depends on being independent."[25] I turn next to some of those writers and the fiction that foregrounds such issues.

Sono Ayako: "Good Luck for Everybody!!"

Sono Ayako's 1955 story "Good Luck for Everybody!!"[26] (the original title is in English) is particularly striking for the manner in which the women protagonists (not all of whom are sex workers) identify equally with the occupiers and the occupied. Frustration and disenfranchisement, poverty even, are not strangers to Sono's Japanese characters nor, we find, to the American servicemen and their families. In the preceding year Sono had published "Enrai no kyaku tachi" ("The Guests from Afar," which I touched on above) in *Mita bungaku,* and that story was nominated for the Akutagawa Prize. The prize, that year, went to Yoshiyuki Jun'nosuke,[27] but the attention given to this story launched Sono's career. The jury, almost to a man, remarked that she writes in a crisp style that flows with ease; it is unforced in both writing and characterization; and it offers a "fresh atmosphere."[28] Her ability to deftly present a wide range of characters with a light comic touch (without being lightweight) shares much with the fiction of Kojima Nobuo. In particular, her portrayals of the foibles and eccentricities, the complexes and anxieties, afflicting both Japanese and Americans, are striking for the time. The story published subsequently, "Good Luck for Everybody!!" contains a more powerful charge of sexual politics than "Enrai no kyaku tachi," which is why I concentrate on it here.

Kumiko and Yōko work as live-in maids for a US military family. This domestic situation focuses a number of themes where romance and marriage intersect with various issues: race and ethnicity; equality and discrimination, both in Japan and in the United States; the choices open (and closed) to men and women, Japanese and American alike. A pervasive sense of resignation envelops both occupied Japanese and occupying Americans. The women from both cultures share anxieties resulting from lack of power. Further, we find that sex work and domestic work appear on a continuum, not as mutually exclusive identity markers, as the male portrayals would have it. That is, "prostitute" does not form an identity role here. Kumiko works as a maid now, but when this military family returns to the United States in the next few weeks, she will be unemployed, with sex work as one of her unattractive options. Indeed, even now, her colleague works as a *pan-pan* in the evenings. Sono deftly captures individual person-alities regardless of racial background. She does not elide race and nationality – just the opposite – but she writes with a subtlety rare in this period.

Sono captures both the Japanese and the Americans in difficult and straitened circumstances. This is a rare achievement, most noticeable in her portrayal of the GI's wife, who claims that her experience in Japan is like a vacation: she has the means to hire domestic help, and her life in the Washington Heights section of Tokyo allows her a mobility she cannot enjoy in the United States. So much so, in fact, that she faces her impending return with some dread, for her future is uncertain. It is not stated, but hinted, that her life in the United States is significantly more constricted, both economically and socially, than the one she currently enjoys in Japan. This transitional situation parallels Kumiko's now uncertain future, for her employment and living situ-ation will change dramatically when the GI employer leaves Japan. Sono's biography reveals that she had worked in a similar situation after the war, and her portrayal is nuanced as she depicts the equivalencies of position (i.e. powerlessness) experienced by these women on very different power scales.

Such uncertainty in the daily lives of all women, both occupied and occupying, is recurrent in the women's fiction. Powerlessness binds them as women, and national boundaries are secondary (although still critical). Future location and employment is uncertain and the women, both GI wives and Japanese, must navigate finicky and often indecipherable bureaucracies controlled by men who make their decisions else-where and arbitrarily, following a different logic. Kumiko and Yōko have little control over their surroundings, yet in the narratives they seem only slightly less in control of their fates than the woman who is their occupier–employer.

Their work as maids is integral to the efficient running of the American household; it also affords the women access to the occupying world unavailable to their country-men. In this tale, they are insiders through domestic service, literally "at home" in the occupiers' domestic space. Such access is often the object of envy and anxiety in male writers: they are envious of the access while anxious about their concomitant loss of masculine power, because they lack such access. The Japanese women, by virtue of their domestic and subservient roles, can exercise control in a sphere their countrymen cannot even enter. Power has been usurped from the Japanese men. At the same time, the occupying soldiers are often revealed to be inept children who need the women to get them through everyday tasks: "The Americans are made to look like children, easily manipulated by their Japanese subjects. This infantilization of the occupiers is not uncommon in women's writing but is rarely, if ever, encountered in men's narra-tives about the era."[29] Women are assumed to be innately attuned to the needs of caring for children; the GI men in whose homes they serve often become children under their care as well. For example, Kumiko is not comfortable with the domestic duties she is expected to understand "naturally" as a woman: she must rely on Yōko's advice on handling the American family's children. Being a woman has not given her any innate understanding of childcare. The female caretaking roles, usually subservient, now afford them employment and a certain power at the same time that the once dominant males have lost their position of command. This reversal of roles is one source of the anxiety expressed by male writers.

Race is introduced in the initial scenes when Kumiko awakes early in the morning as the wan sunlight eases over the "Washington Heights" neighborhood of Tokyo in a smoky haze. She struggles to look out across the neighborhood and sees something come into view in her window that she cannot quite make out – "somehow familiar yet looking for all the world like just-baked black bread. But, a very strange black bread, for it is covered with white icing" – until it hits her that she is looking at her GI boyfriend in his white MP hat. That this African-American soldier blends into the hazy morning light and first strikes her as black, burnt bread develops the impending mystery of the story. Starting here and continuing throughout, his existence is hazy and nebulous, almost non-existent, erased from the white landscape. In a further irony, he goes by the name of Shakespeare, a name given to his grandfather, a slave, by his owner, precisely because he was illiterate. In a story that is attuned to the subtleties of race and class, these ironic pairings contain poignant meaning.

Kumiko talks of marrying Shakespeare as a way to extricate herself from the uncertainty of postwar Japan. While America extends the promise of material wealth and societal liberation, she wonders, in a phrase repeated more than once, what kind of life would be available to her, an Asian woman in Arkansas, married to a black man who is not himself able to share a park bench with a white man. Yōko chides her: "If you want to go live in the middle of nowhere, cut off from other people in a backward society, there is no reason to go all the way to America: We have many places like that right here in Japan." This tempered vision of American reality is consistent with the perspective these female characters bring to the realities of postwar Japanese society.

The conflict in the story is provided by Mrs Wilcox, the family friend who has stayed over the night before. As she awakens in the morning, Kumiko hears Mrs Wilcox talking on the phone. She then tries to process the meaning of Shakespeare's visage in the window while readying herself to begin the morning breakfast tasks; there comes a crash from the kitchen as Mrs Wilcox crumples to the floor. The MPs come, apparently at Mrs Wilcox's request. While talking on the phone, Mrs Wilcox saw a face in the window and then she felt an unknown hand brush hers. A perceived sexual threat had caused her to faint. When the MPs arrive to question the household – was anyone seen on the premises this morning? – Kumiko is in a quandary: should she reveal that she saw Shakespeare in the window? He was on duty and should not have been away from his post. Is there any point in bringing up his name? She is saved from having to make a decision when Mr Mahoney, her employer, pulls the MP aside to explain. What caused her to faint was the family pet nuzzling her hand with its wet nose, a pet pig that had been given to the family as a gift by the Japanese. "They always give too many gifts anyway," he says to the MP, continuing,

> That pig sticks its nose in everything. If you are sitting it noses your shoes. If you are standing, well, you can imagine . . . The pig brushed Mrs Wilcox's hand with its nose, that's all. But look, let's keep this a secret because she will be devastated if

she realizes that she called the MPs for a pig that brushed against her. Besides, the kids love this pig and we don't want anything to happen to it.[30]

With this "sensible" explanation they decide to leave the case "unsolved."

Kumiko's experiences of American racism further complicate her thoughts about marriage to Shakespeare. In her subordinate position she realizes she has almost turned in her boyfriend by revealing his presence. If his presence were known, he would be charged with dereliction of duty, and there would be no end of difficulty for a black officer found outside the home of a white officer, hoping to meet his Japanese girlfriend. Furthermore, had she revealed his presence, the blame for Mrs Wilcox's fright would very likely have fallen on Shakespeare and the problem would have been "solved" in this way. That is, he would have been jailed or discharged, essentially sacrificed for a pig, all in order to preserve a family pet. Mr Mahoney has been very concerned that the children be spared any distress should their cherished pig be punished. This nearly fatal irony is compounded by the fact that the children are not in the least fooled. They cannot wait to get to school the next day to tell all their friends what their pig has done. The dilemmas are much more practical, and much more serious in their ramifications for these women, than those confronting the characters in the men's fiction.

That this sometime prostitute, now working as the trusted maid to a family of the occupying force, is in a sexual relationship with a black soldier layers this story with transgression and complications. Nowhere does any of this offer liberation and freedom, however, or any support for optimism concerning sexual freedom or the change in power structures; it describes only the straitened circumstances of limited postwar choices. Sono's depiction of the situation is but one of the ways that this story, and others by her contemporaries, differ from men's writing I have considered thus far. In this work, as in her "Enrai no kyaku tachi," she shows herself to be a master of characterization. We see in these characters the oppressive sexually discriminatory systems shared by both Japanese society and "democracy." The broad range of characters, imbued with a sophisticated subtlety and irony, reveal the difficulties in navigating survival and deciphering the maze of systems, but none fully escape – or change – it.

Hiroike Akiko: "Onrii tachi" ("The Only Ones")

Hiroike Akiko's "Onrii tachi" ("The Only Ones") was one of ten contenders for the 1954 Akutagawa Prize (as was Sono Ayako's "Enrai no kyaku-tachi"). Hiroike would be awarded the Naoki Prize the following year for *Zeroka no mure*. "Onrii tachi" is so centered on a boarding house, and the woman who owns it, that the house seems a character in the story. The landlady has recently renovated her house to accommodate boarders. She "loves [this house] completely . . . As far as she was concerned the house was a husband who did not eat, a husband who did not beat her."[31] The frame for the story – a group of *pan-pan* who live together in a boarding house – is reminiscent of Tamura's "Nikutai no mon." In contrast to Tamura, however, this space is not occupied by women exercising their freedom and liberty to form a new society, but marks the intersection of desperate lives, none of them attractive, none of them liberating.

The *pan-pan* who take rooms in the house, their GI lovers, and their milieu provide the material for the story. The women all go by English names and they are described among daily squalor, with none of the romantic overtones that Tamura, for example, gives his characters. Kelly, for one, is hasty and impetuous, while friendly and affable. She exhibits an unhealthy pallor and is not especially pretty. She prefers loud colors, the red shoes and leather jackets stereotypical for *pan-pan*, "amidst the many women who wear sandals on their dirty darkened feet": bright colors, that is, in a time when most of the populace are dressing in subdued ones.[32] The landlady, it is hinted, has rented the room to Kelly less because of Kelly than because of her interest in Kelly's GI boyfriend. The young GI with beautiful skin, shining hair, and a bright countenance is kind and courteous to her. He seems the picture of health and youth, in marked contrast to the young Japanese women, who are careworn and undernourished.

The prevailing images are of the turbulence and instability of this lifestyle, the precariousness of existence that results from reliance on handouts from men. For all the glamour associated with sex workers in the writing by men and in the popular imagination generally, and for all the freedom of choice and authority over one's destiny that these women represented, what we find in stories such as this is simply the poverty and squalor of lives constrained both materially and spiritually (*seishinteki*, a word used throughout, which suggests psychological health and well-being, and which overlaps with the *seishin–nikutai* dialectic I explored in the first chapter).

Kelly, for example, lacks proper nightclothes and even a futon; she sleeps in her chemise. In place of curtains, her ten sets of clothing – her entire wardrobe, cycled through the four seasons – hang across her window. The poverty of her life forms another insistent theme: while her friends enjoy going to the bicycle race track, for example, she has never gone because her mother stands in front of the track doing her best to sell a few newspapers, calling to customers desperately as she wipes the sweat from her brow with a soiled handkerchief. Her younger sister, at sixteen, has dropped out of school, taken the name Julie, and established herself in a hotel to take in soldiers. As the oldest, Kelly reasons, it is acceptable for her to be in this profession as a way to help support the family – invoking the long-suffering, responsible female – but there is no reason for the younger daughter to be careless with her life and take up this lifestyle. That two *pan-pan* come from the same family does not go unnoticed in the neighborhood and is a source of shame to them all. Completing the picture of postwar desperation, Kelly's twelve-year-old brother is responsible for the two youngest sisters, one whom displays signs of malnutrition.

This work also highlights the capitalist and societal changes at the end of the occupation era. Fewer and fewer American soldiers in Japan means that the competition among the women has grown increasingly fierce, prices drop, and the women's lives become even more desperate. Mary, even though she cannot speak English very well – which is to say she cannot register displeasure or express refusal – irons, does laundry, and cooks as well as providing sexual services for the soldier supporting her. She cannot afford to do otherwise. The tenuousness of capitalist exchange is an everyday experience.

Like Kelly, we find, Susie also comes from an impoverished family of seven children. She has a Japanese boyfriend, Kawamura, who is kept secret from Larry, her GI boyfriend (who, in turn, is not known to the young Japanese man). Larry has two sons in the United States but promises that he will take Susie back with him. She was recently fired from the bar where she worked when they discovered she was an "only"; with the decrease in business, we are told, the bars use any excuse to get rid of the women. (An "only" is supported by one man, in contrast to a "butterfly" who must flit from one customer to another.) As the end of the year approaches, the winter cold emphasizes the loneliness of the Christmas and New Year holidays – the latter being the more important and nostalgic for the women – and Larry does not appear. She has no way of knowing if he has abandoned her, was transferred suddenly, or if his plane has gone down on a bombing run over the Korean peninsula. Either way it leaves her destitute and lonely at what should be the most festive time of the year. In this way the postwar experience of the Japanese women replicates the war experience: they still wait for men who have gone to the front and not returned, with no means to discern if they have been shot down, are alive or dead, or if they have left for another woman. The powerful irony of this postwar scene is that while the politics of the everyday has changed dramatically – the soldiers on whom they depend are not Imperial soldiers but occupying soldiers – the daily emotional and physical burdens of the women are unchanged.

"Given this material, a full-length novel is called for," wrote Niwa Fumio in his judgment on the Akutagawa Prizes for that year.[33] For all the story's interest and authority, too many characters means none are fully developed, he suggests. Many of the judges (who included such luminaries as Uno Kōji, Satō Haruo, Kawabata Yasunari, and Sakaguchi Ango[34]) critiqued the work for thinness of characterization. A number commented on the unusual subject matter, which I take to refer to the harsh light cast on the usually glamorous image of these women, highlighting a desperate aspect of their lives that is not found in the fiction by men. The catalogue of lifestyles correlates to themes of this study; each woman displays a different personality and situation, and we find tales of survival, rather than liberation and freedom, in a milieu where the women are constricted, not empowered, lonely and sad, tied to soldiers for survival. The cast of characters provides scenarios to narrate the various relationships of the women, while revealing the consistent powerlessness and uncertainty of their hand-to-mouth existence. The shared work does not, however, draw the women into a community; rather, they are rivals for the same customers, which often leads to violence and the threat of violence among themselves. The reader is left with little doubt that most of them will be crushed by these demands, unable to survive solely on the strength of personality, with no liberation apparent.

Nakamoto Takako: "Kichi no onna" ("Military Base Women")

Nakamoto Takako writes of *pan-pan* who rely on GIs in her "Kichi no onna" ("Military Base Women").[35] Nakamoto (1903–91), who was jailed for her writings and leftist activities during the 1930s, lived underground for much of that prewar decade. Her concerns as a Proletarian writer are readily apparent as she uses this portrait of *pan-pan* to introduce a range of societal issues. Most interesting is her decision to make the central character, Sumiko, a member of the discriminated-against *burakumin* caste and to layer the discrimination against sex workers atop this class discrimination. In the story, derogatory cries of "*pan-pan*" overlap with the cries of "*eta*" she remembers from her youth. Although sometimes heavy-handed, this overlap of class discrimination, gender, and poverty provides a sharp indictment of society.

The story opens as two women discuss marriage and the future, prompted by the news that one of their group, Rose, is to marry an American serviceman and go to the United States. The debate turns to whether being an "only" is the same as being married. The grand dream that they share – marriage to a serviceman who will take them from Japan to the United States – can be read, by its extreme unlikelihood, as a marker of the desperation in which they find themselves. They place hope for liberation and freedom, both material and physical, in marriage and life in a new country, and the United States in particular, in a dream at least as old as the Meiji era (Tōson's conclusion in *The Broken Commandment* comes to mind), albeit the country is that of their occupiers.

Two of the women go to a theater to see a local performance of a play. The feuding cruelty of the mother-in-law on stage towards her son's wife affects Sumiko powerfully, reminding her of her own situation before the war when she suffered similar abuse at the hands of her mother-in-law. A boy in the crowd sees her tears and cries out: "Imagine, a *pan-pan* who cries. I didn't think they had emotions." Nakamoto will offset these negative stereotypes of *pan-pan* as cold-hearted and greedy, bent on the destruction of men, by providing a fuller picture of their lives and difficulties.

Sumiko's life has followed a path predicated on her poverty and her *burakumin* class status. She followed her brother and left her home in rural Gunma Prefecture to work in a munitions factory. Such jobs were plentiful as the conflict with China escalated. She fell in with some activists who were jailed and interrogated by the "war machinery." She married one of the activists, who wanted to marry so that they might share their life together for the short time remaining until he was called up. He left for the front three days after the wedding and Sumiko remained to suffer the wrath of her mother-in-law, who claimed at one point that she was glad that there were no children from this union, thus preventing the blood of the family from becoming polluted. When Sumiko could no longer endure the abuse, she returned to her parents' home to wait out the rest of the war. Miserable and disgusted by the lack of opportunities and the discrimination that prevented her from obtaining good jobs, she grew to hate her family history and background. Following the end of the war, she attempted to get work at the same munitions factory, but they had all been closed down. She then traveled to Tokyo where her brother was now working in the black market. At this point her story offers a history of prostitution in Japan:

> The collapse of the social order after the war, together with the freedoms that were promptly made available, meant that there were waitresses at the coffee shops that would without a second thought take money in exchange for their ultimate possession if only taken by the hand by a customer . . . Sumiko saw this [exchange] again and again. Embarrassed, she would look away.[36]

Nakamoto's phrasing is stereotypical. Sumiko displays only contempt for those who would accept money for sex. This turns melodramatic as Nakamoto frames the conflict as one of immediate sacrifice motivated by faithfulness to a husband who has still not been repatriated: Sumiko is committed to enduring the poverty of her situation and to awaiting the return of her husband, no matter how fatigued and grimy he might prove to be, nor how desperate she might become in the interim. For this the other waitresses criticize her as being hopelessly behind the times. "You will immolate your youth," they chide; "How long are you going to wait?" they ask her. By this point Nakamoto has provided a catalog of stereotypes: a *burakumin* youth involved in underground activity and the black market, with a sister who is a *pan pan*. She takes a job as a café waitress, which is understood as the first step towards full-fledged prostitution. Tamura describes similar scenes, but Nakamoto focuses on the despair, poverty, and powerlessness of the women rather than the possibility of liberation in such communities.

For example, Sumiko is initiated into prostitution when tricked by a fellow waitress. She is led to a party where she meets a bear of a GI who promptly wraps her in his arms as though she were a rabbit – it is a rape, although Nakamoto leaves the sexual violence to the imagination of the reader. The GI gives her money that "bewitches" her; her "friend" appropriates half of it as her fee. Sumiko returns home and promptly burns the picture of her husband. Enthralled by the stack of money on her nightstand, she begins her "decline" into full-time prostitution:

> From there Sumiko slid down the stairs of degradation with great speed. The next time [she was invited] she consciously followed Machiko to the same hotel. No past and no future, no responsibilities and no constraints, [she went] following the desire for freedom.[37]

She embarks on a new path, jettisoning her past for "freedom" from her husband's family and from her poverty. This marks the second time she rejects her past, the first being when she left home to deny her *burakumin* identity.

The difference in time represented in these changes is reflected in the difference of space. After the war, her brother gives up the black market and takes over a meat shop in Kanda (layering another stereotypic *burakumin* association). He reports that her husband has returned, but Sumiko cannot face him. The distance between them has "become as vast as the East and West of the Pacific Ocean," which parallels phrasing often encountered in these postwar works, and also reflects the national/political distinctions that impinge upon these characters. This chasm between individuals cannot be crossed, a chasm that separates one not from liberation – as we found in Noma Hiroshi's fiction, for example – but only a semblance of normalcy, here represented as a traditional family. She has now been living as an "only" with a GI named Robert for over a year, "living in a foreign country within the borders of the country of her ancestors."[38] This unifies the disparate strands of her life and collapses the spaces between all the people in her life, between her and her past, and between the reality of a *burakumin* identity and the life she envisioned for herself. At every level and in every situation the country and society betray her and she is cast out, helpless, without support, and driven to the brink. Even her brother throws her employment and associations into her face, casting doubt on her "Japaneseness." She is alienated from society as a prostitute in the same way that she is alienated by virtue of being *buraku-min*. That this connection is made by a family member makes it that much harsher. It also reflects the contradictory responses to sex work: needed as a "comfort" to the soldiers during wartime and as a "floodwall" to protect the homeland afterwards, Sumiko's association with the nation is questioned, along with that of her country-women. Fulfilling the patriotic duty requested of her, she is simultaneously rendered Other.

Space between Sumiko and her boyfriend is collapsed physically and figuratively as well. She and Robert are close together in an embrace: "In the space between these two bodies [*futatsu no nikutai*], with nothing, neither history nor family relations between them, is contained the breadth of the entire Atlantic Ocean."[39] This phrasing exhibits a surprising overlap of vocabulary and concern with Noma Hiroshi's fiction. Elsewhere, we have a line that reads as though directly from Noma, but it is out of place in this story: "She was searching for her own liberation by drawing close to this accumulation of men."[40] Sex is portrayed as a drug to forget the past, while the most compelling desire is financial security. The "liberation" for which Sumiko searches is nothing more than a comfortable life among her countrymen, without prejudice, and with some economic stability. Nakamoto's proletarian concerns for workers and for societal discrimination yields a tone and eye similar to Noma's Marxism: that is, a concern for the economic structures of these situations, although the liberation she desires is of quite a different sort – nothing transcendent, only material.

In plotting Sumiko's trajectory as prostitute (imagined as decline), and with it a history of prostitution in Japan, Nakamoto portrays Sumiko descending to ever less desirable short-term hotels. In a final crisis and an emblematic scene, she refuses a young GI who has no money. As she attempts to shepherd him out of this hotel after he tries to force himself on her, he resists violently and flings her away with a deroga-tory cry of "Jap." This rings in her ears in the same tone as the *eta* that was flung at her in childhood, and she is cast from all communities at once, despised simultaneously as Japanese, prostitute, and *burakumin*. She cannot reject one society to construct a utopian one, for none exist. No liberation will be found.

Nakamoto highlights the historical importance of the Korean conflict in the background. While the post-Pacific War experience she portrays is different from that portrayed by the flesh writers – theirs is in the immediate postwar years of US occupa-tion and Nakamoto's is a decade later, during the US conflict on the Korean peninsula – the themes of loss and trauma are unchanged. Thus, for example, Sumiko's boyfriend is gone in the same way, still on bombing raids, perhaps dead. Nakamoto also connects the experience of postwar Japanese with those (Koreans) living under bombs dropped from US planes. The Koreans are in a situation that was Japan's a few years before. Thus, while the historical difference is noted, in that a different war is being fought, the role of these women in relation to the US soldiers remains fixed, and parallels the position of Asians under the aggressive Americans.

Nakamoto's attempt to draw together different issues into a coherent whole topples under its own weight, however, for she tries to make this work a ground to discuss a full gamut of racial and societal issues. She succumbs to the temptation of melodrama and predictability in both story line and phrasing. With the loss of her boyfriend, Sumiko slides deeper and deeper into depression, and the story ends with a pregnant ellipsis as she prepares to plunge a dagger into her throat. Writing according to her political commitments seems to embroil Nakamoto in the same trap that plagued the male writers: the Proletarian political ideology, which undergirds her writing, crushes her final project. Nakamoto does not claim to abolish ideologies, nor does her ideology detract from her vision of a more equitable society. Her ideological understanding does constrict the success of her fictional representations, however. While she offers no hope for utopia in these writings, her equation of the structural nature of the impediments to the characters' **happiness** is crucial. Changing the structures of society would, presumably, free these characters from their oppression, which is to say, she places the issues and their solutions in contexts much larger than the individual. "Liberation" from such bonds will not be found solely in individual action, nor is it suggested that it will be found in a primal community. Her attention to larger structural connections that constrict the choices of these women is welcome, yet the work suffers under its own ideological load.

Shibaki Yoshiko: "The Susaki Paradise" and "Yakō no onna"

Shibaki Yoshiko (1914–91) was born the daughter of a cloth and clothing merchant in the *shitamachi* section of Asakusa, an area long associated with traditional crafts and the pleasure quarters. This area forms the setting for many works where she explores human relations by focusing on the love, jealousy, and attraction in relationships between men and women. She began her literary career before the Asia-Pacific War and, in 1936, received the Akutagawa Prize for "Seika no ichi" ("The Fruit Market"). The main character of that story, a twenty-six-year-old woman named Yae, is a natural in the wholesale fruit business the family maintains in the bustling Tsukiji market. A central conflict of the work is her "masculinity," compounded by her lack of interest in marriage and her predilection for the "masculine" talents of bidding and haggling over domestic tasks. The reality of a nation at war impinges from the background, for rationing goes into effect as the government sets prices for commodities, making the family retail business nearly impossible.

As Senuma Shigeki notes below, one would have anticipated that the Akutagawa Prize would have left Shibaki poised for a successful career as a writer. War quashed all those hopes. There were government restrictions on the freedom to exercise one's talent and one's voice, and, further, the number of outlets for publication were severely constricted by the war.

> She received no special fanfare of welcome as an Akutagawa-Prize-winning author, nor was the situation such that she could capitalize on the popularity of "Seika no ichi" by writing successful work following on successful work. She was left with no choice but to endure the bad conditions, refine her writing, and wait out the times.[41]

Her postwar works are set in the pleasure quarters emblematic of the postwar milieu and concentrate on the women working there, even as those neighborhoods evoke a more traditional milieu. Ōshima Kiyoshi quotes Shibaki to the effect that she produced these works one after the other, writing as her spirit took her. Thus, in his words, "one gets the sense that [Shibaki] confronts these works having submerged the sadness and despair, and the anger and frustration, of her experiences as a woman."[42]

The experience of a woman is consistently equated with sadness, frustration, and powerlessness in this literature. Shibaki also, however, displays nostalgia for the disappearing world of the past by focusing on the romantic entanglements of love and family among laborers in this traditional downtown neighborhood that evokes prewar Taishō society. Financial instability adds an edge to her characters' lives, but Shibaki does not write from a political sensibility. The Susaki/Mukojima/Kiba area, all surrounded by water, provides the location for exploring individuality as relationships progress and disintegrate. The stories recreate the prewar world of this small community tucked away in the bustle of Tokyo, physically cut off from larger currents: in these works a man and a woman, sometimes with four or five acquaintances from the neighborhood gathered at the local restaurant, comprise "society." Shibaki's focus on the intersection of romance and nostalgia pushed many of her works towards stereotypes and eventually led her to being linked with melodramatic Romance novels (*ren'ai shōsetsu*). I wish to consider here two of the early stories, "Susaki paradaisu" ("The Susaki Paradise," 1954) and "Yakō no onna" ("Women of the Night Lights," 1955) which are more successful in skirting the shoals of melodrama (i.e. stereotypes and predictability), while presenting the issues of sex work and woman's experience that are most relevant to this study.

"Susaki paradaisu" takes its name from the street of bars in the Asakusa area; the entrance to the drinking area was graced by a blue neon arch that spelled out "Susaki paradaisu" over the entrance of the street. Customers reached it after crossing a bridge, just beyond Kiba. Neon and cheap sake amidst empty lots and piles of rubble remaining from wartime bombings identify the setting as postwar. The story opens as Tsutae and Yoshiharu are wandering towards Kiba, having emptied their pockets to pay for the previous night's lodgings. They alight at a bar just inside the entrance to the "Susaki Paradise." Tsutae orders a beer, followed by another. In conversation with the young proprietress – known only by O-kami san, i.e. as "owner" – their story unfolds and develops. They wanted to get married, but their families back in provincial Tochigi Prefecture refused them permission. He will search for work, having recently been a foreman at a warehouse; O-kami san notes that while there are many warehouses in this part of the town, it is unlikely that any comparable positions remain unfilled. She suggests that he could probably get work as a laborer, and makes inquiries, and he begins delivering for a local noodle restaurant. Tsutae proves herself a natural at the entertaining of customers and quickly makes herself indispensable at the bar. Two steady incomes and a place to live: they should have all they need.

The narrative crisis arrives with a self-employed businessman who frequents the bar. He promises Tsutae an apartment and they leave together, not returning until the following morning. Tsutae has a new hairstyle, fashionable new clothes, and the apartment. Her happiness is contagious and genuine; she has long entertained images of domestic happiness, dreaming of herself amidst the simple pleasures of sitting in an apartment with striped wallpaper, fresh tea in the pot, listening to the radio, waiting for a husband to come back. Yoshiharu will not be able to provide this for her, while Ochiai, the businessman, can.

Yet her affection towards Yoshiharu is unshakable. He has no way of knowing what is taking place; from his bicycle, delivering noodles in the rain, he sees Tsutae alight from a grand car, with her new clothes and radiant countenance. When Tsutae had not returned the night before, O-kami san had a premonition and closed the bar early. She locked the shutters and retreated to the small back room with her two children. Yoshiharu eventually arrives in a rage, banging on the grate and threatening physical harm. The next morning O-kami san relates to Tsutae that she is glad they had not met the previous night for there would have been bloodshed had she been within his reach. Yoshiharu sends a message that arrives shortly after Tsutae does: I am at a hotel; bring money. All the happiness Tsutae felt a moment before dissipates. She knows he has no money to pay for the room and is probably planning suicide. "I need to go to him, even if only to give him money for the room," she says. O-kami san advises her not to go, for how will she be able to return? Flying to his side portends death for them both. She feels drawn to him, bound by their past and their promises. She cannot leave him. She takes off to deliver the room money and, of course, never returns.

Poverty unites all these characters and nurtures their destruction. Shibaki, however, focuses on visions of a romantic poverty, of two people simply happy to be together even if destitute. The lack of stable incomes drives her characters into difficult situations. O-kami san, for example, runs the small bar by herself, supporting the two children in the small room, with a husband who, we hear, in answer to a query if he is dead, "might as well be." O-kami san had worked as a prostitute before and during the war, serving as a comfort woman, then as a *pan-pan,* before opening this shop. (We encounter this trajectory again.) Tsutae herself had worked as an unlicensed prostitute until one month before in a nearby area unflatteringly referred to as "Pigeon street" (*Hato no machi*), a name associated with the area because the women sat at open windows and called to potential customers; their voices were likened to the cooing of birds. For O-kami san, like so many of these characters, "prostitute" is not an identity label, but is no model for freedom either; it is simply an employment choice among many unsatisfactory and low-paying jobs.

"Susaki Paradaisu" is the lead story in a series focused on the lives of women working in the Susaki area. "Yakō no onna," also in this series, is of interest here because of its treatment of women caught in cycles of financial and physical oppression. Yōko, for example, works in one of Shinjuku's unregulated areas (*aoisen*, "blue-line") of prostitution. She has become a prostitute not because of irrepressible spirit and a commitment to individuality, but from the need to pay the rent and buy food. She is successful in this business, able to command higher fees than other women in the quarter. Yet her loneliness is extreme. As she stands in front of the house where she works, saying nothing, her limbs seem to emit a light, a phosphorescent allure. A man passes, looks back, and returns to talk. He follows her upstairs where she finds, much to her surprise, that he wishes only to talk. We discover that they have a shared past, rooted in shared memories of the locale, better days before the war, and past loves. Comments on changes in the neighborhood, seemingly no more than passing remarks, consistently hint at the passage of time. Her memories of the early postwar years are vague and dreamlike; even sketchier are her childhood wartime memories. This past is best forgotten: parents killed in wartime bombings, struggles to survive thereafter, and her eventual introduction to sex work.

The man remembers meeting her in an earlier time when she worked as a "geisha." He wants to know how she has "fallen" to this current condition. She responds, "What do you mean [fallen]? Geisha, prostitute [in this time and place], are all the same." As the story unfolds we find just how different it is, however, for work as a "geisha" was much like indentured servitude, and Yōko was constantly tied to debt by the expensive kimono and other accoutrements of the trade. As an unlicensed prostitute she can keep the money she makes, with apparent autonomy to make independent choices. This characterization could have been developed into a celebration of a fierce independence in the face of adversity, as we found with Tamura; Shibaki, however, portrays the instability and violence of this work. The women are all long-suffering in adverse situations, which is to say that Shibaki draws from the standard palette of Japanese melodrama in a manner that does not indict the structures governing women's lives. Resolving to "endure" the situation is given as a legitimate and common response to such situations.

Whereas Borneo Maya was transported away in ecstatic death at the end of Tamura's "Nikutai no mon" following punishment for her transgression, no transcendence accompanies the beating that Yōko receives for transgressing the rules of her community. She has become involved with another prostitute's lover. The jealous woman and a group of friends trap her in an abandoned lot and attack her. The beating she receives for her infraction – the women encircle her and then start in with fists and feet – is obviously not motivated by any commitment to community solidarity, however nobly characterized in Tamura's fiction. Yōko disappears without a trace, and the man who has come to visit her is left to wonder what has become of her.[43] He appears at her door to keep a prearranged appointment after Yōko has called him in desperation – which marks for her an unusual degree of intimacy and trust. She has contacted him even though, in her experience, initiating non-business meetings causes the men to flee. Her disappearance is left unresolved, and the reader anticipates the worst for her; in contrast to other works discussed here, the story does not even hint at liberation, enlightenment, or ecstasy. Liberation was never really anticipated, and it is not delivered. Like many of Shibaki's stories, "Yakō no onna" concludes in solitude and broken promises, in loves lost, and a dose of melodrama.

In Shibaki's stories of this area, the desperation of prostitution as survival and the narrow choices available to women are consistently highlighted, and seem fated, given the women's past histories of working as "comfort women" in wartime or as hostesses and prostitutes in postwar pleasure quarters. The physical destruction of the war lurks in the background, apparent to anyone just outside who might look through the windows. The women try very hard to ignore this destruction, which is repressed along with many other associated memories. The ruins of war are immediately visible, however, and they usually prompt memories of prewar life without constrictions and shortages. Conspicuously absent in the narrow focus of Shibaki's fictional world are either occupation or Japanese soldiers. Shibaki is nostalgic for the mythic past of Tokyo's Shitamachi area; perhaps this causes her to elide the disruptive wartime history and try to recreate a Taishō world in the Shōwa ruins. Consistent with the other fiction I am considering, however, is the depiction of the long shadows that economic difficulties cast over women's lives. The men are laborers in a constricted job market (*fukeiki*, "recession," is a word she often uses). Jobs have been lost or wages cut, and the same jobs no longer support the former lifestyles. More often than not, the men have disappeared and the women must get on alone. The women are also laborers, but without technical skills they are forced to rely on sex work and waitressing. But because Shibaki concentrates on the emotional attachments and complications of love, the sources of that economic disparity are not explored in her stories. It seems that poverty, rather than war, prevents the connections between persons.

Saegusa Kazuko

To close this review of the counterpoint provided by women's postwar fiction, I want to consider briefly a trilogy of novels that appeared in the late 1980s. I introduce Saegusa Kazuko's work at this point, separated as it is in time, for the manner in which her fictional project overlaps with, and comments on, many of the issues developed in this study.[44] Three of her novels, *Sono hi no natsu* (*That Day's Summer*, 1987), *Sono fuyu no shi* (*That Winter's Death*, 1989), and *Sono yoru no owari ni* (*In the Final Moments of that Night*, 1990), summarize the themes I have discussed and develop many of them. She makes these novels a forum to explore the meanings of being a woman in the context of war, of being a woman writing the war experience, and of the varied generational responses to the war. These issues determine, and often prevent, community sharing. Stated another way, they often suggest, while simultaneously preventing, human interaction. These stories come close to the liberation envisioned by the male writers of earlier chapters, but there is no utopian optimism here, but simply the sharp awareness that war experiences are radically individual and ultimately unshareable. This trilogy lies close thematically to many of the works discussed throughout this study, mainly because of Saegusa's exploration of the similarities and equivalencies of a woman's experience of war in comparison to the men's.

These intertwined concerns form a provocative, while complex, nexus of issues. Saegusa's primary consideration is, however, the meaning of being a woman. As she expressed it a few years before the first of these novels was published:

> My thinking has been gradually changing. It is not so much that my thinking [about "being a woman"] has changed; rather, I have tried to write novels more consciously aware of the feminine [*joryū*] because this seems a method to more clearly grasp events.[45]

A catalyst moment was when she received the Tamura Toshiko Prize for literature, an award reserved for female writers: "I guess this makes me a *woman* then," she stated, prompting a guffaw from the novelist Takeda Taijun, one of the selection committee members, the point being that even with her natural antipathy towards prizes for "women's writing" – there being none for "men's writing," she reminds us – the process was instructive and heightened her awareness of herself as a "woman." She had not thought of herself as a "woman writer," but simply as a "writer."[46] Earlier in life, she continues, she would have reacted less to being contrasted as a "woman" in relation to the "male" but would have insisted that all are people, that the important aspects are the human ones, and that the divisions, in literature at least, of male and female are simply prejudice and bias. As she paid closer attention to the differing experiences of men and women in fictional representations, however, she found she was concentrating on the lived experience of being a woman, of how a woman's situation is, in fact, constructed differently within society, and was therefore more consciously aware how her responses to situations diverged from those of her male counterparts. In her work, such differences are revealed in detailed relief under the harsh light of war and postwar realities. The experience of gender is the key to unlocking the differing aspects of men and women, i.e. what is expected of one as woman and allowed as a man. "I wonder," she wrote in the afterword to *Sono hi no natsu*, "if the ideas [*shisō*] and details attendant on the war's end can only be clarified from the woman's experience."[47]

This introduces the next level of issues in her writing, the meanings attendant upon being a woman writing about war. Saegusa had moved from an awareness of the crucial differences that sex and gender exert on understanding experience to suggesting that a woman's experience will most fully encompass and may therefore be the *best*, perhaps the *only*, method to describe those experiences. A woman's experience is qualitatively superior to a man's, she is arguing. That she only turned her gaze to gender and war after thirty years of writing fiction was not, she notes as well, from lack of interest earlier in her career, but from lack of ability: the method for portraying war and related experiences long eluded her. The war experience may be most clearly articulated – it certainly is in this trilogy – at the interface of the "male" and the "female." A woman's body acts as a prism that separates differing strands of the war experience. Saegusa's trilogy examines the differences that might, or might not, result when the power structures emphasized during war and occupation are refracted not only through the enemy soldiers but also through the soldiers of one's own country. The dynamics cannot be divorced from the situation of one's countrymen who, defeated and stripped of their roles, mark a clear contrast to the confident virile occupation soldiers. In exploring such dynamics, Saegusa reflects many of the gender anxieties we found in the male writers while rooting them in a different gendered response.

The first novel of the three highlights the precise moment when one army is defeated and the other is victorious. *Sono hi no natsu* (*That Day's Summer*) captures, as the title conveys, the odd expanse of time marked by the summer day when the emperor announced the end of the war over the radio. We follow a high-school girl's experiences and reactions from the time of the emperor's announcement through the ten days (or so) following, until she returns to her family from the boarding school and munitions factory where she had been evacuated during the war. (This reflects the reality that women and girls could be drafted, from 1944, for factory work in domestic munitions plants.) In that span of time both armies are still unknowns: in the eyes of the sixteen-year-old Yoshii, the returning soldiers do not resemble the high-minded, virtuous, and sacrificial men of the newspaper reports but seem dispirited and ragged; as readers, we also know that the coming occupation army will not be the rapacious horde that she has been led to expect. Worse, the sexual threat anticipated from the invading army proves instead to be embodied in one of her countrymen: a returning soldier on the crowded trains ejaculates onto the back of her skirt. Yoshii has been defiled not by "them" but by one of "us." This experience overlaps with the end of the war and would not have happened, of course, had there been no war and surrender. Thus, her transfer to adulthood is marked by the end of war and the change of armies, anxieties concerning roles in a new society, and displaced sexual energy. The fact of war is indelibly marked in her history. Her coming-of-age is tied to a very specific historical experience; the waves that emanate from this disruption will flow across years of her life and affect future decisions. Her experience is then as equally foundational as that of any young male soldier; tracking the different ramifications, in the case of a young woman, organizes the subsequent novels.

Not only does Saegusa posit the experience of a woman as fundamental, she claims a growing appreciation for the fundamental nature of the war experience in determining an individual's view of life. The experience of war and the experience of being a woman are each, separately, fundamental to the development of an individual and are both exceedingly hard to narrate; paired, they threaten to render experience untransmissible. "The experience of war, and particularly the experience of defeat in war, is, to me at least, an elemental experience."[48] The war and its aftermath have proven to be a core experience for her and her generation, yet, by that very definition, subsequent generations (of women) who do not share that experience will know society in ways essentially different and mutually incomprehensible. The third level she explores – in addition to the experience of war and the experience of being a woman – is how the war experience varies across generations. Men may be prevented by gender from understanding the experiences of women, but that same gender dynamic should enable women to share such experience among themselves. She suggests that war, however, is an experience that cannot be transmitted. If one generation of women knows war and another does not, the experience can no longer be shared even among women, whose experience as women has historically united members of varied generations. The war has again proven to be the experience that prevents human interaction, and renders individuals cut off and quarantined by their experiences. The defining understandings of life, inextricably braided with gender, cannot be passed on.

Saegusa illustrates this as she follows characters through the postwar decades. Experience as a woman is individual and cannot be taught; she suggests that one feels compelled to try teaching and telling nonetheless. But later generations have not experienced the war and this colors their understanding and experience of being "woman," making it essentially different for characters and their generation who lived through the war. The final novel of the trilogy portrays characters of two different generations side by side. Women who worked as *pan-pan* after the war now work together with women young enough to be their daughters. Indeed, they may in fact be their daughters from wartime liaisons, and the contrast of the experience and understanding of society highlights their differences. Saegusa suggests, in these novels, that war is foundational to an individual's identity – not just this particular war, but any war. We encounter the situations war forced on the older women, twenty years earlier, and the ramifications such history has for young women's lives in the "present," the further suggestion being that even if this younger generation has not experienced war, that lack of experience, thrown into relief by the experience of their foremothers, sets parameters to identity that are, as a result, also defining. Womanhood is a shared experience for these characters; thus, for example, if the particulars of one generation resist transmission to the next, a foundational aspect of personality is impacted. Here, too, the need to relate an experience, however impossible it may be to do so, forms a primary theme of the book.

Saegusa explores the interface of gender and war while engaging the literary history and issues I have discussed in the first chapters, in particular the confessional style of *watakushi shōsetsu* fiction. In order to write her personal experience of the war – an experience of the "I" (*watakushi*) – Saegusa found she needed to write the first novel of the trilogy as a *watakushi shōsetsu*, an "I" fiction, because of the manner in which these issues organize the war experience: the war is firstly "my" issue, and at the same time, "an issue of the self." As a result, the first novel is cast in the form of autobiographical fiction, recounting a schoolgirl's life and reactions, as well as those of her dorm mates, at the time of the surrender. Saegusa writes with an assumption that "war tales" valorize the male experience; she takes the *watakushi shōsetsu* as equally (not without controversy, I think) male. She acknowledges that writing of the war experience has been a male prerogative (for many of the reasons I have discussed earlier). Thus, representing war as a woman forces a confrontation with historical practice. Insisting, as she does, that it may be *only* through a woman's view that the war can be fully understood, complicates and enriches her inquiry. Addressing the male dominance of war fiction becomes one key to unlocking the experience. The "I fiction" of the late nineteenth and early twentieth centuries was, Saegusa explains, so clearly a male enterprise, so completely imagined in a male domain, that no applicability to a woman's experience seemed possible. Indeed, the very idea of a woman writing a *watakushi shōsetsu* seemed an oxymoron.[49] This series of novels therefore entailed scaling the bastions of male experience and privilege to overcome male dominance of the representational prerogatives.

Tamura, Noma, Ango and many others worked, consciously, against the confessional *watakushi shōsetsu* tradition; Saegusa finds she must first invoke that (masculine) style of story-telling in order to move beyond it. The first of the trilogy reads autobiographically while the subsequent novels develop the themes of the development of a sense of self across time; the subsequent two novels move "beyond" that character while continuing her story. Saegusa captures a broader expanse of the postwar situation as her women live out the ramifications of their youth during the war. Saegusa weaves the experience of war, the experience of development as a woman, and fictional/literary history together in this trilogy.

The naïveté of a young girl focuses imagery that we do not find in other fiction. While much of the imagery is consistent with that of other postwar literature – the unknown quality of an emperor who had always been distant, the confusion upon hearing this voice, the nation unified under his image and working towards a common goal, the chaos of soldiers and evacuees returning to their homes, the sexual threat and violence now associated with soldiers, the difficulties of daily existence – this young girl lacks the maturity to evaluate the situations. Yoshii had believed most of what was relayed through her school officials, so the abrupt manner in which the wartime values were shown to be false was especially shocking: the nation appears not so unified after all, individual goals and national goals may not be transparently synonymous. Furthermore, as students prepare to return to their homes, she realizes the differing family situations of classmates, some of whose houses have been bombed and destroyed, some of whose parents are killed or missing, scattered across the former empire. In the concentrated light of *Sono hi no natsu*, the sacrifices and destruction of individuals are spotlighted, and they are always referenced by the announcement of the emperor she had naively (she realizes by novel's end) taken to be more than human. This mutability of values parallels the hypocrisy revealed in her school officials.

A number of story lines intersect and overlap across the three books: a young woman who has her hopes set on finishing school even while disparaged and chided by her father for wasting her time; a variety of women who are involved in sex work in one form or another, willingly (but not without reservation) as *pan-pan*; a young woman who uses her fluency in English for an office job with the occupying forces, which is viewed by a returning soldier as prostitution of a different sort; the repatriated soldier who must confront the postwar chaos; a middle-aged man who has amnesia, unable to remember who he is or what he did during the war; and the girl of four or five who seems to have adopted him. The majority of characters are women and their lives turn on the experiences of sex between Japanese women – most often sex workers – and the occupying soldiers, who are rarely welcome.

Nationality, which here correlates to a power differential, marks a fundamental difference in these experiences, dependent on whom the partner is. Saegusa explains that difference in the context of unwanted sex:

> There is, to me, "something" that occurs in the rape by an enemy soldier and the rape by a man on the street that prevents thinking about them both in the same way. Young women of today's generation may insist that they are the same. But I must disagree. How the woman will continue with life after being raped is funda-mentally different.[50]

That is, the options available are profoundly different if one is raped by, and defiled by, occupying soldiers, as opposed to becoming pregnant after sex with a young soldier set to be mobilized the following morning (to refer to two images from the novels); Saegusa explores these differences at length. The young woman who is raped by GIs finds her options rearranged and her choices limited: she is convinced she will be rejected by her family (whose response to this "defilement" all but suggests suicide), meaning that she must abandon all her dreams of schooling and marriage. The irony here is that the promise of equality and possibility introduced by American democracy and embodied in the US soldiers is, in the short space of time it takes for the sexual violence to be committed, swept away by the very persons charged with providing it for her. The betrayal of trust at this level amplifies the transgression; it scars as profoundly as incest. She runs from her family, buries the transgression within her, and begins the life of the prostitute, the only life that seems open to her. Whether "in fact" this is the sole choice or not, Saegusa is able convincingly to portray these options. Democratic ideals of freedom are being reversed, with the apparent support of the Japanese government institutions that are providing sexual services to the occupying soldiers. All trust is transgressed, for even those around the young woman seem tacitly to support this objectifying of her body (self) as sex object.

Saegusa is very pointed in her portrayals of this history: Yoshii of *Sono hi no natsu* and Chikako of *Sono fuyu no shi* form two halves of the historical and societal realities of prostitution after the war when the government, together with the occupation forces, helped establish, for example, the Recreation and Amusement Association (RAA) that organized "dancers" in cafés open only to the American GIs. Is it not odd, Saegusa has her characters ask, how the government seems to need us both in victory and loss, disparaging our roles all the while? Someyo, in the third of the novels, knows this history well, having responded to the army's call for "special nurses" and consequently being sent to South Asia in 1938 when she was eighteen years old. "Special nurse" however, meant "comfort woman." She was encouraged by the promise that the army would take on her debts and pay them off for her. With the defeat and her return to Japan, she finds in place the Recreation and Amusement Association, almost "as if it had been waiting for her there." Looking back some decades later, former comfort women and current prostitutes recall their initial introductions to the RAA. One introduces it in conversation:

> – Can't get my tongue around that one.
> Someyo laughed. – What is that, the RAA?
> – According to Sute-san it is to be a facility that makes "comfort women" available for use by the American troops, as a way to protect the women of Japan from the violence of the stationed troops; they are advertising for prostitutes to construct a floodwall for Japan.
> – Floodwall?
> – That's what everyone is calling it. And the powers-that-be are giving lots of [financial] assistance to it.
> – What? Why would the government be building brothels for enemy soldiers?
> – Well, if they don't . . .
> It made Someyo sick.
> – I get it: we thought we had come back from giving comfort and encouragement to Japanese soldiers only to find that now we were going to be, in order to protect the soldiers' wives and daughters, a what? A floodwall? So now, we are being told to hold back, now with our bodies, what we were unable to hold back during the war. Is that it?[51]

This question focuses a number of the themes crucial to this study. A woman's body is consistently offered as marking the boundaries, and as such her body provides the entryway or the exit from current realities and pressure, the rampart to be crossed or the defensive earthwork. Her body can mark the passage to release and liberation; that same body can also function as a limit, the border to keep men away from protected areas, i.e. the proper young women of Japan. The women's disbelief captures the surprise: it is not the women who have structured it in this manner. This is a male imagining of their bodies: in this trilogy women are able to articulate the government's role in structuring this masculine ideology/sexuality. The women's writings mark semiotic points of access or refusal, which have been assigned to them by others. "Commonsensical" to the men and also ideal, the system must be uncovered and deciphered by the women. In all the works I have examined, then, no matter how constructed, the foundational issues center on the physical body and its role in supporting or solving the immediate concerns of society. So basic was it to the writing of men that it gave rise to an expanded set of nuances attached to "body." These issues have become issues because of the war that simultaneously accentuated and threatened the roles and existence of those very bodies.

Conclusion

I have focused in this study on the centrality of body imagery in postwar Japanese fiction. In the fiction of postwar writers a number of issues appear with obsessive consistency, all refracted through the prism of physicality. For the men, in particular, that physicality was imagined as sex with a woman, sex that offered liberating possibilities. Tamura, Noma, and Ango each imagined the liberation of the body in slightly different ways; they refracted it through a number of prisms: changing societal and gender roles, national and individual identity, the meaning of the individual and its Others. A sexually available woman, and sex workers in particular, formed the most consistent of refracting lenses. The ramifications of this body imagery and the issues propelling it are, we have seen, significantly different for male writers than for female. The flesh writers consistently placed a transcendent value on a woman's body. The contradiction ensnared them in the end.

We found that Tamura Taijirō imagined a society in which all could forge a new identity based on their individual desires; however, the imagery he employed proved that these desires would proceed from a sexualized traditional economy: women provide sex to men, thereby providing them the liberation and the means to the individual wholeness that they seek. He wrote of prostitutes (that is, *pan-pan* and "comfort women") who inhabit a community of their own making, free from societal strictures and mores. He, like many, wished to be free to determine his own identity and he wrote from the assumption that a similar freedom was available to all individuals – men and women alike – in the postwar years. This "liberation" is based on the sexualized activity of commodified women and a system built upon male dominance, however. Furthermore, as we realize from the fiction itself, the society the women inhabit in his fiction is not free from strictures.

Noma Hiroshi's characters hope to establish individual identity via the body of a woman, to crawl inside and share her body. He wrote of his search for a release from the oppression of the body which led to another cycle: the oppression of the body that drives one closer and into the (woman's) body, but that body resists transgression and the individual is repelled. We find that each desires to burrow inside the partner but he can draw only as close as the barrier of skin. The recently experienced battlefield has made these men more painfully aware of the weakness of their bodies. Their relations with women also highlight their weaknesses and inabilities, as "men," to perform as male. They expect to find liberation in the body of another, but that same body prevents the necessary connection.

Sakaguchi Ango's women also occupy the place of liberation, only to disappear and lead men to ruin at the crucial moment, often obliterating the man at the same time. Ango's images and descriptions of decadence captured his readers' imagination and became part of the postwar cultural landscape. Defining the individual and the body is central to almost all of his work published in the late 1940s and after. In these postwar years, Ango's antidote to the war and its propagandistic national culture is a return to the individual, a recovering of individual desires and needs, which he too found necessary following decades of state oppression and control. The imagery and the impetus is also "masculine" in many of the same ways as the other male writers, in that it posits salvation and identity as discoverable in and through the sexualized body of a woman.

The obsession with women as guides (or as the path itself) to a utopia seems more than a legacy of the war – the image provided by the standard canon of postwar Japanese fiction – for so many women writers do not find this topic compelling enough to write about. The fiction by women that looks at this milieu draws lines in different, damning directions: namely, finding that Japanese men and the occupying GIs are similar in their treatment of women. It highlights the oppressive structures, of both Japan and the United States, that confine women. Thus, Tamura placed women at the center of his ideal existence, the tattoos and other marks of men guide us in our readings of them, and the story lines turn on men's access to the women. Noma tends to be even more focused, and his women serve as both guide and locale for perfection in the symbolic order. Desire for woman forms the plot of his novels, a "story of success or failure in gaining access to the body" of the woman, in Peter Brooks' words.[1] Noma's characters desire not only access, but also possession, by crawling into her body. Ango's characters pursue women who promise the same liberation and physical understanding of the universe. This search always ends in failure, for the woman disappears, even as she promises to "pierce the mysteries of life" via her body.[2]

While the men seem blind to these structures, many women could not help but see their place within it. Their fiction often highlights the social constraints that prevent the liberation that the men seek and, ultimately, reinforces oppressions much older than wartime. Women writing in the postwar period reflect the same sense of lack and possibility, and also a concern for the individual self and its Others. Like the male writers, they explored, in their fiction, individual identity and possibilities of agency. What they do not share, however, is a sense that the times brought liberation; we find no suggestion in the women's fiction that gender relations had changed at all.

These fictional representations provide one of the substantial foundations on which subsequent generations of writers will construct their fiction. I have noted the relevance of works by writers such as Nosaka Akiyuki, Kojima Nobuo, Ōe Kenzaburō, Mishima Yukio, Abe Kōbō, and Kurahashi Yumiko who came of age in the 1950s and 1960s and absorbed much from the writers discussed in previous chapters. The flesh writers and the women writing after the war provided a foundation for those writers who did not know war as adults. The writers of this later generation were too young to serve as soldiers but not too young to have experienced the war and its aftermath. The sexuality described by them, i.e. those in elementary school during the war, continues the themes of physicality expressed by the flesh writers. In contrast, sex is almost always violent and political power structures are prominent concerns in the next generation of writers, soft-focus romanticism has gone from their writing, and one finds little suggestion of utopian possibility. We have seen the hopefulness of Tamura, Noma, and Ango belied by the imagery of their fiction; the next generation, however, will not begin with any such hopefulness. The dull pain of nihilism and despair found in so many writers that came of age in the late 1950s has clouded the optimism expressed in the 1940s and early 1950s by the flesh writers. Indeed, Tamura's later work, "Inago," correlates to this shift: similar scenarios no longer allow liberating possibilities.

Of that next generation, Ōe Kenzaburō, for example, has written much concerning what he learned from Noma and the influence of and sense of connection he feels to the wartime generation. Ōe has been consistently enamored of the previous, postwar generation of writers and has expressed the desire to be counted among their number. In his telling, the postwar writers were motivated by social issues, political activism, and a sense of responsibility.[3] Ōe's work also magnifies another stream refracted through many of these writers, namely the influence of Sartre's fiction and Existentialism. Ōe's early fiction displays his reading and absorption of Sartre's philosophy; it builds on and continues the discussions that were articulated by Noma, Tamura, Ango, and others immediately after the end of the war. His obsession with the physical continues a line-age articulated by the previous, postwar, generation.

This lineage continues into the present in images of the body in sex work and sexual possibility, with depictions of US soldiers as Other, in the work of writers such as Murakami Ryū and Yamada Eimi. The imagery of the body in these works, consonant with (while working against) the previous fiction, continues the dialogue between liberating practice and oppressive structure. The place that the flesh writers have in this dialogue is foundational to a palette of images that continues to energize imaginaries of the body, and the ramifications of this conceptualization extend to the fiction being produced at the end of the twentieth century.

Notes

Introduction

1 This information is taken from Yamaoka Akira, *Shomin no sengo: fūzoku hen – sengo taishū zasshi ni miru*, Tokyo: Taiheishuppansha, 1973, 265–6; Sekii Mitsuo, "Sengo fūzoku jiten," *Tokyojin* (August 1995): 74–5; and Edward Seidensticker, *Tokyo Rising: The City Since the Great Earthquake*, New York: Alfred A. Knopf, 1990, 181; for a representative picture of the "picture frame show," see John W. Dower, *Embracing Defeat: Japan in the Wake of World War II*, New York: W.W. Norton & Company, 1999, 151–3.

2 Isoda Kōichi, *Sengoshi no kūkan*, Tokyo: Shinchōsha, 1983, 125.

3 A number of current critics and thinkers insist on calling it the Asia-Pacific War in order not to overlook the nations of Asia that were invaded; that is, to call attention to the nations involved rather than simply the body of water. See Kawamura Minato *et al.*, *Sensō wa dono yō ni kataretekita ka*, Tokyo: Asahi Shinbunsha, 1999, 7–9. Further, the "Second World War" referred to in the United States (at least) is also known in Japan as the "fifteen-year war," and dated from the Japanese invasion of China in 1931. Suzuki Yūko, in her close attention to women's history at this time, writes of the "Second World War" (*dainijitaisen*) defined parenthetically as "the fifteen-year war that covers the Manchuria incident, Sino-Japanese war, Asia-Pacific War." *Feminizumu to sensō*, Tokyo: Marujusha, 1997, 19ff.

4 For further detail, see Tsurumi's chapter entitled "Everyday Life During the War," in *An Intellectual History of Wartime Japan, 1931–45*, New York: KPI, 1986, 85–93. For comparison, one can look to France:

> The rations were meagre, falling below basic physiological needs for the poorest members of the urban population. Given that the minimum daily requirement, depending on age, sex and occupation, is in the order of 2,400 calories, the size alone of the official rations goes a long way to explaining the attraction of, and perhaps even the necessity for, the black market: just 900 calories per adult in Paris in August 1944, 1,210 in September, and 1,515 in May 1945. To obtain them there was the endless queuing, and often kowtowing to shopkeepers to whom the system of ration cards bound entire families.
>
> (Jean-Pierre Rioux, *The Fourth Republic, 1944–58*, trans. Godfrey Rogers, Cambridge: Cambridge University Press, 1987, 23–4)

5   Oda Makoto recounts that the postwar experience reduced everyone to a primitive aboriginal existence, planting vegetables in every available space, for example. "Oda Makoto ni suite," in *"Korosuna" kara*, Tokyo: Chikuma Shobō, 1976, 401. See also Dower, *Embracing Defeat*, 87–97, and Igarashi Yoshikuni, *Bodies of Memory: Narratives of War in Postwar Japanese Culture, 1945–70*, Princeton: Princeton University Press, 2000, esp. 52–5.

6   As in the recent article by Eleanor H. Kerkham, "Pleading for the Body: Tamura Taijirō's 1947 Korean Comfort Woman Story, *Biography of a Prostitute*," in Marlene J. Mayo *et al.*, *War, Occupation and Creativity: Japan and East Asia, 1920–60*, Honolulu: University of Hawai'i Press, 2001, 310–59, and Igarashi, *Bodies of Memory*, and, in Japanese, the essays contained in *Kōza shōwa bungakushi*, ed. Yūseidō Henshūbu, 5 vols, Tokyo: Yūseidō, 1988.

7   "Nikutai ga ningen de aru," *Gunzō*, 5 (1947): 12.

8   Honda, *Monogatari sengo bungakushi*, 2 vols, Tokyo: Iwanami Shoten, 1990, 1: 131. Keene echoes Honda when he writes: "Noma Hiroshi is often treated as the emblematic postwar writer" (Donald Keene, *Dawn to the West*, 2 vols, New York: Holt, Reinhart, and Winston, 1984, 1: 974). Likewise, a Japanese literary dictionary reiterates that, "With *Kurai e* (1946) Noma appeared on the literary stage as the standard bearer for the 'first wave of postwar writers'" (Kindai Sakka Kenkyū Jiten Kankokukai, *Kindai sakka kenkyū jiten*, Tokyo: Ōfusha, 1983, 315).

9   "Kao no naka no akai tsuki," in *Zenshū*, 22 vols, Tokyo: Chikuma Shobō, 1969, 1: 119.

10 "Zoku darakuron," in *Nihon bunka shikan: Sakaguchi Ango essai shū*, Tokyo: Kodansha, 1996, 240.

11 I employ a scholarly convention here, referring to Noma Hiroshi and Tamura Taijirō by their family names, while referring to Sakaguchi Ango by the pen name that functions as a given name.

12 "Nikutai jitai ga shikō suru," in *Teihon Sakaguchi Ango zenshū*, 13 vols, Tokyo: Tōjusha, 7: 237–8.

13 Nina Cornyetz, *Dangerous Women, Deadly Words: Phallic Fantasy and Modernity in Three Japanese Writers*, Stanford: Stanford University Press, 1999, 9.

14 In, for example, "This Sex Which Is Not One," in *Writing on the Body*, ed. Katie Conboy, Nadia Medina, and Sarah Stanbury, New York: Columbia University Press, 1997, 248–56.

15 Anne McClintock, *Imperial Leather: Race, Gender, and Sexuality in the Colonial Contest*, New York: Routledge, 1995.

16 I thank Michael Molasky for noting this; I refer the reader to his work for extended discussion of the ramifications of this.

17 See, for example, Oka Yoshitake, "Generational Conflict after the Russo-Japanese War," in *Conflict in Modern Japanese History*, ed. Victor J. Koschmann and Tetsuo Najita, Princeton: Princeton University Press, 1982, 197–225.

18 Nishikawa Nagao and Nakahara Akio, *Sengo kachi no saikentō*, Tokyo: Yūhikaku, 1986, esp. Chapter 8. Ben-Ami Shillony draws important contrasts between these various "postwars" as well. Ben-Ami Shillony, *Politics and Culture in Wartime Japan*, Oxford: Clarendon Press, 1981, esp. Chapter 5.

19 Noma Hiroshi, "Jibun no sakuhin," in *Zenshū*, 14: 256.

20 Nakamura Shin'ichirō, *Zōho sengo bungaku no kaisō*, Tokyo: Chikuma Sōsho, 1983, 44–5, 100ff.

21 Furubayashi Takashi, *Sengoha sakka ha kataru*, "Noma Hiroshi," Tokyo: Chikuma Shobō, 1971, 8.

1 The discourse on the body

1 And, at that point, it also overlaps with the *shutaisei* debates concerning the basis for subjectivity and agency, as explored in detail by Victor Koschmann, among others.

2 Quoted in Okuno Takeo, "Tamura Taijirō," in *Okuno Takeo sakka ron shū*, 5 vols, Tokyo: Tairyusha, 1977, 3. 250.

3 As Tsuge Teruhiko writes, "Of the [postwar] writers who made an issue of existentialism, there are, first, those who described the postwar situation in terms of the body [*nikutai*, with *shintai* provided as synonym], Oda Sakunosuke, Sakaguchi Ango, and Tamura Taijirō." This gloss of *shintai* to highlight the meaning of *nikutai* is not uncommon. That they are distinct and that *nikutai* gains new currency in everyday speech is one of my points; the need to provide a gloss for it supports this argument. The distinction is indeed important and central to both Tsuge's, and my own, arguments. Tsuge Teruhiko, "Jitsuzonshugi," in *Nihon bungaku shinshi*, ed. Hasegawa Izumi, vol. 6, Tokyo: Shibundō, 1994, 132.

4 See Ueno Kōshi, *Nikutai no jidai: taikenteki 60-nendai bunkaron*, Tokyo: Gendai Shokan, 1989, for a discussion of the 1960s through the trope of the *nikutai*/body.

5 See also the essay by Kojima Nobuo, "Nikutai no seishin," in *Kojima Nobuo zenshū*, vol. 6, Tokyo: Kōdansha, 1971, for a discussion of this dialectic that seems to approach these two terms from a different tradition: e.g. "I have written at various places in my fiction of the pitiful [state] where the *seishin* is spurned in order to foster the *nikutai*" (93). I also suggest the reader consult the essays by Kamei Hideo and Yoshida Hiroo, all of whom borrow heavily from Merleau-Ponty in their conceptualization of the body. Kamei is one of many who rely on Merleau-Ponty; that is, *shintai* is body and spirit/personality, the amalgam of *seishin* and *nikutai*. *Nikutai* is the physical object, *seishin* that which is aware of the Other. See, for example, Merleau-Ponty's *Signs*, trans. Richard C. McCleary, Evanston, IL: Northwestern University Press, 1964, 227–32.

6 Chou Wan-yao, "The *Kōminka* Movement in Taiwan and Korea: Comparisons and Interpretations," in *The Japanese Wartime Empire, 1931–45*, ed. Peter Duus, Ramon H. Myers, and Mark R. Peattie, Princeton: Princeton University Press, 1996, 42.

7 See the discussion by Igarashi for examples, especially page 14, and also Chapter 2. The thrust of his argument concerns the manner in which the "healthy body of the nation was dismembered as Imperial Japan experienced a radical transformation, and these dismembered bodily images were assembled again in the postwar period in order to articulate the new nationhood" (14). The nation forms the argumentative focus of Igarashi's study, while I focus on these writers' articulation of an individual within that nation. Igarashi, *Bodies of Memory*.

8 Saeki Junko, *"Iro" to "ai" no hikaku bunkashi*, Tokyo: Iwanami Shoten, 1998, 9–10.

9 Igarashi, *Bodies of Memory*, 13. Seiji Lippit employs this distinction in an analysis of Yokomitsu Riichi's novel from the 1930s, *Shanhai*; see his *Topographies of Japanese Modernism*, New York: Columbia University Press, 2002, 105.

10 Igarashi, *Bodies of Memory*, 49. For more on this correlation between fit bodies and fit nation, see 49–52.

11 Maruyama Masao, "From Carnal Literature to Carnal Politics," in *Thought and Behaviour in Modern Japanese Politics*, ed. Ivan Morris, London: Oxford University Press, 1963, 246–8. This article was originally published in 1949, in *Tenbō*, as "Nikutai bungaku kara nikutai seiji made."

12 Tsurumi Shunsuke, *An Intellectual History of Wartime Japan, 1931–45*, New York: KPI, 1986, 23. Tsurumi goes on to give a historical account of the origins of the term; see especially 23–32. I also refer the reader to Carol Gluck, *Japan's Modern Myths: Ideology in the Late Meiji Period*, Princeton: Princeton University Press, 1985, for an extended discussion of this process, and to Tsurumi's "Kotoba no omamoriteki sayōhō ni tsuite," in *Tsurumi Shunsuke chosakushū*, 5 vols, Tokyo: Chikuma Shobō, 1972, 3: 12–25.

13 George M. Wilson, *Patriots and Redeemers in Japan: Motives in the Meiji Restoration*, Chicago: University of Chicago Press, 1992, 42. See as well the discussion that Bob Wakabayashi gives to the mystical nature of the *kokutai* in early conceptualizations of Aizawa Seishisai in *Anti-Foreignism and Western Learning in Early-Modern Japan: The New Theses of 1825*, Cambridge, MA: Council on East Asian Studies, Harvard University, 1986, esp. 123.

14 Michel Foucault, *Discipline and Punish*, trans. Alan Sheridan, New York: Vintage Books, 1995, 25.

15 Dorinda Outram, *The Body and the French Revolution*, New Haven, CT: Yale University Press, 1989, 7. Outram goes on to discuss how manipulation of bodies is of particular concern to fascist regimes. This connection has been explored by many. The first is perhaps the study of fascist German literature by Klaus Theweleit, *Male Fantasies*, trans. Stephen Conway, 2 vols, Minneapolis: University of Minneapolis Press, 1987. For the Japanese context see Peter Duus, "Introduction: Japan's Wartime Empire: Problems and Issues," in *The Japanese Wartime Empire, 1931–45*, especially the photographs on pp. xxviii and xxx that remind this reader, at least, of mass demonstrations and exhibitions of the sort associated with Nazi and fascist regimes.

16 According to the preface, this work was prepared in English and later translated into Japanese. The words in brackets are those that appear in the Japanese text. This is especially critical in that "bodyism," a non-Japanese construction, becomes *nikutai bungaku* in the Japanese version, corresponding to my discussion here.

17 Tsurumi, *An Intellectual History*, 31–2. I have chosen to focus on Noma Hiroshi in this study, along with Ango and Tamura, rather than writers such as Tanaka, because of the wider continued readership of the former authors.

18 Wakabayashi, *Anti-Foreignism*, 69. See also Inoue Hideaki, "Kokutai, kokudo, seibetsu: Nihon shinwa no shintaikan," in *Nihon ni okeru shintai*, Tokyo: Ōbunsha, 1964, 55–97.

19 Germaine A. Hoston, *Marxism and the Crisis of Development in Prewar Japan*, Princeton: Princeton University Press, 1986, 29–31.

20 Inoue Hideaki, "Kokutai, kokudo, seibetsu," 56–8. John Dower has explored this conceptualization extensively in his *War Without Mercy*, New York: Pantheon, 1986.

21 Particularly in the immediate postwar years which were even more difficult, in terms of food supplies, than the constricted war years themselves. I refer the reader to John W. Dower's detailing of these shortages in his *Embracing Defeat*.

22 Alan Wolfe, "From Pearls to Swine: Sakaguchi Ango and the Humanity of Decadence," in *War, Occupation, and Creativity: Japan and East Asia*, 363.

23 "The American School" and "American *Hijiki*" can be found, in English translation, in

Contemporary Japanese Literature: An Anthology of Fiction, Film, and Other Writing since 1945, ed. Howard Hibbett, Tokyo: Tuttle, 1978. Michael Molasky analyzes "The American School," in *The American Occupation of Japan and Okinawa: Literature and Memory*, London and New York, Routledge, 1999, 30 and following, as does Van Gessel in *The Sting of Life: Four Contemporary Japanese Novelists*, New York: Columbia University Press, 1989, Chapter 3. Yoshikuni Igarashi discusses "American *Hijiki*" in his *Bodies of Memory*, 164 and following

24 This does not seem to make the national body feminine, even though they are fleeing from the national body, and even though the national body was often reconstructed as female under Occupation.

25 This was one of the defining criticisms against the Japanese state. See, for example, the works of Oda Makoto.

26 Isoda Kōichi, *Sengoshi no kūkan*, Tokyo: Shinchōsha, 1983, 122.

27 I have hinted at English equivalents to these terms above. As *Kenkyusha's Japanese–English Dictionary* (fourth edition) has it, *kokka* refers to "a state; a country; a nation; a body politic; a polity." *Kokutai* is "the national structure; the fundamental character (of a country); a national polity." *Kazoku kokka* refers to the *kokka* constructed discursively as an organic family unit (*kazoku*). In all cases it is a national entity that contains more than simply the laws of a political entity, but a sense, in the Japanese context of this time, of a "body" that comprises these elements.

28 See Dower, *Embracing Defeat*, for concrete examples of this.

29 Isoda, *Sengoshi no kūkan*, 122.

30 Ibid., 122. This seems to connect, in imagery, with Oda Sakunosuke's desire to tear apart the veil of postwar society, as noted below.

31 "*Nikutai no sengen*," *Nikutai*, 1, 1: 4–5 (n.d.) [1947].

32 Tamura Taijirō, *Nikutai no bungaku*, Tokyo: Kusano Shobō, 1948, 48.

33 Kamiya Tadataka, "Yokuatsu kara kaihō e," in *Kōza Shōwa bungakushi*, ed. Yūseido henshūbu, 5 vols, Tokyo: Yūseido, 1988, 3: 6.

34 Senuma Shigeki made a similar contemporary critique, pointing out the "feudalistic elements" remaining in the literature of the body, "Nikutai bungaku no yukikata," in *Sengo bungaku nōto, jō*, Tokyo: Kawade Shobō, 1975, 57–9.

35 See, for example, Inagaki Masami, *Heieki o kyohishita Nihonjin: todai sha no senjika teikō*, Tokyo: Iwanami Shoten, 1973, and Nihon sayoku bungeika sorengo, eds, *Sensō ni taisuru sensō: anchi miritarizumu shōsetsushū*, Tokyo: Fuji Shuppan, 1984.

36 A further complication in this nexus of images is that the conception of the victimized male overlaps with, and supports, a postwar Japanese reconstruction of the war as one wherein Japanese were victims of aggression while downplaying the aggression of their own nation and the armies they served. The flesh writers wished to highlight the oppression and aggression of the Japanese state, but lost in this portrayal is the aggression towards those of neighboring countries. Obsessive concern with "we" as victims elides the victimization of others, and with it the responsibility shared as Japanese aggressors in that victimization. For more on the construction of postwar memory, see Norma Field, "War and Memory: Japan, Asia, the Fiftieth, and After," *Positions*, 5, 1 (Spring 1997): 1–50 and Carol Gluck, "The Past in the Present, in *Postwar Japan as History*, ed. Andrew Gordon, Berkeley: University of California Press, 1993, 64–95.

37 Togaeri Hajime cannot explain Ango's rapturous description of Tokyo being bombed, insisting that had he suffered as a soldier he could never have written in so positive a vein, *Nise no kisetsu*, Tokyo: Kōdansha, 1954, 53.

38 Quoted in Sone Hiroyoshi, "Kaisetsu: shōfuteki nikukan," in *Nikutai no mon*, by Tamura Taijirō, Tokyo: Chikuma Shobō, 1988, 240.

39 See Cathy Caruth, ed., *Trauma: Explorations in Memory*, Baltimore: Johns Hopkins University Press, 1995, 3ff., for definitions and history of this disease.

40 Honda Shūgo, quoted in Alan M. Tansman, *The Writings of Kōda Aya: A Japanese Literary Daughter*, New Haven, CT: Yale University Press, 1993, 61.

41 Kimura Yoshinaga, *Mishima Yukio no naka no Mishima Yukio*, Tokyo: Hobunkan Shuppan, 1988, 9.

42 Kamiya Tadataka, "Yokuatsu kara kaihō e," 3: 4.

43 For more on the genre, in English, see the work of Tomi Suzuki, Dennis Washburn, Irmela Hijiya-Kirschneiret, and Edward Fowler. In Japanese, see Takahashi Hideo, Yamada Teruo, Nakamura Mitsuo, and Ōe Kenzaburō.

44 Horii Ken'ichi, "Baihin to shite no shintai," in *Kōza Shōwa bungakushi*, ed. Yūseido henshūbu, 5 vols, Tokyo: Yūseido, 1988, 127.

45 Nakamura Miharu, "Ryutsu suru shintai," in *Kōza Shōwa bungakushi*, ed. Yūseido henshūbu, 5 vols, Tokyo: Yūseido, 1988, 1: 139.

46 Ichiko Teiji, *Nihon bungaku zenshū*, 6 vols, Tokyo: Gakutosha, 1978, 4: 451–4.

47 Isoda Kōichi, *Sajō no kyōen*, Tokyo: Shinchōsha, 1972, 191.

48 Ibid., 191. Isoda further insists that when the Naturalists assume that the "nature" they uphold opposes the established order, they are being overly simplistic. They posit a rationalized Nature to oppose a rationalized establishment, when nature is often irrational and unpredictable, where the weak are eaten, and only the physically strong survive. He asks, rhetorically, if movements such as Fascism or Nazism, by whatever name, are not simply frightening religious-tinged festivals that invoke the most powerful, because most uncontrollable, of natural forces, unfettered human activity. In this, he reminds one of Georges Bataille's writings on festival and group dynamics.

49 Ibid., 190.

50 Ibid., 192.

51 Sakaguchi Ango, "Nikutai jitai ga shikō suru," in *Teihon Sakaguchi Ango zenshū*, 13 vols, Tokyo: Tōjusha, 1975, 7: 239.

52 Togaeri, *Nise no kisetsu*, 70.

53 Sakaguchi Ango, "Nikutai jitai ga shikō suru," 7: 239.

54 Sekine Hiroshi, "Watashi no Sarutoru," *Gendai no me* (October 1966): 98.

55 For more of these particulars, see my "When Sartre was an Erotic Writer: Body, Nation, and Existentialism in Japan after the Asia-Pacific War," *Japan Forum* (Spring 2002): 77–103.

56 There is a parallel suggestive of further study here: Sartre's prewar fiction had some of its most pronounced applicability, in France as well, to the postwar situation. Likewise, much "postwar" fiction in Japan was set in and/or conceived before the war. This is the force of Shirai Kōji's comment that whatever the similarities – and there are many – between the postwar situation in France and Japan, postwar phenomena, such as Camus' *The Stranger* and Sartre's *Nausea*, are prewar in conception and execution ("Atogaki," in *Sarutoru zenshū*, vol. 6, Tokyo: Jinbun Shoin, 1951, 280). The impetus comes from the sense of crisis of the

prewar years, to be sure, but in Japan it took the war to bring these forces to the fore, a point made earlier by Honda Shūgo, in *Monogatari sengo bungakushi*, 228.

57 Ishizaki Hitoshi, "Jitsuzon to hōkai kankaku," in *Kōza Shōwa bungakushi*, ed. Yūseido henshūbu, 5 vols, Tokyo: Yūseido, 1988, 3: 120.

58 Shirai Kōji, "Jitsuzonshugi ni tsuite," in *Nihon kindai bungaku to gaikoku bungaku*, ed. Nihon Kindai Bungaku Kan, Tokyo: Yomiuri Shinbunsha, 1969, 216–31.

59 Kikuchi Shōichi, "Jitsuzon e no kanshin," *Bungaku*, 15, 11 (1947): 41. Shirai Kōji's article "Jitsuzonshugi ni tsuite" is also pertinent in this regard.

60 The work of Shiina Rinzō is important here. He may be the first "Existentialist" in Japan. If he is the first, he was writing as such *before* Sartre's work was even known in Japan. *Omoki nagare no naka ni* (*In the Sluggish Stream*) was first published in *Tenbō*, in 1947, but only after the editor, Usui Yoshimi, left it to languish in a desk drawer for a year and a half. Shiina wrote an angry letter to Usui motivated by the frustration of not seeing the work in print and also spurred on by a small notation in the *Asahi shinbun* dedicated to notes from abroad introducing Sartre's work. In Shiina's recollection, "When I read that, I realized that [Sartre and I] were writing about very similar things. I was angry about this and shot off an abrupt letter to Usui the editor." A telegram accepting the initial story promptly came back. Usui commented on the story in his editor's column:

> I imagine there are many negative as well as positive responses to this piece by Shiina Rinzō, *In the Sluggish Stream*. I think he should fearlessly follow this ambitious path he has forged. I wait with expectation further developments from this chosen path. There is one thing I would like to say at this juncture, however: before any readers come to hasty conclusions, it should be noted that this work was completed before all the recent chatter about the work of Sartre.
> (In Saitō Suehiro, *Sakuhinron: Shiina Rinzō*, Tokyo: Ofūsha, 1989, 11)

61 And perhaps sharing the lineage of Tanizaki as well. See Asabuki Tomiko, *Sarutoru Bovowaru to no nijuhachinichikan, Nihon*, Tokyo: Dohōsha Shuppan, 1995, on Sartre's fascination with Tanizaki's fiction.

62 For a further development of these overlaps, see my "Sartre's Fiction in Postwar Japan," in *Confluences: Postwar Japan and France*, Ann Arbor: University of Michigan Center for Japanese Studies, 2002, 86–109.

63 Oda Sakunosuke, "Kanōsei no bungaku," in *Oda Sakunosuke*, Chikuma Nihon bungaku zenshū, Tokyo: Chikuma Shobō, 1998, 452. The imagery of nation-as-body is relevant in its own right.

64 Ibid., 454.

65 Ibid., 456.

66 Aono, Suekichi, "Saikaku no kōshoku bungaku to nikutaiha bungaku," *Yomiuri hyōron*, 10 (1949): 75–9.

67 Oda, "Kanōsei no bungaku," 457.

68 Sekine, "Watashi no Sarutoru," 99.

69 Noma Hiroshi, "Jōkyō," in *Sarutoru techō/ Carnet Sartrien*, Tokyo: Jinbun Shoin, 1952, 1.

70 Ibid., 1–2.

71 See, for example, Mori Arimasa, "Sarutoru in okeru nikutai no mondai," *Kosei*, 10, 2 (1949).

72 And also of Merleau-Ponty; see note 42.

73 Hazel E. Barnes, "Introduction," in Jean-Paul Sartre, *Being and Nothingness*, New York: Philosophical Library, 1956, xxxix.

74 Ibid., xl.

75 Maruyama Masao, "The Ideology and Dynamics of Japanese Fascism," in *Thought and Behaviour in Modern Japanese Politics*, ed. Ivan Morris, London: Oxford University Press, 1963, 35–6.

2 The (gendered) discourse and a (woman's) body

1 Peter Brooks, *Body Work: Objects of Desire in Modern Narrative*, Cambridge, MA: Harvard University Press, 1993, 8. For a Japanese treatment of these themes I refer the reader to the work of Mizuta Noriko, which I refer to in more detail in Chapter 5.

2 For the importance of "womb imagery," see Rebecca Copeland, "Mother Obsession and Womb Imagery in Japanese Literature," *Transactions of the Asiatic Society of Japan*, 3 (1988): 131–50; Tsuruta Kin'ya, *Nihon kindai bungaku ni okeru "mukogawa": hahanaru mono sein-aru mono*, Tokyo: Meiji Shoin, 1986.

3 "Hirabayashi Taiko," in *Gendai josei bungaku jiten*, ed. Watanabe Sumiko *et al.*, Tokyo: Tokyodo Shuppan, 1990, 300.

4 Igarashi Yoshikuni also explores the gendered symbols of postwar occupation society: "The relationship between the United States and Japan in the postwar melodrama is highly sexualized": *Bodies of Memory*, 29.

5 Dower, *Embracing Defeat*, esp. Chapters 14 and 16.

6 Molasky, *The American Occupation of Japan and Okinawa*, 28.

7 Ibid., 27.

8 Albeit within a discourse that emphasized the maternal aspects of their societal roles. Miyake Yoshiko quotes from Jerome Cohen to note that "The mobilization of Japanese women for war work, while 'greater than in the case of Germany . . . [was] far less than the strenuous effort in Britain.'" "Doubling Expectations: Motherhood and Women's Factory Work under State Management in Japan in the 1930s and 1940s," in *Recreating Japanese Women, 1600–45*, ed. Gail Lee Bernstein, Berkeley: University of California Press, 1991, 267.

9 Mizuta Noriko has outlined the parameters of this history in a cogent discussion of Hayashi Fumiko's work. See "In Search of a Lost Paradise: The Wandering Woman in Hayashi Fumiko's *Drifting Clouds*," in *The Woman's Hand: Gender and Theory in Japanese Women's Writing*, ed. Paul Gordon Schalow and Janet A. Walker, Stanford: Stanford University Press, 1996, esp. 334–7.

10 In but one example, this is the position that Yukiko of Hayashi Fumiko's *Drifting Clouds* finds herself in: in Mizuta Noriko's words, the prewar understandings of her uncle constitute "an order that supports only two choices for a woman in relation to a man: she can either marry or become a prostitute." Ibid., 338.

11 Nishikawa Nagao, *Nihon no sengo shōsetsu*, Tokyo: Iwanami Shoten, 1988, 63.

12 Ibid., 63.

13 Susan Bordo and Alison M. Jaggar, eds, *Gender/Body/Knowledge: Feminist Reconstructions of Being and Knowing*, New Brunswick, NJ: Rutgers University Press, 1989, 4.

14 Ibid., 4. Judith Butler outlines a similar history; see her *Gender Trouble: Feminism and the Subversion of Identity*, New York: Routledge, 1990, esp. 10 and following.

15 Contemporary writers such as Saegusa Kazuko, and critics such as Mizuta Noriko, will regularly draw from such Western theorists. I am not unaware of the problematics of reading Western (i.e. North American and European) theory in parallel with these Japanese writers. The experience of modernism, the spread of commodity capitalism, the experience of imperialism, colonialism, and expansion, are rooted in the experience these writers have of Japanese society, to be sure, yet are also filtered through their own wide and sophisticated readings in many language traditions. Nina Cornyetz broaches this subject in her introduction, *Dangerous Women, Deadly Words: Phallic Fantasy and Modernity in Three Japanese Writers*, Stanford: Stanford University Press, 1999, 3 ff.

16 Ann Sherif, *Mirror: The Fiction and Essays of Kōdo Aya*, Honolulu: University of Hawai'i Press, 1999, 73. Desire in capitalist consumption of commodified objects – "as objects of desire and consumption" – structures much of the fiction under consideration in this study.

17 Sharalyn Orbaugh, "The Body in Contemporary Japanese Women's Fiction," in *The Woman's Hand: Gender and Theory in Japanese Women's Writing*, 151.

18 Shibaki Yoshiko, *Susaki paradaisu*, Tokyo: Shūeisha, 1994, 44.

19 Julia Kristeva, "Women's Time," in *The Feminist Reader*, ed. Catherine Belsey and Jane Moore, London: Macmillan Press, 2nd edition, 1997, 208.

20 As is often noted, after the surrender, the literary magazines promptly featured works of established older writers such as Shiga Naoya, Masamune Hakuchō, Nagai Kafū, Tanizaki Jun'ichirō, and Uno Kōji. "Shōwa ga hiraita josei bungaku," in *Gendai josei bungaku jiten*, 17.

21 See, in particular, *Monogatari to hanmonogatari no fūkei*, Tokyo: Tabata Shoten, 1993.

22 Andrew E. Barshay, *State and Intellectual in Imperial Japan*, Berkeley: University of California Press, 1988, xiii.

23 Maeda Ai's work, especially as collected in *Toshi kūkan no bungaku*, Tokyo: Chikuma Shobō, 1982, explores the importance, and the new configurations, of space in literature starting in the Meiji era. Another important discussion of these issues, from a different angle, can be found in the essay by R. Radhakrishnan, "Nationalism, Gender, and the Narrative of Identity," in *Nationalisms and Sexualities*, ed. Andrew Parker, Mary Russo, Doris Sommer, and Patricia Yaeger, New York and London: Routledge, 1992.

24 Miyake Yoshiko, "Doubling Expectations," 270.

25 Ibid., 271.

26 Mizuta Noriko, *Monogatari to hanmonogatari no fūkei*, 66.

27 Luce Irigaray, *The Irigaray Reader*, ed. Margaret Whitford, Oxford: Basil Blackwell, 1991, 53.

28 Ibid., 169.

29 Mizuta, *Monogatari*, 67.

30 Ibid., 63.

31 Kanda Fuhito, *Senryo to minshushugi*, Tokyo: Shōgakkan, 1989, 58.

32 Susaki Takashi *et al.*, *Sengoshi daijiten*, Tokyo: Sanseido, 1991, entry for "*pan-pan.*" These explanations appear to have been taken from Ono Tsunenori's history of sex in the Shōwa era, *Angura Shōwa shi: sesoura no ura no hiji hatsukokai*, Tokyo: Minami Shuppanbu, 1981, 78–9. Ono bases his explanations, sensibly, on *Gendai yōgo no kiso chishiki 1948 nenpan* (the 1948 edition of *Contemporary Language Usage*).

33 Molasky, *The American Occupation*, 103.

34 Sone, "Kaisetsu," 242–3.

35 Susaki, *Sengoshi daijiten*, entry for "*pan-pan.*" This dictionary goes on to note that the women who dealt exclusively with the GIs became known as *yōpan*, as will be reflected in the fiction considered in Chapter 5. See also the discussions in Ono, *Angura Shōwa shi*, 78–80, and Michael Molasky's study.

36 This history is detailed in Molasky's study, *The American Occupation*, especially Chapter 4, and Tanaka Toshiyuki, *Japan's Comfort Women: Sexual Slavery and Prostitution During World War II and the US Occupation*, New York: Routledge, 2002.

37 Harada Hiroshi, *MP no jiipu kara mita Senryōka no Tōkyō*, Tokyo: Sōshisha, 1994, 169. He notes as well that the arrival of WACs in Japan further complicated official Occupation support for prostitution facilities among the troops, since one of the contemporary rumors reported the WACs were a US version of the "comfort women."

3 Tamura Taijirō

1 Okuno Takeo, "Tamura Taijirō," in *Okuno Takeo sakka ron shū*, 5 vols, Tokyo: Tairyūsha, 1977, 3: 249.

2 See David Desser, "Gate of Flesh(tones): Color in the Japanese Cinema," in *Cinematic Landscapes: Observations on the Visual Arts and Cinema of China and Japan*, ed. Linda C. Ehrlich and David Desser, Austin: University of Texas Press, 1994, 312–17 for a helpful discussion of the movie.

3 Okuno, "Tamura Taijirō," 249.

4 There is no discernible connection, but it seems suggestive that the translation of Raymond Radiguet's *Le diable au corps* by Shinjo Yoshiakira into Japanese in 1954 bears this same title – *Nikutai no akuma* – (Tokyo: Shinchōsha). Mishima Yukio, whose work I have not the space to treat here even though he is within the parameters of the discussion, was greatly enamored of Radiguet's novel, and the affinities between it and his *Confessions of a Mask*, for example, are not minor. An obsessive fascination with the body of a woman is a theme shared by both works. There is also a horror of the erotic object that functions in tandem with the fascination and obsession of that body, in a way that Georges Bataille, for one, would lead us to expect.

5 Occupation policies dramatically freed possibilities of expression; even so, sexuality between Japanese and Americans could not be discussed. Criticism of the occupying forces was also strictly forbidden. In particular, "Sensitive social issues such as fraternization, prostitution involving the occupation forces, or mixed-blood children, to say nothing of GI crimes including rape, could not be discussed." Dower, 412. See also Yokote Kazuhiko, *Hisenryōka no bungaku ni kansuru kisōteki kenkyū: ronkōhen*, Tokyo: Musashino shobō, 1996, esp. 9–43. Again, the hypocrisy and onerousness of these arbitrary restrictions, especially initiated by those forces associated with, and self-constructed to represent, democratic freedom, were not lost on the Japanese.

6 For an important discussion of one work, see Eleanor H. Kerkham's recent essay, "Pleading for the Body: Tamura Taijirō's 1947 Korean Comfort Woman Story, *Biography of a Prostitute*," in *War, Occupation, and Creativity: Japan and East Asia*, 310–59.

7 Wolfe, "From Pearls to Swine," in ibid., 366.

8 Ibid.

9 Dower, *Embracing Defeat*, 157.

10 J. Victor Koschmann, *Revolution and Subjectivity in Postwar Japan*, Chicago: University of Chicago Press, 1996, 59.

11 Igarashi Yoshikuni, *Bodies of Memory*, 56.

12 Tamura Taijirō, *Waga bundan seishunki*, Tokyo: Shinchōsha, 1963, 219.

13 Takami Jun, "Panpan reisan," *Shinchō*, 10 (1953): 116.

14 Tamura, *Waga bundan seishunki*, 228–9.

15 Sone Hiroyoshi, "Kaisetsu: shōtuteki nikukan," 241.

16 "Nikutai ga ningen de aru," 14.

17 Tamura Taijirō, "Nikutai no mon," in *Tamura Taijirō, Kane Tatsuo, Ōhara Tomie shū*, Tokyo: Chikuma Shobō, 1978, 34.

18 Mori Eichi, "Fūzoku shōsetsu to chukan shōsetsu," in *Kōza Shōwa bungakushi*, ed. Yūseido henshūbu, 5 vols, Tokyo: Yūseido, 1988, 3: 238.

19 "Nikutai ga ningen de aru," 12.

20 "Nikutai bungaku no kiban," in *Nikutai no mon*, Tokyo: Chikuma Shobō, 1988, 228.

21 Ibid.

22 "Kore kara no watakushi," in *Nikutai no mon*, Tokyo: Chikuma Shobō, 1988, 231.

23 "Nikutai ga ningen de aru," 12.

24 Tamura, "Nikutai kaihō ron," in *Nikutai no bungaku*, Tokyo: Kusano Shobō, 1948, 143.

25 *Nikutai no bungaku*, 55–62.

26 Eleanor H. Kerkham suggests that Occupation censorship is largely responsible for Tamura's move to less artistically satisfying work, "Pleading for the Body."

27 *Nikutai no bungaku*, 48–9.

28 "Nikutai no kiban," 44–5.

29 Developed in his essay "Ideology as Conflict," in *Conflict in Modern Japanese History*, 25–61.

30 This is the ideology that Eric Wolf explores, and defines, as an anthropologist, in ways fruitful for studies such as this: Eric R. Wolf, *Envisioning Power*, Berkeley: University of California Press, 1999. See especially page 25 and following.

31 Louis Althusser, *Lenin and Philosophy, and Other Essays*, trans. Ben Brewster, London: New Left Books, 1971, 149.

32 "Nikutai ga ningen de aru," 12–14.

33 Tamura, *Waga bundan seishunki*, 219.

34 These issues are themselves part of a blatantly gendered discourse, as Alan Tansman has noted:

> The discourse of modernity in Japanese intellectual life employs the language of gender: that which resists the modern – the anti-rational, non-Western, native core of Japanese culture – has figured in the culture as feminine, and femininity has been the trope used to evoke the authentic, unsullied native genius. "Feminine" literature – where *feminine* implies subtle gradations of psychological states and evocations of "Japanese" beauty within a confined sphere – has been invoked as an alternative to the baleful effects of a Western, male, overly intellectual, and unrooted modern sensibility.
>
> (Tansman, *The Writings of Kōdo Aya*, 2)

35 Kamiya Tadataka, "Yokuatsu kara kaihō e," 3: 6.

36 Ken Ito, *Visions of Desire: Tanizaki's Fictional Worlds*, Stanford: Stanford University Press, 1991, 1–2.

37 Togaeri Hajime, *Nise no kisetsu*, 74.

38 Ibid., 74.

39 Ibid., 9.

40 In Tamura's telling, Yokomitsu Riichi wanted to see this story receive the Natsume Sōseki Prize. Also, he continues, Aono Suekichi preferred this story to "Nikutai no mon." This follows the passage where he notes how "Nikutai no akuma" led to numerous requests and commissions. Tamura, *Waga bundan seishunki*, 216–17.

41 "Nikutai no akuma," in *Nikutai no mon*, Tokyo: Chikuma Shobō, 12. This concern for the eyes and the gaze of the Other I am tempted to call "Sartrean," given the importance of Sartre's fiction at this time, as I have discussed.

42 Ibid., 13.

43 Ibid.

44 Ibid., italics added.

45 Ibid., 44.

46 Togaeri, *Nise no kisetsu*, 82.

47 Tamura, "Nikutai no akuma," 46. There is in this phrase a resonance with Noma Hiroshi's work, as we shall see, wherein two bodies grope and search for each other independently of any rational volition. The compound used for "irony" here is a combination of the characters skin and flesh, thus Tamura is able to attain a double-entendre (although not one that would strike Japanese) by seeming to say as well "what a cruel flesh."

48 Isoda, *Sengo*, 123–4; this failing did not go unnoticed by Tamura's contemporaries, and was criticized by his friend Togaeri Hajime, *Nise no kisetsu*, 78.

49 Igarashi, *Bodies of Memory*, 60. Igarashi goes on to trace the invocation of Western/Christian imagery in this story as pointing to "a salvation to be found through identification with the victors." I find this an over-reading. I am arguing that the identification is not with the victors so much as a resurrection of and identification with a masculinist tradition.

50 For one discussion, see William Hauser, "Women and War: The Japanese Film Image," in *Recreating Japanese Women*.

51 "Nikutai no akuma", 58.

52 Ibid., 43.

53 "Nikutai no mon," 33.

54 Ibid.

55 Yet in an important way it is not unreal. The division of Tokyo into territory, turf, by the *pan-pan,* and the instances of corporal punishment exacted by the women, who did indeed work in gangs, conforms to contemporary recollections and imagery (although it is difficult to determine how much is "imagery" how much "actual"). See the descriptions in Shiomitsu Kazu, *Ameyoko 35 nen no gekishi*, Tokyo: Tokyo kobo shuppan, 1982, esp. 204 ff. See also Molasky, *The American Occupation of Japan and Okinawa*, who argues that this reflects a largely constructed imagery. This imagery is also included in a story I discuss in the final chapter, "Susaki Paradaisu."

56 Sakaguchi Ango, "Discourse on Decadence," trans. Seiji M. Lippit, *Review of Japanese Culture and Society*, 1, 1 (1986): 1.

57 "Nikutai no mon," 34.

58 Ibid., 35–6.

59 *Takumashii* is a word that I often hear in discussions of this work.

60 "Nikutai no mon," 54.

61 Ibid.

62 Although this precise phrase does not appear in these stories, there is no question that this describes their situation. Much recent scholarship explores the situation of these women forced into sexual slavery. It is also clear from other essays that this institution forms the imagery Tamura has in mind. See, for one extended discussion, the special issue of *Positions*, Spring 1997. For the specifics of this censorship of terms during the Occupation, this story, and the "comfort women," see Kerkham, "Pleading for the Body."

63 Quoted in Kerkham, ibid., 310.

64 For one discussion of this possibility, in wider contexts, see Kevin Doak, "Narrating China, Ordering East Asia: The Discourse on Nation and Ethnicity in Imperial Japan," in *Constructing Nationhood in East Asia*, ed. Chow Kai-wing, Kevin Michael Doak, and Poshek Fu, Ann Arbor: University of Michigan Press, 2001, 85–113, esp. 105.

65 Tamura, *Waga bundan seishunki*, 220–1.

66 Kerkham, "Pleading for the Body," 336. Kerkham suggests, in her important articulation of the background to this work, that the publicity lost from this incident had wide ramifications for Tamura's career as a writer. I think it may also suggest the source of the animosity Tamura expresses towards Ango's work, as I discuss later. For a fuller discussion of censorship issues see John Dower, especially Chapter 14 of *Embracing Defeat*, and the work of Yokote Kazuhiko, *Hisenryōka no bungaku ni kansura kisōteki kenkyū: ronkōhen*, Tokyo: Musashino Shobō, 1996.

67 Tamura Taijirō, "Shunpuden," in *Tamura Taijirō shū*, Tokyo: Kōdansha, 1953, vol. 13 of *Gendai chōhen meisaku zenshū*, 437. Tamura wrote in the preface of the collection of short stories of which "Shunpuden" was the title, that "I wrote this [collection] with a longing, on the verge of tears, for the young women [of the continent] in the service of the army, with only desires for revenge on the women of Japan" because the Japanese women, at the front and shortly after the return, had only contempt for the foot soldiers and gave all their attention to the officers of the armed forces. Quoted in Kerkham, "Pleading for the Body," 340.

68 "Shunpuden," 437.

69 Ibid., 438.

70 According to John Dower there was a bitter pun in circulation at this time, where the Imperial army (*kōgun*) was referred to as an army of locusts (*kōgun*), *Embracing Defeat*, 507.

71 Tamura, Taijirō, "Inago," in *Nikutai no mon*, Tokyo: Chikuma Shobō, 1988, 189.

72 Ibid., 170.

73 Ibid., 176–7.

74 Ibid., 163–5.

75 Ibid., 163–5.

76 Ibid., 216.

4 Noma Hiroshi

1 A number of the stories discussed here have been translated by James Raeside in *"Dark Pictures" and Other Stories*, Ann Arbor: Center for Japanese Studies, University of Michigan, 2000.

2 According to the *Gendai Nihon hungaku daijiten*, Noma Hiroshi, Umezaki Haruo (1915–65), Shiina Rinzō (1911–73), and Nakamura Shin'ichirō, (1887–1924), make up the "first [wave] of new postwar writers," and Hotta Yoshie (1918–) and Abe Kōbō (1924–83), among others, make up the second wave. The third wave (*daisan no shinjin*) is perhaps most often referred to as a group, and includes such writers as Yasuoka Shōtarō (1920–), Yoshiyuki Junnosuke (1924–94), Kojima Nobuo (1915–), Shōno Junzō (1921–), and Endō Shūsaku (1923–96) (Hisamatsu Sen'ichi *et al.*, *Gendai Nihon bungaku daijiten*, Tokyo: Meiji Shoin, 1965, 635).

3 "Kao no naka no akai tsuki," in *Noma Hiroshi zenshū*, 22 vols, Tokyo: Chikuma Shobō, 1969, 1: 119.

4 Noma Hiroshi, "Jibun no sakuhin ni tsuite (I, II)," in *Zenshū*, 14: 255.

5 Skin is a powerful border metaphor that is richly explored in Noma's fiction. Atsuko Sakaki has initiated some recent theoretical inquiries into this palette of images in the context of Abe Kōbō's *Tanin no kao* (presentation "Scratch the Surface, Film the Face: Obsession with the Depth and Fascination with the Surface in Abe Kōbō's 'The Face of Another'," 1 March 2003, University of Kentucky). The recent study by Claudia Benthien, although generated from the cultural milieu of Germany, is a path-breaking work on these topics: *Skin: On the Cultural Border Between Self and the World*, trans. Thomas Dunlap, New York: Columbia University Press, 2002.

6 Yohana Keiko groups this story with others of insatiable desire. I am situating it in the context of Noma's soldiers' experience/characters who have found themselves in a femininized position, rather than as the initiators of heterosexual desire. "Onna no shintai/onna no ishiki," in *Kōza Shōwa bungakushi*, 5 vols, ed. Yūseidō henshūbu, Tokyo: Yūseidō, 1988, 5: 117.

7 Ōe Kenzaburō, "Kaisetsu," in *Zenshū*, 1: 367.

8 Okuno Takeo, "Sengo bungaku to sei," in *Bungakuteki seiha*, Tokyo: Kamakura Insatsu, 1964, 101.

9 Nishikawa, *Nihon no sengo shōsetsu: haikyo no hikari*, 258.

10 Noma Hiroshi, "Futatsu no nikutai," in *Zenshū*, 1: 64. Unless noted otherwise, all translations are my own.

11 "Kurai e," in *Zenshū*, 1: 31.

12 Ibid., 4.

13 Noma Hiroshi, "Nikutai wa nurete," in *Zenshū*, 1: 75.

14 "Kurai e," 9.

15 "Futatsu no nikutai," 64.

16 Nishikawa Nagao, *Nihon no sengo shōsetsu*, 256–8.

17 Noma does not explore the counterpoint, the very permeability of skin and the damage that can be caused by the single bullet sufficient to render this entire physical mass into stinking putrid putty. As the soldier also knows only too well, the steel wall of a canteen may survive a bullet, but the skin will not. My phrasing here is prompted by Klaus Theweleit's analysis

of the warrior ethic; there is much of the fascist concern for violence as antidote to stifling cerebral concerns in the fiction of the flesh writers.

18 Nishikawa, *Sengo shōsetsu*, 259.

19 Ibid., 262.

20 Noma, "Futatsu no nikutai," 61.

21 This is not so distant from Foucault's description of the "body of the condemned," in *Discipline and Punish*, as I suggested in the Introduction.

22 Noma Hiroshi, "Kurai e," 28. Unless otherwise noted, all translations are my own.

23 "Nikutai wa nureru," 81–2.

24 "Kurai e," 28.

25 Yamada Minoru, "Jitsuzon ishiki to naizo kankaku – Noma Hiroshiron," in *Noma Hiroshi kenkyū*, ed. Watanabe Hiroshi, Tokyo: Chikuma Shobō, 1969, 124.

26 Ibid., 125. Yamada borrows G. H. Mead's definition of salvation as "a sense of tranquility in one's surroundings."

27 Tomioka Kōichirō, *Sengo bungaku no arukeorojii*, Tokyo: Fukutake Shobō, 1986, 99–100.

28 Ibid., 97.

29 Noma Hiroshi, "Jibun no sakuhin ni tsuite," 260.

30 Ibid., 253.

31 Or, as John Nathan retells Ōe Kenzaburō's boyhood experience, few were quite so eager to die for the cause as they often acted:

> Once a day [Ōe's] turn had come to be called to the front of the classroom and asked, "What would you do if the Emperor commanded you to die?" and Ōe had replied, knees shaking, "I would die, Sir, I would cut open my belly and die." In bed at night, he had suffered the secret guilt of knowing, at least suspecting, he was not truly eager to destroy himself for the Emperor.
> (John Nathan, "Introduction," in Ōe, Kenzaburō, *Teach Us To Outgrow Our Madness: Four Short Novels*, New York: Grove Press, 1977, xiii)

32 Togaeri Hajime, *Nise no kisetsu*, 34–5.

33 When asked by a journalist in 1975 whether Japanese values had changed, the emperor expressed the same sentiment in plainer language. "I understand that since the conclusion of the war people have expressed various opinions," he responded, "but, looking at this from a broad perspective, I do not think there has been any change between prewar and postwar." Dower, *Embracing Defeat*, 556.

34 Miyamoto Yuriko, "Senkyuhyakuyonjyurokunen no bundan," in *Zenshū*, 14 vols, Tokyo: Kawade Shobō, 1952, 11: 68. *Kindai bungaku* is the journal published by the *Kindai bungakukai*, the first issue of which appeared in 1946, and the last in 1964. The original board of editors was comprised of Honda Shūgo (1908–), Hirano Ken (1907–78), Haniya Yutaka (1909–97), Ara Masahito (1913–79), Sasaki Kiichi (1914–93), Odagiri Hideo (1916–2000), and Yamamuro Shizuka (1906–2000), critics often referred to in this essay. *Kindai bungaku* was less strident in its political aims than was the rival journal, of which Miyamoto was closely associated, *Shin Nihon bungaku*. The first issue of *Shin Nihon bungaku* was also on newsstands in 1946 and continues to be published in 2003. It is an organ of the Japan Communist Party. Noma joined both the Japan Communist Party and

the *Shin Nihon bungakukai* in 1946 and served on the editorial board of *Shin Nihon bungaku* from 1947, along with other Party figures such as Tsuboi Shigeji, Kubokawa Tsurujiro, Nakano Shigeharu, Kubota Masafumi, and Nakajima Kenzo. One detects thinly veiled Party sentiments creeping into Miyamoto's judgments, which is how her comments were understood by contemporaries (like Honda Shūgo) (Hisamatsu Sen'ichi *et al., Gendai Nihon bungaku daijiten*, 348–9, 588–9; Donald Keene, *Dawn to the West*, 2 vols, New York: Holt, Rinehart, and Winston, 1984, 1: 970–4; Miyamoto, "Senkyuhyakuyonjyurokunen no bundan," 82.

35 "Senkyuhyakuyonjyurokunen no bundan," 81.

36 These details do not mean the work is autobiographical – it is not – but biographical elements do remain close to the surface of this work.

37 Noma, "Kurai e," 7.

38 Ibid., 8.

39 Ibid., 23.

40 Ibid., 25.

41 Ibid., 54–5.

42 Ibid., 54.

43 Ibid., 55.

44 Ibid., 31.

45 "Nikutai wa nurete," 95.

46 "Kurai e," 3.

47 Ibid., 7. I note only in passing that Georges Bataille's understanding of sex and death asserts its relevance in Noma's fiction as well. The simultaneous attraction and repulsion felt in the face of both orgasm and death, as in religious ecstasy, is erotism and is a characteristic common to both Noma and Bataille. This erotism offers the space where one individual may connect with another, in Bataille's formulation, the only space shared by all humanity. This also strikes me as an apt description of the liberation which Noma's characters seek (George Bataille, *Erotism: Death and Sensuality*, trans. Mary Dalwood, San Francisco: City Lights Books, 1986, 1–62).

48 This may sound parodic of Existentialist rhetoric. At this time, there was nothing ironic in this phrasing. Further, I find that it helps explain the appeal of Existentialism in the early postwar years, as mentioned in the first chapter. See also my "When Sartre was an Erotic Writer: Body, Nation, and Existentialism in Japan after the Asia-Pacific War," *Japan Forum* (Spring 2002): 77–103.

49 Ōe Kenzaburō, "Kaisetsu," 371.

50 See, for example, Donald Keene's discussion, *Dawn to the West*, 1: 975–6.

51 "Jibun no sakuhin ni tsuite," 253.

52 "Kurai e," 53. This translation is slightly abridged.

53 Honda Shūgo, "'Kurai e' to tenkō," in Noma Hiroshi, *Zenshū*, 1: 351.

54 Furubayashi Takashi, *Sengoha sakka ha kataru*, "Noma Hiroshi," Tokyo: Chikuma Shobō, 1971, 17.

55 And also the philosophy of the Kyoto school, which would have been his undergraduate environment. As Furubayashi Takashi describes it, the three legs on which Noma's work rested, in the early works at least, are Marxism, Symbolism, and Nishida (Kyoto University) philosophy, *Sengoha sakka ha kataru*, 18. James Raeside gives a fuller account of these issues,

particularly the "total novel" and the Symbolist interactions, in "Afterword," in *"Dark Pictures" and Other Stories*, 167 ff.

56 This is, curiously, the criticism most often leveled at the *watakushi shōsetsu* tradition.

57 Noma Hiroshi, "Shōsetsuron," in *Zenshū*, 14: 34–5.

58 Noma Hiroshi, "Jōkyō," 1.

59 Noma essentially cut his teeth on the Symbolists. See the discussion in the "Prose style" section below.

60 "Jōkyō," 1–2.

61 Suzuki Sadami, "Noma Hiroshi no ichi," in *Isuito Noma Hiroshi*, ed. Bungei Henshūbu, Tokyo: Kawade Shobō Shinsha, 1991, 146, 154; see also Oda, Makoto, "'Sono ato' no 'sengo bungaku' – Noma Hiroshi no baai," *Gunzō*, 7 (1991): 194–5.

62 Nishikawa, *Nihon no sengo shōsetsu*, 261.

63 "Jibun no sakuhin ni tsuite (I, II)," 253.

64 "Hōkai kankaku," in *Zenshū*, 1: 184.

65 Ibid., 181.

66 "Kurai e," 28.

67 "Hōkai kankaku," 185.

68 "Kao no naka no akai tsuki," 35–6. Unless noted otherwise, the translations from "Kao no naka no akai tsuki" are by Kin'ya Tsuruta.

69 Ibid., 136; my translation; ellipses original.

70 Watanabe Hiroshi, *Noma Hiroshiron*, Tokyo: Shinbisha, 1969, 109.

71 Nishikawa, *Sengo shōsetsu*, 230.

72 Miyamoto, "Senkyuhyakuyonjyurokunen no bundan," 82.

73 "I'm suffocating: existence penetrates me everywhere, through the eyes, the nose, the mouth." Jean-Paul Sartre, *Nausea*, trans. by Lloyd Alexander, New York: New Directions, 1964, 126.

74 Iwasaki Kunieda, "Noma Hiroshi no buntai," *Shinchō*, 88, 3 (1991): 258.

75 Honda, *Monogatari sengo bungakushi*, 134.

76 Nishikawa, *Sengo shōsetsu*, 262.

77 Okuno Takeo, "Sengo bungaku to sei," 100. This follows his discussion of the new plane of discourse to which Ango, Tamura, Oda, and others had taken sex after the war.

78 "Jibun no sakuhin ni tsuite," 256.

79 Furubayashi, *Sengoha sakka ha kataru*, 18.

80 Jay Rubin, "From Wholesomeness to Decadence: The Censorship of Literature under the Allied Occupation," *Journal of Japanese Studies*, 11, 1 (1985): 80; Keene, *Dawn to the West*, 1: 975. I do not think, however, that Noma would find in this a criticism. He was hardly the lone twentieth-century writer assuming that art should demand effort of the reader. Nishikawa, *Sengo shōsetsu*, 233, 263.

81 Keene, *Dawn to the West*, 1: 976.

82 In fact, as Noma goes on to explain, his goal was not so much to push or challenge the grammatical structures and features of the language but to "save" and "rescue" the language. He wishes to rescue the language from what he calls its traditional weakness of expression and infuse it with "thought": "My goal is to add thought [*shikō*] to the abstraction of expression currently found in Japanese" ("Buntai, kao, sono hoka," in *Zenshū*, 14: 294).

83 "Jibun no sakuhin ni tsuite," 252–6.

84 "Watakushi no kotoba," in *Zenshū*, 15: 292.
85 Watanabe, *Noma Hiroshiron*, 96.

5 Sakaguchi Ango

1 Okuno Takeo echoes many when he notes that the prose style of the short story "Hakuchi" ("The Idiot") has direct bearing on the subsequent works of writers like Shiina Rinzō, Takeda Taijun, Yasuoka Shōtarō, and Kaiko Ken. Okuno Takeo, *Sakaguchi Ango*, Tokyo: Bungei Shunjū, 1972, 156.
2 This title phrasing is Alan Wolfe's.
3 Karatani Kōjin deserves much of the credit for this, starting with his 1996 volume (a collection of essays written over a twenty-year span), *Sakaguchi Ango to Nakagami Kenji,* Tokyo: Ōta Shuppan, 1996. Karatani is also editing the most recent of Ango's *Complete Works*, with Sekii Mitsuo. Sekii has been active in this regard, recently as editor of a special volume (*bessatsu*), in which Karatani figures prominently, in the series put together by the journal *Kokubungaku kaishaku to kanshō, Sakaguchi Ango to Nihon bunka*, Tokyo: Ibundo, 1999.
4 Carolyn Dean suggests, in the context of reading Lacan, that the tendency to posit a symbolic patriarch in the face of a discredited father figure, and likewise the theorizing of a self in the face of a non-existent one, suggests the structural necessity of such figures, even with the acknowledgment that they cannot exist. This prompts me to ask if the flesh writers are implicitly acknowledging the need for some ideological structure in the face of one dissolving before their eyes. The issue here lies with their proposed alternative ideology and concept of self, which prove no less restrictive than that which they wish to replace. *The Self and its Pleasures: Bataille, Lacan, and the History of the Decentered Subject*, Ithaca, NY: Cornell University Press, 1992.
5 Dean, again, suggests that the interwar and postwar crises in France provided the cultural specificities that led to the theorizing of the decentralized subject in thinkers such as Lacan, Foucault, and Bataille. These are thinkers helpful in working through the issues of these Japanese writers, as well. She notes how the cultural particularities of France undergird this development. The Japanese war experience suggested to the flesh writers as well that the only coherent self is the dissolved self. Modernism and the experience of war seem to foster similar anxieties and literary responses.
6 Karatani, and Nishikawa Nagao as well, note the correspondences to current thinking about Japanese culture and find in Ango keys and clues to get beyond culture-bound essentialist thinking. There is something of a contradiction here, given the temptation that essentialism holds for Ango, that I will explore more fully later. See Karatani's discussion in *Sakaguchi Ango to Nakagami Kenji*, especially 35 and following, and again on 63 and following. Nishikawa is clearest on this in Chapter 9 of his *Kokkyō no koekata*, Tokyo: Chikuma Shobō, 1992.
7 "Darakuron," in *Gendai Nihon bungaku zenshū*, vol. 78: *Ishikawa Jun, Sakaguchi Ango, Dazai Osamushū*, Tokyo: Chikuma Shobō, 1961, 224. All translations are my own, unless otherwise noted.
8 Karatani, *Sakaguchi Ango to Nakagami Kenji*, 11.
9 "Darakuron," 224.
10 Ibid., 224.

11 Karatani ties this method of narrative to Nakagami Kenji, which is important as well, *Sakaguchi Ango*, 96ff.

12 The "irony" that Kevin Doak (*Dreams of Difference,* Berkeley: University of California Press, 1994) has explicated in relation to the Romantics is suggestive here. Ango's irony – "farce" – is not unrelated to this tradition.

13 Katō Norihiro takes on many of these themes in recent considerations of the war and its legacies. He conceives of the Japanese as sharing a past, beliefs, and practices by being rooted in the physical attributes of the Japanese archipelago. While this conceptualization draws much from polemic *nihonjinron* discourse, he also draws from thinkers such as Watsuji Tetsurō and Etō Jun. By imagining this shared "body" of knowledge as a body (*shintai*) he suggests a tie to the visceral, innate imagery of the flesh writers. I would suggest that his thinking as developed in a book such as *Nihon to iu shintai* (Tokyo: Kōdansha, 1994) represents a radical, although logical, result of lines of thinking that tempted Ango: the individual body anchors identity; that body is part of a larger political/cultural body necessary for individual identity; and that cultural entity is unique and closed to those not physically members of the group. Ango does not develop his thinking with the rigor and single-mindedness of Katō, but when I suggest that Ango was tempted by essentialism, Katō articulates the logical conclusions of the "temptation" I have in mind, where individual body and national body overlap.

14 Wolfe, "From Pearls to Swine," 369; emphasis original.

15 "Zoku Darakuron," in *Nihon bunka shikan: Sakaguchi Ango essai shū*, Tokyo: Kodansha, 1996, 240.

16 Ibid., 241.

17 "Darakuron," 224.

18 "Nyōtai," in *Teihon Sakaguchi Ango zenshū*, 13 vols, Tokyo: Tōjusha, 1975, 3: 13. This language replicates the title of Ango's discussion of Sartre, and suggests that Lulu was the idea behind this "Woman's body."

19 Igarashi documents the oft-told tale of a Tokyo District Court judge who died of starvation when he rigidly followed the rationed allotments. Igarashi, *Bodies of Memory*, 53.

20 Okuno Takeo, *Sakaguchi Ango*, 14.

21 Tsurumi Shunsuke and Kuno Osamu are perhaps the most extreme in the way they tie the postwar experience to the prewar, positing in their classic study of postwar Japanese thought (*Gendai Nihon no shisō*) that the reversal of values concomitant with the surrender made existentialism an experience common to all Japanese in the postwar years. This is straightforward enough, but they subsequently equate the angst and anguish of the prewar *tenkō* experience – the mass movements of the 1930s, especially, when intellectuals renounced their Marxism in the face of police pressure and interrogation – with the reversal of values at the end of the war to argue that these also constitute a *tenkō* experience for the populace at large. Since in this description all Japanese are *tenkōsha*, and since *tenkō* is a prototypical Existentialist experience, Tsurumi and Kuno go on to state that all Japanese are thereby existentialists. This seems, from my perspective, to be overstated. Nonetheless, they are correct in noting that postwar issues are not divorced from the concerns of prewar society; the disillusion engendered by the surrender continues that which accompanied the mass arrests and *tenkō* of the 1930s. Tsurumi, Shunsuke and Kuno Osamu, *Gendai Nihon no shisō*, Tokyo: Iwanami Shoten, 1969.

22 Okuno, *Sakaguchi Ango*, 14.
23 Translation by James Dorsey, in *The Critical Mischief of Sakaguchi Ango*, ed. James Dorsey and Douglas N. Slaymaker, forthcoming.
24 Karatani, *Sakaguchi Ango to Nakagami Kenji*, 67.
25 "Bungaku no furusato," in *Nihon bunka shikan: Sakaguchi Ango essaisen*, Tokyo: Kōdansha (bungeibunkō), 1995, 93.
26 "Zoku Darakuron," 245.
27 Foucault, *Discipline and Punish*, 25; Michel Foucault, *The History of Sexuality*, trans. Robert Hurley, New York: Pantheon Books, 1978, 95.
28 "Bungaku no furusato," 88.
29 Ibid., 92.
30 "Watashi wa umi wo dakishimetai," in *Zenshū*, 6: 237.
31 "Zoku darakuron," 242.
32 "Bungaku no furusato," 93.
33 "Watashi wa umi wo dakishimetai," 236.
34 Okuno, *Sakaguchi Ango*, 26.
35 "Watashi wa umi wo dakishimetai," 237.
36 Ibid., 241.
37 Ibid., 239.
38 Ibid., 237.
39 Yajima Michihiro, "'Watashi wa umi wo dakisimete itai' nikutai no seishinka," in *Sakaguchi Ango kenkyū*, ed. Moriyasu Masafumi and Takano Yoshitomo, Tokyo: Nansōsha, 1973, 345.
40 It is this essay-story pair that helped secure his fame and for which most remember him. I note this distinction of essay and story while aware that it is a false one, particularly in the Japanese context, where essay and story are part of a single continuum, as Miyoshi Masao has so forcefully written.
41 This will be a repeated pattern in Ango and one that mirrors the style of Sartre, an overlap that proves increasingly suggestive. This match of essay and fiction reflects a reading practice extended to Sartre's initial reception in Japan, and marks an important component of the construction of the public intellectual in Japanese society. At the same time, as noted previously, to distinguish between "fiction" and "essay" is to set up a false dichotomy.
42 "The Idiot," trans. George Saitō, in *Modern Japanese Stories: An Anthology*, ed. Ivan Morris, Rutland, VT: Charles E. Tuttle, 1962, 384.
43 I am thinking of "Shisha no ogori" ("Lavish are the Dead," 1957).
44 "The Idiot," 405.
45 Ibid., 400.
46 "Hakuchi," in *Sakaguchi Ango Dazai Osamu shū* (*Gendai Nihon bungaku taikei* 77), Chikuma Shobō, 1969, 273, my translation; "Watashi wa umi wo dakishimetai," 239.
47 "The Idiot," 396; translation modified.
48 Tsurumi notes, however, that the charge given these surveillance posts was rarely carried through with any consistency; Tsurumi Shunsuke, *An Intellectual History of Wartime Japan*, 89–90.
49 "Hakuchi," 385–6.
50 Okuno Takeo, *Sakaguchi Ango*, 15–16.
51 "Watashi wa umi wo dakishimetai," 239. The imagery of flight in the context of Ango's

modernist sensibilities suggests other lines of inquiry, particularly when overlapped with thinking about the sublime:

> The role of the sublime in this study [*The Female Grotesque*] is highly qualified "aerial" – a term I use to designate a zone that is at once historical and imaginary. As historical, it belongs to the late-nineteenth and twentieth century preoccupation with modernity and the specific technological contents of those futurist aspirations for progress, associated with spectacle. As imaginative 'the aerial sublime' posits a ream of freedom with the everyday. For latecomers to the scene of political identity, freedom as expressed in boundless flight is still an almost irresistible image.
>
> (Mary J. Russo, *The Female Grotesque: Risk, Excess, and Modernity*, New York: Routledge, 1995, 11)

52 Karatani, *Sakaguchi Ango to Nakagami Kenji*, 35.
53 "Dekadan bungakuron," in *Nihon bunka shikan: Sakaguchi Ango essai sen*, Tokyo: Kōdansha (bungeibunkō), 1996, 233.
54 Ibid.
55 "Ossified forms" is a borrowing from John Whittier Treat's writing about popular culture. Richard Torrance has noted provocatively that if a mark of the popular in culture is measured by the numbers of people practicing it, then perhaps it is precisely the oldest of cultural forms – tea ceremony, *haiku* and *waka*, *nagauta* – that are practiced by the largest numbers of people in contemporary Japan that are the most "popular." Richard Torrance, "Pre-World War Two Concepts of Japanese Popular Culture and Takeda Rintarō's 'Japan's Three Penny Opera,'" in *A Century of Popular Culture in Japan*, ed. Douglas N. Slaymaker, Lewiston, NY: Edwin Mellen Press, 2000, 20.
56 "Dekadan bungakuron," 232.
57 Okuno, *Sakaguchi Ango*, 14; Karatani, *Sakaguchi Ango to Nakagami Kenji*, 67.
58 "Darakuron," 221–2.
59 "Dekadan bungakuron," 220.
60 Ango is hardly a feminist, but this critique of patriarchal institutions shares much in analysis with later critiques of patriarchy by thinkers such as Komashaku Kimi, Mizuta Noriko, and Saegusa Kazuko.
61 "In the Forest, Under Cherries in Full Bloom," trans. Jay Rubin, in *The Oxford Book of Japanese Short Stories*, ed. Theodore W. Goossen, Oxford: Oxford University Press, 1997, 205.
62 Ibid., 224.
63 Matsuda Yumi, "'Sakura no mori no mankai no shita' no oni," in *Sakaguchi Ango kenkyū*, 381–2.
64 "Dekadan bungakuron," 223–4.
65 Ibid., 223.
66 Ibid., 226.
67 Karatani, *Sakaguchi Ango to Nakagami Kenji*, 66.
68 Keene, *Dawn to the West*, 1: 1077.
69 As Jay Rubin has explained.
70 Okuno, *Sakaguchi Ango*, 146.
71 See, for example, Chapters 8 and 9 of *Kokkyō no koekata*. Nishikawa charts how Ango

emphasizes *daraku*, individuality, and the quotidian, to valorize the everyday people and "culture" he knows from bars and back streets, in contrast to the essentialized and ideologized Japanese culture found (but never seen) in Bruno Taut. Taut, the architect of international renown who crossed national boundaries, followed the European paradigms of static culture and was unable to traverse the cultural barriers marked by those same borders. In contrast, Sakaguchi Ango, famous nowhere, disciple of the decadent, traversing only neon-lit back streets, conceived of a model of flexible culture by pursuing the individual and was able to set the groundwork for theorizing on culture that traversed cultural boundaries. I have developed this connection in my "Sakaguchi Ango's Individual Cult(ure)," in *The Critical Mischief of Sakaguchi Ango*.

72 Okuno, *Bungakuteki seiha*, 100–4.

73 Philopon was a drug used widely for its energizing effects during wartime, especially in the munitions factories, becoming very widespread in use following the war: in 1954 more than 200,000 persons were reported as addicts injured by its use, and 550,000 persons were identified as users, at all levels of society. Susaki Takashi *et al.*, *Sengoshi daijiten*, Tokyo: Sanseido, 1991, entry for "hiropon."

74 Keene, *Dawn to the West*, 1: 1065.

75 Sahashi Bunju, *Sakaguchi Ango: Sono sei to shi*, Tokyo: Shunjūsha, 1980, 5.

76 Karatani Kōjin, in personal correspondence, insists that Ango "was a novelist, but the type of novelist who denied the novel as a genre. I think [one] should not distinguish his so-called novels from essays or detective stories." We are better to speak then of his "writing." 5 March 2000. See as well his essay in *The Literary Mischief of Sakaguchi Ango*.

77 Hyōdo Masanosuke, *Noma Hiroshiron*, Tokyo: Shinchōsha, 1971, 5. Togaeri Hajime is even less positive in his response to Ango, blasting him for his lack of soldiering experience. Ango writes, for example, of being in Tokyo during the war, and of watching the bombings from atop a building in the Ginza, in which Togaeri sees a voyeur of the first order. Togaeri finds him to be all wind and no substance. In an uncharacteristic burst of patriotism, Togaeri asserts that for all those Japanese who served as soldiers and were treated inhumanely by the army (Togaeri being one, having been called up late in life), Ango's account of "glory under the bombs" can only seem as a slap in the face. Togaeri Hajime, *Nise no kisetsu*, 51 ff.

78 Okuno, *Sakaguchi Ango*, 22.

79 See Karatani's introductory essay, forthcoming in *Sakaguchi Ango's Critical Mischief*.

80 Okuno, *Sakaguchi Ango*, 23–4.

81 Ibid., 11.

82 Karatani, *Sakaguchi Ango to Nakagami Kenji*, 21.

83 Okuno, *Sakaguchi Ango*, 250.

84 For more on this issue, see Mori Eichi, "Fūzoku shōsetsu to chukan shōsetsu," esp. 3: 235–40. Odagiri Susumu, ed., *Nihon kindai bungaku daijiten*, 6 vols, Tokyo: Kōdansha, 1977–8, 3: 90, emphasis added.

85 Oda Sakunosuke provides, albeit rather obliquely, I admit, a parallel set of images in his "Kanosei no bungaku." He recalls a night of drinking with Ango (and Dazai Osamu). He writes of frustration with overrated culture, reminiscent of Ango's writing, in a passage that also connects these all to Sartre. To paraphrase, there is a show of the great treasures at Nara's *Shōsōin* near Oda's residence. People pack themselves like sardines into trains to be trampled and poked by the crowds of travelers and tourists flocking to see the exhibit. They

are no doubt interesting individuals of respectable position, but they allow themselves to be ordered around by bus drivers, who check their personalities at the door. They get to Nara, stream through the exhibit, make a big fuss of "oohs" and "aahs," and are herded out again. If this is the way to value culture, I do not need it, he says. He stays at home, looking at *Life* magazine in bed, looking for all the world like something the cat dragged in (*doraneko*). On the cover of *Life* is a picture of a wall-eyed Jean-Paul Sartre. Oda uses this as a springboard to discuss Sartre, in a series of images that connect him back to Ango and the ironic tradition of aesthetics. Oda Sakunosuke, "Kanōsei no bungaku," 446.

86 Tsuge Teruhiko, "Jitsuzonshugi," 6, 141.

87 I have developed this history more completely in "When Sartre was an Erotic Writer," 77–103.

88 Hyōdo Masanosuke, *Sakaguchi Angoron*, Tokyo: Tojūsha, 1972, 145. Hyōdo, echoing others I have mentioned, goes on to note that it no longer needs to be pointed out that only in the postwar was this sort of inquiry, where a work's action was based on physical activity and attraction, possible.

89 Tamura Taijirō, "Nikutai bungaku to ningen no jiyū," in *Nikutai no bungaku*, Tokyo: Kusano Shobō, 1948, 47.

90 Ibid., 48–9.

6   When women write postwar Japan

1   As I noted in the introduction, mainstream literary magazines featured works of established, older writers such as Shiga Naoya, Masamune Hakuchō, Nagai Kafū, Tanizaki Jun'ichirō, and Uno Kōji after the war. Watanabe Sumiko, "Shōwa ga hiraita josei bungaku," 17.

2   Ueno Chizuko, "Ishi wo nageru," in *Danryū bungakuron*, ed. Ueno Chizuko, Ogura Chikako, and Tomioka Taeko, Tokyo: Chikuma Shobō, 1992, 400. Ueno identifies Saegusa Kazuko, whom I discuss in the final section of this chapter, as one who has taken up the latter project, as does the groundbreaking volume in which Ueno's essay appeared. Sharalyn Orbaugh has suggested a similar paradigm for reading women's fiction; see, for example, her "The Body in Contemporary Japanese Women's Fiction," 119–64.

3   I feel the need, defensively perhaps, to posit my own awareness that putting the "woman's chapter" at the end of the study looks suspiciously like a postscript or an afterthought. My intent, however, is to explore the perspectives that these women writers bring to men's fiction and offset, rather than reinforce, traditional imbalances.

4   Shibaki Yoshiko, "Yakō no onna," *Bungei*, 19 (1955): 172.

5   Saegusa Kazuko, *Sono fuyu no shi*, Tokyo: Kodansha, 1989, 17.

6   Jean Bethke Elshtain, *Women and War*, n.p.: Basic Books, 1987, 165.

7   Nakagawa Shigemi, "Hayashi Fumiko: onna wa sensō wo tatakau ka?," in *Nanpō chōyō sakka: sensō to bungaku*, ed. Tadataka Kamiya and Kazuaki Kimura, Kyoto: Sekai Shisōsha, 1996, 242. For a discussion of Nakagawa's contributions to these issues, see Mizuta Noriko's "Hijiki no seibetsu to Feminizumu hihyō," in *Senjika no bungaku*, ed. Kimura Kazunobu, Tokyo: Inpakuto Shuppankai, 2000, 297–9.

8   Molasky, *The American Occupation of Japan and Okinawa*, 287.

9   Wartime discourses had clear roles for *mothers*: the household was a public space where the mother of the family was also the mother of the nation: "The Shōwa mother was regarded as

the mother of the nation, while the Meiji mother had been recognized merely as the mother *within* the state." Miyake, "Doubling Expectations," 277.

10 I refer the reader to Noriko Mizuta's cogent discussion of this work, "In Search of a Lost Paradise: The Wandering Woman in Hayashi Fumiko's *Drifting Clouds*," 329–51.

11 Hayashi Fumiko, *The Floating Clouds*, Tokyo: Hara Publishing, 1965, 39. Yukiko's response to this is ambivalent and I find it hard to characterize: it is clearly a rape at the outset, yet Yukiko also looks forward to her uncle's coming in the night, and is nostalgic for his touch while she is far from home. Melodrama seems to win out, downplaying the violence of this scene.

12 Ibid., 55.

13 Morosawa Yōko, *Onna no sengoshi*, Tokyo: Miraisha, 1971, 48. Suzuki Yūko, *Feminizumu to sensō*, Tokyo: Marujusha, 1997, 15. Suzuki also provides a detailed synopsis of the policies undergirding this structure, including those that require high-school-age women (of certain classes) to work in factories in the manner of Saegusa's protagonist. This ground is covered as well by, for example, Miyake Yoshiko, "Doubling Expectations." The experiences of high-school students, such as those described in Saegusa's first novel, can be found in many oral history collections, such as Asahi Shinbunsha, ed., *Onnatachi no taiheiyō sensō*, 3 vols, Tokyo: Asahi Shinbunsha, 1991, and Shōgakkan, ed., *Onnatachi no hachigatsu jūgonichi: mō hitotsu no Taiheiyō sensō*, Tokyo: Shōgakkan, 1995.

14 Morosawa, *Onna no sengoshi*, 50 ff.; also Molasky, *The American Occupation*.

15 Joan Ericson, *Be a Woman: Hayashi Fumiko and Modern Japanese Women's Literature*, Honolulu: University of Hawai'i Press, 1997, 9. This is also explored by Phyllis Lassner, *British Women Writers of World War II*, New York: St Martin's Press, 1998, esp. 3 and following.

16 The imagery of the *yamamba* is central in this project, as is the exploration of the *majō* by critics such as Mizuta Noriko and Komashaku Kimi. Reproductive imagery is also integral to this; see Vera Mackie's discussion of Fukuda Hideko in *Creating Socialist Women in Japan*, Cambridge: Cambridge University Press, 1997, esp. 7 and following.

17 Mizuta Noriko develops these ideas in her *Monogatari to hanmonogatari no fūkei*.

18 It is not insignificant that the first writer discussed in Ueno Chizuko, Ogura Chikako, and Tomioka Taeko, *Danryū bungakuron*, is Yoshiyuki Jun'nosuke, whose story "Shūu" ("Hard Shower") was awarded the Akutagawa Prize over Sono Ayako's 1954 submission, which I discuss below. In Ueno, Ogura, and Tomioka's discussion of this work, the "masculine" elements relevant to my study become even more obvious.

19 Quoted in Saegusa Kazuko, *Ren'ai shōsetsu no kansei*, Tokyo: Seidosha, 1991, 20–1. Saegusa's preface to Komashaku's volume expands themes I suggest here.

20 In the context of contemporary discussions regarding an essential identity "core," see Judith Butler, *Gender Trouble*, esp. 12 and following.

21 Saegusa, *Ren'ai shōsetsu no kansei*, esp. 9–26.

22 When not plain wrong-headed for its complicity in ghettoizing women's writing; see the introductory chapters of Rebecca Copeland's recent study, *Lost Leaves: Women Writers in Meiji Japan*, Honolulu: University of Hawai'i Press, 2000, and also the discussion in Joan Ericson's consideration of *joryū bungaku* in the context of her study of Hayashi Fumiko, *Be a Woman*.

23 Mara Miller, "Canons and the Challenge of Gender," *Monist*, 76, 4 (October 1993): 484.

24 Ibid., 484.

25 Elise K. Tipton, ed., *Society and the State in Interwar Japan*, London and New York: Routledge, 1997, 258.

26 First appearing in *Gunzō*, 10 (October 1955): 61–79, this story has not been reprinted in any other collections.

27 The reader is referred to note 18 above for more on the significance of this choice of prize-winners.

28 Quoted in the entry under her name in Odagiri Susumu, ed., *Nihon kindai bungaku daijiten*.

29 Molasky, *The American Occupation*, 300.

30 "Good Luck for Everybody!!," *Gunzō* (October 1955): 66.

31 Hiroike Akiko, "Onrii tachi," *Bungei shunjū* (March 1954): 278.

32 Ibid., 279.

33 Niwa Fumio, "Dokugokan," *Bungei shunjū*, 3 (1954): 273–4.

34 Ango's critique is also at this point: "The matron of the house is not fully realized [*kaket-einai*]. [She] looks at the *onrii* with a sharp eye, but the vision of the matron lacks definition. Therefore, this does not constitute a complete [fully-realized] work of fiction," ibid., 277.

35 *Gunzō* (July 1953): 102–27. This story has a circuitous history that almost ensured its anonymity. See the discussion and recovery of the authorship of this work by Mike Molasky, *The American Occupation*, 309 and following, and esp. note 25.

36 Nakamoto Takako, "Kichi no Onna," *Gunzō* (July 1953): 111.

37 Ibid., 112.

38 Ibid., 113.

39 Ibid., 105.

40 Ibid., 124.

41 Senuma Shigeki, "Kaisetsu," in *Shibaki Yoshiko sakuhinshū*, 5 vols, Tokyo: Yomiuri Shinbunsha, 1975, 5: 335.

42 Ōshima Kiyoshi, "Kaisetsu," in Shibaki Yoshiko, *Susaki paradaisu*, Tokyo: Shūeisha, 1994, 215.

43 This imagery of the *pan-pan* working as violent, self-policing gangs would seem to be largely a constructed imagery, with little basis in reality. See Chapter 3, note 55.

44 Michael Molasky also comments on these works.

45 Saegusa Kazuko, *Sayōnara otoko no jidai*, Kyoto: Jinbun Shoin, 1984, 124.

46 Ibid., 123–5.

47 *Sono hi no natsu*, Tokyo: Kodansha, 1987, 194.

48 *Sono fuyu no shi*, 206.

49 These arguments can be found in Saegusa, *Sayōnara otoko no jidai*, esp. 79–140.

50 Ibid., 207.

51 *Sono yoru no owari ni*, Tokyo: Kodansha, 1990, 9–11.

Conclusion

1 Peter Brooks, *Body Work*, 8.

2 Ibid.

3 For a more complete discussion of this confluence, see the work of Tsukiramu Toshiyuki, "Sedairon no gyakusetsu," in *Ōe Kenzaburō, Abe Kōbō*, Tokyo: Yūseidō, 1974, 167–83 and Ichijo Takao, *Ōe Kenzaburō no sekai*, Osaka: Izumi Shōin, 1985.

References

Althusser, Louis. *Lenin and Philosophy, and Other Essays*. Trans. Ben Brewster. London: New Left Books, 1971.

Aono Suekichi. "Saikaku no kōshoku bungaku to nikutaiha bungaku." *Yomiuri hyōron* 10 (1949): 75–9.

Arima Tatsuo. *The Failure of Freedom: A Portrait of Modern Japanese Intellectuals*. Cambridge, MA: Harvard University Press, 1985.

Asabuki Tomiko. *Sarutoru Bovowaru to no nijuhachinichikan, Nihon*. Tokyo: Dohōsha Shuppan, 1995. Translation of *Vingt-huit jours au Japon avec Jean-Paul Sartre et Simone de Beauvoir: 18 septembre–16 octobre 1966*. Paris: Langues & Mondes/L'Asiathèque, 1996.

Asahi Shinbunsha, ed. *Onnatachi no taiheiyō sensō*. 3 vols. Tokyo: Asahi Shinbunsha, 1991.

Bakhtin, Mikhail. *Rabelais and his World*. Trans. Helene Iswolsky. Bloomington: Indiana University Press, 1984.

Barnes, Hazel E. "Introduction." In Sartre, Jean-Paul. *Being and Nothingness*. New York: Philosophical Library, 1956.

Barshay, Andrew E. *State and Intellectual in Imperial Japan*. Berkeley: University of California Press, 1988.

Barthes, Roland. "Striptease." In *A Barthes Reader*. Ed. Susan Sontag. New York: Hill and Wang, 1982. 85–8.

Bataille, George. *Erotism: Death and Sensuality*. Trans. Mary Dalwood. San Francisco: City Lights Books, 1986. Rpt. of *Death and Sensuality: A Study of Eroticism and the Taboo*, 1962.

Benthien, Claudia. *Skin: On the Cultural Border Between Self and the World*. Trans. Thomas Dunlap. New York: Columbia University Press, 2002.

Bordo, Susan. "The Feminist as Other." *Metaphilosophy* 27, 1–2 (1996): 10–27.

——, and Alison M. Jaggar, eds. *Gender/Body/Knowledge: Feminist Reconstructions of Being and Knowing*. New Brunswick, NJ: Rutgers University Press, 1989.

Brooks, Peter. *Body Work: Objects of Desire in Modern Narrative*. Cambridge, MA: Harvard University Press, 1993.

Butler, Judith P. *Gender Trouble: Feminism and the Subversion of Identity*. New York: Routledge, 1990.

Bynum, Caroline. "Why all this Fuss about the Body? A Medievalist's Perspective." *Critical Inquiry* 22, 1 (1995): 1–33.

Camus, Albert. "Interview au <Diario> de Sao-Paulo." Trans. Jean Coste. In *Essais*. Ed. R. Quilliot and L. Faucon. (Bibliothèque de la Pléiade.) Paris: Gallimard, 1967. 1697–9 (cf. p. 1752).

——. *The Plague*. Trans. Stuart Gilbert. New York: Vintage International, 1991.

Caruth, Cathy, ed. *Trauma: Explorations in Memory.* Baltimore: Johns Hopkins University Press, 1995.

Chou, Wan-yao. "The *Kōminka* Movement in Taiwan and Korea: Comparisons and Interpretations." In *The Japanese Wartime Empire, 1931–1945.* Ed. Peter Duus, Ramon H. Myers, and Mark R. Peattie. Princeton: Princeton University Press, 1996. 40–68.

Collins, Margery L., and Christine Pierce. "Holes and Slime: Sexism in Sartre's Psychoanalysis." In *Women and Philosophy: Toward a Theory of Liberation.* Ed. Carol C. Gould, and Mary W. Wartofsky. New York: G. P. Putnam, 1976. 112–27.

Cook, Haruko Taya, and Theodore F. Cook. *Japan at War: An Oral History.* New York: New Press, 1992.

Copeland, Rebecca. *Lost Leaves: Women Writers of Meiji Japan.* Honolulu: University of Hawai'i Press, 2000.

———. "Mother Obsession and Womb Imagery in Japanese Literature." *Transactions of the Asiatic Society of Japan* 3 (1988): 131–50.

Cornyetz, Nina. *Dangerous Women, Deadly Words: Phallic Fantasy and Modernity in Three Japanese Writers.* Stanford: Stanford University Press, 1999.

Coward, Rosalind, and John Ellis. *Language and Materialism: Developments in Semiology and the Theory of the Subject.* London: Routledge and Kegan Paul, 1977.

Culler, Jonathan. "Five Propositions on the Future of Men in Feminism." In *Men Writing the Feminine: Literature, Theory, and the Question of Genders.* Ed. Thaïs E. Morgan. Albany: State University of New York Press, 1994.

Dean, Carolyn J. *The Self and Its Pleasures: Bataille, Lacan, and the History of the Decentered Subject.* Ithaca, NY: Cornell University Press, 1992.

Demetz, Peter. *Postwar German Literature: A Critical Introduction.* New York: Pegasus, 1970.

Desser, David. "Gate of Flesh(tones): Color in the Japanese Cinema." In *Cinematic Landscapes: Observations on the Visual Arts and Cinema of China and Japan.* Ed. Linda C. Ehrlich, and David Desser. Austin: University of Texas Press, 1994.

Doak, Kevin Michael. *Dreams of Difference: The Japan Romantic School and the Crisis of Modernity.* Berkeley: University of California Press, 1994.

———. "Narrating China, Ordering East Asia: The Discourse on Nation and Ethnicity in Imperial Japan." In *Constructing Nationhood in East Asia.* Ed. Kai-wing Chow, Kevin Michael Doak, and Poshek Fu. Ann Arbor: University of Michigan Press, 2001. 85–113.

Dorsey, James, and Douglas N. Slaymaker, eds. *The Critical Mischief of Sakaguchi Ango.* Forthcoming.

Dower, John W. *Embracing Defeat: Japan in the Wake of World War II.* New York: W.W. Norton & Company, 1999.

———. *War Without Mercy: Race and Power in the Pacific War.* New York: Pantheon Books, 1986.

Duus, Peter. "Introduction: Japan's Wartime Empire: Problems and Issues." In *The Japanese Wartime Empire, 1931–1945.* Ed. Peter Duus, Ramon H. Myers, and Mark R. Peattie. Princeton: Princeton University Press, 1996. xi–xlvii.

Elison, George. *Deus Destroyed: The Image of Christianity in Early Modern Japan.* Cambridge, MA: Harvard University Press, 1973.

Elshtain, Jean Bethke. *Women and War.* Basic Books, 1987.

Ericson, Joan. *Be a Woman: Hayashi Fumiko and Modern Japanese Women's Literature.* Honolulu: University of Hawai'i Press, 1997.

Etō Jun. *Sakka wa kodō suru, sono hoka*. Tokyo: Kōdansha, 1969. Vol. 5 of *Etō Jun chosaku shū*. 6 vols. 1967–73.

———. *Zen bungei jihyō*. 2 vols. Tokyo: Shinchōsha, 1989.

Fiddes, Nick. *Meat, a Natural Symbol*. London and New York: Routledge, 1992.

Field, Norma. "War and Memory: Japan, Asia, the Fiftieth, and After." *Positions* 5, 1 (Spring 1997): 1–50.

Foucault, Michel. *Discipline and Punish*. Trans. Alan Sheridan. New York: Vintage Books, 1995.

———. *The History of Sexuality*. Trans. Robert Hurley. New York: Pantheon Books, 1978.

Fowler, Edward. *The Rhetoric of Confession*. Berkeley: University of California Press, 1988.

Furubayashi Takashi. *Sengoha sakka ha kataru*. "Noma Hiroshi." Tokyo: Chikuma Shobō, 1971. 7–28.

Fussell, Paul. *Doing Battle: The Making of a Skeptic*. Boston: Little, Brown and Company, 1996.

Garon, Sheldon. *Molding Japanese Minds: The State in Everyday Life*. Princeton: Princeton University Press, 1997.

Gessel, Van. *The Sting of Life: Four Contemporary Japanese Novelists*. New York: Columbia University Press, 1989.

Gibson, Keiko Matsui. "Noma Hiroshi's Struggle for the Total Novel: Critical Absorption of Balzac, Joyce, and Sartre." Dissertation Indiana University, 1992.

Gluck, Carol. *Japan's Modern Myths: Ideology in the Late Meiji Period*. Princeton: Princeton University Press, 1985.

———. "The Past in the Present." In *Postwar Japan as History*. Ed. Andrew Gordon. Berkeley: University of California Press, 1993. 64–95.

Hanada Kiyoteru. "Mishima Yukio." In *Mishima Yukio: hihyō to kenkyū*. Ed. Shirakawa Masayoshi. Tokyo: Haga Shoten, 1974. 31–9.

———. "Sei Sebasuchan no kao." In *Mishima Yukio kenkyū*. Ed. Hasegawa Izumi *et al.* Tokyo: Ishifumi Shoin. 1970.

Harada Hiroshi. *MP no jiipu kara mita senryōka no Tōkyō*. Tokyo: Sōshisha, 1994.

Harootunian, H. D. "Ideology as Conflict." In *Conflict in Modern Japanese History*. Ed. Najita Tetsuo, and J. Victor Koschmann. Princeton: Princeton University Press, 1982. 25–61.

Hasegawa Izumi, ed. *Mishima Yukio kenkyū*. Tokyo: Ishifumi Shoin. 1970.

———. *Sengo bungaku shi*. Tokyo: Meiji Shoin, 1974.

Hauser, William B. "Women and War: The Japanese Film Image." In *Recreating Japanese Women, 1600–1945*. Ed. Gail Lee Bernstein. Berkeley: University of California Press, 1991. 296–313.

Hayashi Fumiko, *The Floating Clouds*. Tokyo: Hara Publishing, 1965.

Hibbett, H., ed. *Contemporary Japanese Literature: An Anthology of Fiction, Film, and Other Writing since 1945*. Tokyo: Tuttle, 1978.

Higonnet, Margaret Randolph *et al. Behind the Lines: Gender and the Two World Wars*. New Haven, CT: Yale University Press, 1987.

Hijiya-Kirschneiret, Irmela. *Rituals of Self-Revelation: Shishōsetsu as Literary Genre and Socio-Cultural Phenomenon*. Cambridge, MA: Harvard University Press, 1996.

Hiroike Akiko. "Onrii tachi." *Bungei shunjū* (March 1954): 278–95. Reprinted in Enchi Fumiko *et al. Gendai no joryū bungaku*. Vol. 1. Tokyo: Asahi Shinbunsha, 1974. 193–212.

Hisamatsu Sen'ichi *et al. Gendai Nihon bungaku daijiten*. Tokyo: Meiji Shoin, 1965.

Honda Shūgo. "*Kurai e* to tenkō." In *Noma Hiroshi zenshū.* 22 vols. Tokyo: Chikuma Shobō, 1969. 1: 348–53.

———. *Monogatari sengo bungakushi.* 2 vols. Tokyo: Iwanami Shoten, 1990.

———. "Noma Hiroshi." In *Noma Hiroshi kenkyū.* Ed. Watanabe Hiroshi. Tokyo: Chikuma Shobō, 1976. 47–66.

Horii Ken'ichi. "Baihin to shite no shintai." In *Kōza Shōwa bungakushi.* 5 vols. Ed. Yūseido henshūbu. Tokyo: Yūseido, 1988. 1: 119–28.

Hoston, Germaine A. *Marxism and the Crisis of Development in Prewar Japan.* Princeton: Princeton University Press, 1986.

———. *The State, Identity, and the National Question in China and Japan.* Princeton: Princeton University Press, 1994.

Hotate Michihisa. *Chūsei no naka no ai to jūzoku: emaki no naka no nikutai.* Tokyo: Heibonsha, 1986.

Hyōdo Masanosuke. *Noma Hiroshiron.* Tokyo: Shinchōsha, 1971.

———. *Sakaguchi Angoron.* Tokyo: Tojūsha, 1972.

Ibuki Takehiko. "Sarutoru no sekaikan." *Sekai bungaku* 4 (1947): 2–21.

———. "Yakusha no kotoba." In *Kabe.* By Jean-Paul Sartre. Trans. Ibuki Takehiko *et al.* Tokyo: Jinbun Shoin, 1950. Vol. 5 of *Sarutoru zenshū.* Trans. of "Le Mur." 1938. 251–6.

Ichijo Takao. *Ōe Kenzaburō no sekai.* Osaka: Izumi Shōin, 1985.

Ichikawa Hiroshi. *<Mi> no kōzō: shintairon wo koete.* Tokyo: Aonisha. 1997.

———. *Seishin to shite no shintai.* Tokyo: Kōdansha. 1992. (First edition 1975.)

Ichiko Teiji. *Nihon bungaku zenshū.* 6 vols. Tokyo: Gakutosha, 1978.

Igarashi Yoshikuni. *Bodies of Memory: Narratives of War in Postwar Japanese Culture, 1945–1970.* Princeton: Princeton University Press, 2000.

Inagaki Masami. *Heieki o kyohishita Nihonjin: todai sha no senjika teikō.* Tokyo: Iwanami Shoten, 1973.

Inoue Hideaki. "Kokutai, kokudo, seibetsu: Nihon shinwa no shintaikan." In *Nihon ni okeru shintai.* Tokyo: Ōbunsha, 1964. 55–97.

Irigaray, Luce. *The Irigaray Reader.* Ed. Margaret Whitford. Oxford: Basil Blackwell, 1991.

———. "This Sex Which Is Not One." In *Writing on the Body.* Ed. Katie Conboy, Nadia Medina, and Sarah Stanbury. New York: Columbia University Press, 1997. 248–56.

Ishizaki Hitoshi. "Jitsuzon to hōkai kankaku." In *Kōza Shōwa bungakushi.* 5 vols. Ed. Yūseido henshūbu. Tokyo: Yūseido, 1988. 3: 113–23.

Isoda Kōichi. *Sajō no kyōen.* Tokyo: Shinchōsha, 1972.

———. *Sengoshi no kūkan.* Tokyo: Shinchōsha, 1983.

Ito, Ken. *Visions of Desire: Tanizaki's Fictional Worlds,* Stanford: Stanford University Press, 1991.

Iwakami Jun'ichi. "Sarutoruteki jituzon no hōkai." *Sekai bunka* 3, 4 (1998): 16–22.

Iwasaki Kunieda. "Noma Hiroshi no buntai." *Shinchō* 88, 3 (1991): 258–9.

Kamei Hideo. "Shintaironteki na kindai bungaku no hajimari." In *Bungaku ni okeru shintai.* Ed. Sato Yasumasa. Tokyo: Ōbunsha, 1984. 71–80.

Kamiya, Tadataka. "Yokuatsu kara kaihō e." In *Kōza Shōwa bungakushi.* 5 vols. Ed. Yūseido henshūbu. Tokyo: Yūseido, 1988. 3: 3–14.

Kanda Fuhito. *Senryo to minshushugi.* Tokyo: Shogakkan, 1989.

Karatani Kōjin. *Sakaguchi Ango to Nakagami Kenji.* Tokyo: Ōta Shuppan, 1996.

Katō Norihiro. *Nihon to iu shintai*. Tokyo: Kōdansha, 1994.

Kawamura Minato *et al. Sensō wa dono yō ni kataretekita ka*. Tokyo: Asahi Shinbunsha, 1999.

Keene, Donald. *Dawn to the West*. 2 vols. New York: Holt, Rinehart, and Winston, 1984.

Kerkham, Eleanor H. "Pleading for the Body: Tamura Taijirō's 1947 Korean Comfort Woman Story, *Biography of a Prostitute*." In *War, Occupation, and Creativity: Japan and East Asia, 1920–1960*. Ed. Marlene J. Mayo, J. Thomas Rimer, and H. Eleanor Kerkham. Honolulu: University of Hawai'i Press, 2001. 310–59.

Kikuchi Shōichi. "Jitsuzon e no kanshin." *Bungaku* 15, 11 (1947): 41–4.

Kimura Yoshinaga. *Mishima Yukio no naka no Mishima Yukio*. Tokyo: Hobunkan Shuppan, 1988.

Kindai Sakka Kenkyū Jiten Kankokukai. *Kindai sakka kenkyū jiten*. Tokyo: Ōfusha, 1983.

Kobayashi Hideo. *Literature of the Lost Home*. Trans. Paul Anderer. Stanford: Stanford University Press. 1995.

Kojima Nobuo. "Nikutai to seishin." In *Kojima Nobuo zenshū*. Vol. 6. Tokyo: Kōdansha, 1971.

Komashaku Kimi. *Majo no ronri*. Tokyo: Fuji Shuppan, 1984.

——. *Majo no shinpan*. Tokyo: Fuji Shuppan, 1984.

Komori Yōichi. *Kōzō to shite no katari*. Tokyo: Shin'yosha, 1988.

Koschmann, J. Victor. *Revolution and Subjectivity in Postwar Japan*. Chicago: University of Chicago Press, 1996.

Koshiro Yukiko. *Trans-Pacific Racisms and the U.S. Occupation of Japan*. New York: Columbia University Press, 1999.

Kristeva, Julia. "Women's Time." In *The Feminist Reader*. 2nd edition. Ed. Catherine Belsey, and Jane Moore. London: Macmillan Press, 1997.

Kuhn, Annette. "Structures of Patriarchy and Capital in the Family." In *Feminism and Materialism: Women and Modes of Production*. Ed. Annette Kuhn, and Ann Marie Wolpe. London: Routledge & Kegan Paul, 1978. 42–67.

Lassner, Phyllis. *British Women Writers of World War II*. New York: St. Martin's Press, 1998.

Le Doeuff, Michèle. *Hipparchia's Choice: An Essay Concerning Women, Philosophy, etc*. Trans. Trista Selous. Oxford: Blackwell, 1991.

Lippit, Seiji M., trans. "Discourse on Decadence." *Review of Japanese Culture and Society* 1, 1 (1986): 1–5.

——. *Topographies of Japanese Modernism*. New York: Columbia University Press, 2002.

McClintock, Anne. *Imperial Leather: Race, Gender, and Sexuality in the Colonial Contest*. New York: Routledge, 1995.

Mackie, Vera. *Creating Socialist Women in Japan*. Cambridge: Cambridge University Press, 1997.

Maeda Ai. *Toshi kūkan no naka no bungaku*. Tokyo: Chikuma Shobō, 1982.

Maruyama Masao. "From Carnal Literature to Carnal Politics." In *Thought and Behaviour in Modern Japanese Politics*. Ed. Ivan Morris. London: Oxford University Press, 1963. Trans. of "Nikutai bungaku kara nikutai seiji made." *Tenbō* 10 (1949): 6–16.

——. "The Ideology and Dynamics of Japanese Fascism." In *Thought and Behaviour in Modern Japanese Politics*. Ed. Ivan Morris. London: Oxford University Press, 1963. 24–83.

Masuda Koh, general editor. *Kenkyusha's New Japanese–English Dictionary*. 4th edition. Tokyo: Kenkyusha, 1974.

Matsuda Yumi. "'Sakura no mori no mankai no shita' no oni." In *Sakaguchi Ango kenkyū*. Ed. Moriyasu Masafumi, and Takano Yoshitomo. Tokyo: Nansōsha, 1973. 381–97.

Merleau-Ponty, Maurice. *Signs.* Trans Richard C. McCleary. Evanston, IL: Northwestern University Press, 1964.

Miller, Mara. "Canons and the Challenge of Gender." *Monist* 76, 4 (October 1993): 477–93.

Mishima Yukio. "Introduction." In *Young Samurai: Body Builders of Japan.* By Yatō Tamotsu. New York: Grove Press. Trans. of *Taido.* vii–x. 1967.

—— with Nosaka Akiyuki. "Erochishizumu to kokka kenryoku." In *Zenshū.* Vol. 36. Tokyo: Shinchōsha, 1973. 108–18.

Miyake Yoshiko. "Doubling Expectations: Motherhood and Women's Factory Work under State Management in Japan in the 1930s and 1940s." In *Recreating Japanese Woman, 1600–1945.* Ed. Gail Lee Bernstein. Berkeley: University of California Press, 1991. 267–95.

Miyamoto Yuriko. "Senkyuhyakuyonjyurokunen no bundan." In *Zenshū.* 14 vols. Tokyo: Kawade Shobō, 1952. 11: 68–90.

Miyoshi Masao. *Accomplices of Silence.* Berkeley: University of California Press, 1974.

Mizuta Noriko. "Hijiki no seibetsu to Feminizumu hihyō." In *Senjika no bungaku.* Ed. Kimura Kazunobu. Tokyo: Inpakuto Shuppankai, 2000. 297–9.

——. "In Search of a Lost Paradise: The Wandering Woman in Hayashi Fumiko's *Drifting Clouds.*" In *The Woman's Hand: Gender and Theory in Japanese Women's Writing.* Ed. Paul Gordon Schalow, and Janet A. Walker. Stanford: Stanford University Press, 1996. 329–51.

——. *Monogatari to hanmonogatari no fūkei.* Tokyo: Tabata Shoten, 1993.

Moi, Toril. *Simone de Beauvoir: The Making of an Intellectual Woman.* Oxford: Blackwell, 1994.

Molasky, Michael S. *The American Occupation of Japan and Okinawa: Literature and Memory.* London and New York: Routledge, 1999.

Mori Arimasa. "Sarutoru in okeru nikutai no mondai." *Kosei* 10, 2 (1949): 16–18.

Mori Eichi. "Fūzoku shōsetsu to chukan shōsetsu." In *Kōza Shōwa bungakushi.* 5 vols. Ed. Yūseido henshūbu. Tokyo: Yūseido, 1988. 3: 235–46.

Morosawa Yōko. *Onna no sengoshi.* Tokyo: Miraisha, 1971.

Mulhern, Chieko, ed. *Japanese Women Writers: A Bio-Critical Sourcebook.* Westport, CT: Greenwood Press, 1994.

Muramatsu Sadataka, and Sumiko Watanabe. *Gendai josei bungaku jiten.* Tokyo: Tokyodo Shuppan, 1990.

Nakagawa Shigemi. "Hayashi Fumiko: onna wa sensō wo tatakau ka?" In *Nanpō chōyō sakka: sensō to bungaku.* Ed. Tadataka Kamiya, and Kazuaki Kimura. Kyoto: Sekai Shisōsha, 1996. 239–58.

Nakamoto Takako. "Kichi no Onna." *Gunzō* (July 1953): 102–27.

Nakamura Miharu. "Ryutsu suru shintai." In *Kōza Shōwa bungakushi.* 5 vols. Ed. Yūseido henshūbu. Tokyo: Yūseido, 1988. 1: 129–41.

Nakamura Mitsuo. "Senryōka no bungaku." In *Nakamura Mitsuo zenshū.* 16 vols. Tokyo: Chikuma Shobō, 1972. 8: 101–12.

——. "Watashi shōsetsu ni tsuite." In *Zenshū.* Vol. 7. Tokyo: Chikuma Shobō, 1972. 116–40.

Nakamura Shin'ichirō. *Zōho sengo bungaku no kaisō.* Tokyo: Chikuma Sōsho, 1983.

Nathan, John. "Introduction." In Ōe Kenzaburō. *Teach Us To Outgrow Our Madness: Four Short Novels.* New York: Grove Press, 1977.

Newton, Judith, and Deborah Rosenfelt, eds. *Feminist Criticism and Social Change.* New York and London: Methuen, 1985.

Nihon Daijiten Kanko Kai. *Nihon kokugo daijiten.* Tokyo: Shōgaku Kan, Shukusatsuban, 1984–5.

Nihon sayoku bungeika sorengo, eds. *Sensō ni taisuru sensō: anchi miritarizumu shōsetsushū.* Tokyo: Fuji Shuppan, 1984.

Niino Naoyoshi. "Kodai ni okeru shintai ni kakawaru shisō." In *Nihon seikatsu shisō kenkyū.* Ed. Seikatsu Shisō Kenkyūkai. Morioka-shi: Kumatani Insatsu, 1989. 1–18.

"Nikutai no sengen." Nikutai 1, 1 (n.d.) [1947].

Nishikawa Nagao. *Kokkyō no koekata: hikaku bunkaron josetsu.* Tokyo: Chikuma Shobō, 1992.

——. *Nihon no sengo shōsetsu: haikyo no hikari.* Tokyo: Iwanami Shoten, 1988.

——. "Two Interpretations of Japanese Culture." Trans. Mikiko Murata, and Gavan McCormack. In *Multicultural Japan.* Ed. Donald Denon, Mark Hudson, Gavan McCormack, and Tessa Morris-Suzuki. Cambridge: Cambridge University Press, 1996. 245–64.

Nishikawa Nagao, and Nakahara Akio. *Sengo kachi no saikentō.* Tokyo: Yūhikaku, 1986.

Niwa Fumio. "Dokugokan." *Bungei shunjū* 3 (1954): 273–4.

Noma Hiroshi. "A Red Moon in her Face." Trans. Kin'ya Tsuruta. *The Literary Review* 6, 1 (1962): 35–57. Trans. of "Kao no naka no akai tsuki." 1947.

——. "Bungaku nyūmon." *Zenshū.* 20: 3–98.

——. "Bunsho nyūmon." *Zenshū.* 20: 99–252.

——. "Buntai, kao, sono hoka." *Zenshū.* 14: 294–7.

——. "Buntai ni tsuite." *Zenshū.* 15: 339–43.

——. "Dainijitaisengo no bungaku." *Zenshū.* 15: 5–26.

——. *"Dark Pictures" and Other Stories.* Trans. James Raeside. Ann Arbor: University of Michigan Press, 2000.

——. "Futatsu no nikutai." *Zenshū.* 1: 61–73.

——. "Hōhō no mondai." In *Ōe Kenzaburō, Abe Kōbō.* Tokyo: Yūseido, 1974. 154–8.

——. "Hōkai kankaku." *Zenshū.* 1: 175–218.

——. "Jibun no sakuhin ni tsuite (I, II)." *Zenshū.* 14: 251–9.

——. "Jōkyō." *Sarutoru techō/Carnet Sartrien.* Tokyo: Jinbun Shoin, 1952.

——. "Kao no naka no akai tsuki." *Zenshū.* 1: 115–37.

——. "Kurai e." *Zenshū.* 1: 3–60.

——. "Nikutai wa nurete." *Zenshū.* 1: 74–114.

——. "Ōe Kenzaburō: hito to shisō." *Zenshū.* 18: 122–3.

——. "Shōsetsu no bunshō." *Zenshū.* 15: 283–91.

——. "Shōsetsuron (I, II, III)." *Zenshū.* 14: 28–43.

——. "Watakushi no kotoba." *Zenshū.* 15: 292–5.

——. *Zenshū.* 22 vols. Tokyo: Chikuma Shobō, 1969.

——. *Zone of Emptiness.* Trans. Bernard Frechtman. Cleveland: World Pub. Co., 1956. Trans. of *Shinkū chitai.* 1952.

Oda Makoto. "Oda Makoto ni tsuite." In *"Korosuna" kara.* Tokyo: Chikuma Shobō, 1976.

——. "'Sono Ato' no 'sengo bungaku' – Noma Hiroshi no baai." *Gunzō* 7 (1991).

——. "The Ethics of Peace." In *Authority and the Individual in Japan: Citizen Protest in Historical Perspective.* Ed. J. Victor Koschmann. Tokyo: University of Tokyo Press, 1978. 154–70.

Oda Sakunosuke. "Kanōsei no bungaku." In *Oda Sakunosuke.* Chikuma Nihon bungaku zenshū. Tokyo: Chikuma Shobō, 1998. 425–61.

Odagiri Susumu, ed. *Nihon kindai bungaku daijiten.* 6 vols. Tokyo: Kōdansha, 1977–8.

Ōe Kenzaburō. *Dōjidai toshite no sengo.* Tokyo: Kōdansha, 1973.

——. "Kaisetsu." In *Zenshū. Noma Hiroshi.* 22 vols. Tokyo: Chikuma Shobō, 1969. 1: 361–72.

——. "Noma Hiroshi wa hattenteki ni shizoku suru." In *Noma Hiroshi kenkyū*. Ed. Watanabe Hiroshi. Tokyo: Chikuma Shobō, 1976. 104–10.

——. "Watashi shōsetsu ni tsuite." *Gunzō* 9 (1961): 192–7.

Ogawa Kazuo. *Meiji bungaku to kindai jiga: hikaku bungakuteki kōsatsu*. Tokyo: Nanundō, 1982.

Oka Yoshitake. "Generational Conflict after the Russo-Japanese War." In *Conflict in Modern Japanese History*. Ed. Victor J. Koschmann, and Tetsuo Najita. Princeton: Princeton University Press, 1982. 197–225.

Ōkubo Tsuneo. *Gendai bungaku kenkyū jiten 7 vols. Tokyo: Tokyodō Shuppan, 1983*.

——. "Sengo bungakushi no hōhō to kadai." In *Shōwa no bungaku*. Ed. Nihon Bungaku Kenkyū Keikōkai. Tokyo: Yūseido, 1981. 235–40.

Okuno Takeo. *Sakaguchi Ango*. Tokyo: Bungei Shunjū, 1972.

——. "Sengo bungaku to sei." In *Bungakuteki seiha*. Tokyo: Kamakura Insatsu, 1964. 99–106.

——. "Tamura Taijirō." In *Okuno Takeo sakka ron shū*. 5 vols. Tokyo: Tairyūsha, 1977. 3: 249–55.

Ono Tsunenori. *Angura Shōwa shi: sesoura no ura no hiji hatsukokai*. Tokyo: Minami Shuppanbu, 1981.

Orbaugh, Sharalyn. "The Body in Contemporary Japanese Women's Fiction." In *The Woman's Hand: Gender and Theory in Japanese Women's Writing*. Ed. Paul Gordon Schalow, and Janet A. Walker. Stanford: Stanford University Press, 1996. 119–64.

Ōshima Kiyoshi. "Kaisetsu." In Shibaki Yoshiko. *Susaki paradaisu*. Tokyo: Shūeisha, 1994. 215–22.

Outram, Dorinda. *The Body and the French Revolution*. New Haven, CT: Yale University Press, 1989.

Radhakrishnan, R. "Nationalism, Gender, and the Narrative of Identity." In *Nationalisms and Sexualities*. Ed. Andrew Parker, Mary Russo, Doris Sommer, and Patricia Yaeger. New York and London: Routledge, 1992.

Radiguet, Raymond. *Le diable au corps*. Paris: Grasset, 1923.

——. *The Devil in the Flesh*. Trans. Kay Boyle, with an introduction by Aldous Huxley. London: Grey Walls Press, 1949.

Rearick, Charles. *The French in Love and War: Popular Culture in the Era of the World Wars*. New Haven, CT: Yale University Press, 1997.

Raeside, James. *"Dark Pictures" and Other Stories*. Ann Arbor: Center for Japanese Studies, The University of Michigan, 2000.

Remarque, Erich Maria. *All Quiet on the Western Front*. New York: Fawcett Crest, 1958.

Remnick, David. "Reading Japan." *The New Yorker*. 6 Feb. 1995: 38–44.

Rioux, Jean-Pierre. *The Fourth Republic, 1944–1958*. Trans. Godfrey Rogers. Cambridge: Cambridge University Press, 1987.

Roberts, Mary Louise. *Civilization Without Sexes: Reconstructing Gender in Postwar France, 1917–1927*. Chicago: University of Chicago Press, 1994.

Rubin, Jay. "From Wholesomeness to Decadence: The Censorship of Literature under the Allied Occupation." *Journal of Japanese Studies* 11,1 (Winter 1985): 71–103.

——. *Injurious to Public Morals: Writers and the Meiji State*. Seattle: University of Washington Press, 1983.

Russo, Mary J. *The Female Grotesque: Risk, Excess, and Modernity*. New York: Routledge, 1995.

Saegusa Kazuko. *Ren'ai shōsetsu no kansei.* Tokyo: Seidosha, 1991.

——. *Sayonara otoko no jidai.* Kyoto: Jinbun Shoin, 1984.

——. *Sono fuyu no shi.* Tokyo: Kodansha, 1989.

——. *Sono hi no natsu.* Tokyo: Kodansha, 1987.

——. *Sono yoru no owari ni.* Tokyo: Kodansha, 1990.

Saeki Junko. *"Iro" to "ai" no hikaku bunkashi.* Tokyo: Iwanami Shoten, 1998.

Sahashi Bunju. *Sakaguchi Ango: Sono sei to shi.* Tokyo: Shunjūsha. 1980.

Saitō Suehiro. *Sakuhinron: Shiina Rinzō.* Tokyo: Ofūsha, 1989.

Sakaguchi Ango. "Darakuron." In *Gendai Nihon bungaku zenshū,* vol. 78: *Ishikawa Jun, Sakaguchi Ango, Dazai Osamushū.* Tokyo: Chikuma Shobō, 1961. 220–4.

——. "Dekadan bungakuron." In *Nihon bunka shikan: Sakaguchi Ango essai sen.* Tokyo: Kōdansha (bungeibunkō), 1996. 218–33.

——. "Discourse on Decadence." Trans. Seiji M. Lippit. *Review of Japanese Culture and Society* 1, 1 (1986): 1–5. Trans. of "Darakuron." 1946.

——. "Hakuchi." In *Sakaguchi Ango Dazai Osamu shū.* (*Gendai Nihon bungaku taikei* 77.) Tokyo: Chikuma Shobō, 1969. 268–80.

——. "In the Forest, Under Cherries in Full Bloom." Trans. Jay Rubin. In *The Oxford Book of Japanese Short Stories.* Ed. Theodore W. Goossen. Oxford: Oxford University Press, 1997.

——. *Nihon bunka shikan: Sakaguchi Ango essaisen.* Tokyo: Kōdansha (bungeibunkō), 1995.

——. "Nihon seishin." Reprinted in Nishikawa Nagao. *Kokkyō wo koekata.* Tokyo: Chikuma Shobō, 1992. 280–1.

——. "Nikutai jitai ga shikō suru." In *Teihon Sakaguchi Ango zenshū.* 13 vols. Tokyo: Tōjusha, 1975. 7: 237–8.

——. "Nyōtai." In *Teinhon Sakaguchi Ango zenshū.* 13 vols. Tokyo: Tōjusha, 1975.

——. "The Idiot." Trans. George Saitō. In *Modern Japanese Stories: An Anthology.* Ed. Ivan Morris. Rutland, VT: Charles E. Tuttle, 1962. Trans. of "Hakuchi," 1946. 383–415.

——. "Watashi wa umi wo dakishimetai." In *Zenshū.* 6: 153–63.

——. "Zoku darakuron." In *Nihon bunka shikan: Sakaguchi Ango essai shū.* Tokyo: Kodansha, 1996.

Sakai Naoki. "Subject and Substratum: On Japanese Imperial Nationalism." *Cultural Studies* 14, 3/4 (2000): 463–530.

Sartre, Jean-Paul. *Nausea.* Trans. Lloyd Alexander. New York: New Directions, 1964.

Schlant, Ernestine, and Thomas J. Rimer, ed. *Legacies and Ambiguities: Postwar Fiction and Culture in West Germany and Japan.* Washington, DC: The Woodrow Wilson Center Press, 1991.

Seidensticker, Edward. *Tokyo Rising: The City since the Great Earthquake.* New York: Alfred A. Knopf, 1990.

Sekii Mitsuo. *Sakaguchi Ango to Nihon bunka.* Tokyo: Ibundo, 1999.

——. "Sengo fūzoku jiten." *Tokyojin* (August 1995): 74–5.

Sekine Hiroshi. "Watashi no Sarutoru." *Gendai no me* (October 1966).

Senuma Shigeki. "Kaisetsu." In *Shibaki Yoshiko sakuhinshū.* 5 vols. Tokyo: Yomiuri shinbunsha, 1975. 5: 333–9.

——. "Nikutai bungaku no yukigata." In *Sengo bungaku nōto, jō.* Tokyo: Kawade Shobō, 1975.

Sherif, Ann. *Mirror: The Fiction and Essays of Kōdo Aya*. Honolulu: University of Hawai'i Press, 1999.

Shibaki Yoshiko. *Shibaki Yoshiko sakuhinshū*. 5 vols. Tokyo: Yomiuri shinbunsha, 1975.

——. *Susaki paradaisu*. Tokyo: Shūeisha, 1994.

——. "Yakō no onna." *Bungei* (1955): 164–83.

Shiina Rinzō. *Zenshū*. 24 vols. Tokyo: Tōjusha, 1970.

Shillony, Ben Ami. *Politics and Culture in Wartime Japan*. Oxford: Clarendon Press, 1981

Shinmura Izuru. *Kōjien*. 4th edition. Tokyo: Iwanami Shoten, 1991.

Shiomitsu Kazu. *Ameyoko 35 nen no gekishi*. Tokyo: Tokyo kobo shuppan, 1982.

Shirai Kōji. "Atogaki." In *Sarutoru Zenshū*. Vol. 6. Tokyo: Jinbun Shoin, 1951. 279–88.

——. "Jitsuzonshugi ni tsuite." In *Nihon kindai bungaku to gaikoku bungaku*. Ed. Nihon Kindai Bungaku Kan. Tokyo: Yomiuri Shinbunsha, 1969. 216–31.

Shōgakkan, ed. *Onnatachi no hachigatsu jūgonichi: mō hitotsu no taiheiyō sensō*. Tokyo: Shōgakkan, 1995.

Slaymaker, Douglas N., ed. *A Century of Popular Culture in Japan*. Lewiston, NY: Edwin Mellen Press, 2000.

——. "Kaisetsu: shōfuteki nikukan." In *Nikutai no mon*. By Tamura Taijirō. Tokyo: Chikuma Shobō, 1988. 239–43.

——. "Noma Hiroshi." In *The Dictionary of Literary Biography: Modern Japanese Novelists*. Ed. Van Gessel. Detroit: Gale Research, 1998. 154–62.

——. "Sartre's Fiction in Postwar Japan." In *Confluences: Postwar Japan and France*. Ed. Douglas N. Slaymaker. Ann Arbor: University of Michigan Center for Japanese Studies, 2002. 86–109.

——. "When Sartre was an Erotic Writer: Body, Nation, and Existentialism in Japan after the Asia-Pacific War." *Japan Forum* (Spring 2002): 77–103.

Sone Hiroyoshi. "Gendai bungaku ni okeru josei no hakken: Saegusa Kazuko no baai." *Kokubungaku* 5 (May 1986): 57–63.

——. "Kaisetsu: shōfuteki nikukan." In *Nikutai no mon*. By Tamura Taijirō. Tokyo: Chikuma Shobō, 1988. 239–42.

——. *Shōwa bungaku arubamu II*. Bessatsu 4 of Shinchō Nihon bungaku arubamu. Tokyo: Shinchōsha, 1990.

Sono Ayako. "Good Luck for Everybody!!" *Gunzō* (October 1955): 61–79.

Steinhoff, Patricia G. *Tenko: Ideology and Societal Integration in Prewar Japan*. New York: Garland, 1991.

Suleiman, Susan Rubin. "Introduction." In *The Female Body in Western Culture: Contemporary Perspectives*. Ed. Susan Rubin Suleiman. Cambridge, MA: Harvard University Press, 1986. 7–29.

Susaki Kiichi. "'Sengo bungaku' wa gensō datta." In *"Sengo bungaku" ronsō*. 2 vols. Ed. Usui Yoshimi. Tokyo: Banchō Shobō, 1972. 1: 559–71.

Susaki Takashi *et al*. *Sengoshi daijiten*. Tokyo: Sanseido, 1991.

Suzuki Sadami. "Noma Hiroshi no ichi." In *Tsuitō Noma Hiroshi*. Ed. Bungei Henshūbu. Tokyo: Kawade Shobō Shinsha, 1991. 36–161.

Suzuki Tomi. *Narrating the Self: Fictions of Japanese Modernity*. Stanford: Stanford University Press, 1996.

Suzuki Yūko. *Feminizumu to sensō*. Tokyo: Marujusha, 1997.

Takahashi Haruo. "Purotaria bungaku." In *Nihon bungaku shinshi*. Ed. Hasegawa Izumi. Tokyo: Shibundo, 1991. 60–88.

Takahashi Hideo. *Gensō toshite no "watakushi."* Tokyo: Kōdansha, 1976.

Takami Jun. "Panpan reisan." *Shinchō* 10 (1953): 116–20.

Takeda Kiyoko. "Tennō sei shisō no keisei." In *Iwanami kōza. Nihon rekishi*. Vol. 1: *Kindai*. Tokyo: Iwanami Shoten, 1962. 267–311.

Tamura Taijirō. "Inago." In *Nikutai no mon*. Tokyo: Chikuma Shobō, 1988. 161–217.

——. "Kore kara no watakushi." In *Nikutai no mon*. Tokyo: Chikuma Shobō, 1988. 230–2.

——. "Nikutai bungaku no kiban." In *Nikutai no mon*. Tokyo: Chikuma Shobō, 1988. 226–8.

——. "Nikutai bungaku to ningen ni jiyū." In *Nikutai no bungaku*. Tokyo: Kusano Shobō, 1948. 47–50.

——. "Nikutai ga ningen de aru." *Gunzō* 5 (1947): 11–14.

——. "Nikutai kaihō ron." In *Nikutai no bungaku*. Tokyo: Kusano Shobō, 1948.

——. "Nikutai no akuma." In *Nikutai no mon*. Tokyo: Chikuma Shobō, 1988.

——. *Nikutai no bungaku*. Tokyo: Kusano Shobō, 1948.

——. "Nikutai bungaku to ningen ni jiyū." In *Nikutai no bungaku*. Tokyo: Kusano Shobō, 1948. 47–50.

——. "Nikutai no mon." In *Tamura Taijirō, Kane Tatsuo, Ōhara Tomie shū*. Tokyo: Chikuma Shobō, 1978. Vol. 62 of *Chikuma gendai bungaku taikei*.

——. "Shunpuden." In *Tamura Taijirō shū*. Tokyo: Kōdansha, 1953. Vol. 13 of *Gendai chōhen meisaku zenshū*.

——. *Waga bundan seishunki*. Tokyo: Shinchōsha, 1963.

Tamura Taijirō et al. Kitahara Takeo, Inoue Tomoichirō, *Tamura Taijirō shū*. Tokyo: Kōdansha, 1980. Vol. 94 of *Nihon gendai bungaku zenshū*.

Tanaka Ryō. "An Interview with Jean-Paul Sartre." *Orient/West* 7, 5 (1962): 63–9.

Tanaka Toshiyuki. *Japan's Comfort Women: Sexual Slavery and Prostitution During World War II and the US Occupation*. London and New York: Routledge, 2002.

Tansman, Alan M. *The Writings of Kōda Aya: A Japanese Literary Daughter*. New Haven, CT: Yale University Press, 1993.

Theunissen, Michael. *The Other: Studies in the Social Ontology of Husserl, Heidegger, Sartre, and Buber*. Trans. Christopher Macann. Cambridge, MA: MIT Press, 1984.

Theweleit, Klaus. *Male Fantasies*. 2 vols. Trans. Stephen Conway. Minneapolis: University of Minneapolis Press, 1987.

Tipton, Elise K., ed. *Society and the State in Interwar Japan*. London and New York: Routledge, 1997.

Togaeri Hajime. *Nise no kisetsu*. Tokyo: Kōdansha, 1954.

"Tokushū no tame ni – naze, ima, 'shintai' na no ka?" *Shin Nihon bungaku* 26, 10 (October 1971): 74–5.

Tomioka Kōichirō. *Sengo bungaku no arukeorojii*. Tokyo: Fukutake Shobō, 1986.

Torrance, Richard. "Pre-World War Two Concepts of Japanese Popular Culture and Takeda Rintarō's 'Japan's Three Penny Opera.'" In *A Century of Popular Culture in Japan*. Ed. Douglas N. Slaymaker. Lewiston, NY: Edwin Mellen Press, 2000. 17–40.

Treat, John Whittier. "Beheaded Emperors and the Absent Figure in Contemporary Japanese Literature." *PMLA* 109, 1 (1994): 100–15.

——. "Hiroshima Nōto and Ōe Kenzaburō's Existentialist Other." *Harvard Journal of Asiatic Studies* 47 (1987): 97–136.

——. *Writing Ground Zero: Japanese Literature and the Atomic Bomb*. Chicago: University of Chicago Press, 1995.

Tsuge Teruhiko. "Jitsuzonshugi." In *Nihon bungaku shinshi*. 6 vols. Ed. Hasegawa Izumi. Tokyo: Shibundō, 1994. 6: 126–51.

——. "Nichijō to hinichijō no hazama." *Kōza Shōwa bungakushi*. 5 vols. Ed. Yūseidō henshūbu. Tokyo: Yūseido, 1988. 3: 3–13.

"Ōe Kenzaburō." In *Ōe Kenzaburō, Abe Kōbō*. Tokyo: Yūseido, 1974. 214–26.

Tsukiramu Toshiyuki. "Sedairon no gyakusetsu." In *Ōe Kenzaburō, Abe Kōbō*. Tokyo: Yūseido, 1974. 167–83.

Tsurumi Kazuko. *Social Change and the Individual: Japan Before and After Defeat in World War II*. Princeton: Princeton University Press, 1970.

Tsurumi Shunsuke. *An Intellectual History of Wartime Japan, 1931–1945*. New York: KPI, 1986. Translation of *Senjiki Nihon no seishinshi: 1931–1945-nen*. Tokyo: Iwanami Shoten, 1982.

——. "Kotoba no omamoriteki sayōhō ni tsuite." In *Tsurumi Shunsuke chosakushū*. 5 vols. Tokyo: Chikuma Shobō, 1972. 3: 12–25.

Tsurumi Shunsuke, and Kuno Osamu. *Gendai Nihon no shisō*. Tokyo: Iwanami Shoten, 1969.

Tsuruta Kin'ya. *Nihon kindai bungaku ni okeru "mukogawa": hahanaru mono seinaru mono*. Tokyo: Meiji Shoin, 1986.

Ueno Chizuko. "Ishi wo nageru." In *Danryū bungakuron*. Ed. Ueno Chizuko, Ogura Chikako, and Tomioka Taeko. Tokyo: Chikuma Shobō, 1992. 400–1.

Ueno Kōshi. *Nikutai no jidai: taikenteki 60-nendai bunkaron*. Tokyo: Gendai Shokan, 1989.

Ueno Toshiya. "Suiito emōshon." *Bungei* 34, 1 (1995): 301–5.

Umehara Takeshi. "Jitsuzonshugi no jitsuzonteki hihan." *Shisō no kagaku* 9 (1967): 9–16.

Usui Yoshimi. *Kawazu no uta*. Tokyo: Chikuma Shobō, 1965.

——, ed. *"Sengo bungaku" ronsō*. 2 vols. Tokyo: Banchō Shobō, 1972.

Wagenaar, Dick, and Yoshio Iwamoto. "Yukio Mishima: Dialectics of Mind and Body." *Contemporary Literature* 16, 1 (1975): 41–60.

Wakabayashi Bob Tadashi. *Anti-Foreignism and Western Learning in Early-Modern Japan: The New Theses of 1825*. Cambridge, MA: Council on East Asian Studies, Harvard University, 1986.

Washburn, Dennis. *The Dilemma of the Modern in Japanese Fiction*. New Haven, CT: Yale University Press, 1995.

Watanabe Hiroshi. *Noma Hiroshiron*. Tokyo: Shinbisha, 1969.

——. *Ōe Kenzaburōron*. Tokyo: Sanbisha, 1973.

——. "'Seinen no wa' wa ika ni naru imi de zentai shōsetsu ka." *Shin Nihon bungaku* 520 (1991): 84–94.

Watanabe Kazutami. "Sengo shisō no mitorizu." In *Sengo Nihon no seishinshi*. Ed. Najita Tetsuo, Maeda Ai, and Kamishima Jirō. Tokyo: Iwanami Shoten, 1988. 95–112.

Watanabe Sumiko. "Shōwa ga hiraita josei bungaku." In *Gendai josei bungaku jiten*. Ed. Watanabe Sumiko *et al.* Tokyo: Tokyodo Shuppan, 1990. 15–20.

Whiteside, Kerry H. *Merleau-Ponty and the Foundation of an Existential Politics*. Princeton: Princeton University Press, 1988.

Williams, Raymond. *Keywords: A Vocabulary of Culture and Society.* New York: Oxford University Press, 1985.

Wilson, George M. *Patriots and Redeemers in Japan: Motives in the Meiji Restoration.* Chicago: University of Chicago Press, 1992.

Wolf, Eric R. *Envisioning Power.* Berkeley: University of California Press, 1999.

Wolfe, Alan. "From Pearls to Swine: Sakaguchi Ango and the Humanity of Decadence." In *War, Occupation, and Creativity: Japan and East Asia, 1920–1960.* Ed. Marlene J. Mayo, J. Thomas Rimer, and H. Eleanor Kerkham. Honolulu: University of Hawai'i Press, 2001. 360–79.

Yajima Michihiro. "'Watashi wa umi wo dakisimeteitai' nikutai no seishinka." In *Sakaguchi Ango kenkyū.* Ed. Moriyasu Masafumi, and Takano Yoshitomo. Tokyo: Nansōsha, 1973. 337–52.

Yakushiji Noriaki. *Noma Hiroshi.* Tokyo: Fumiizu Shuppan, 1977.

———. *Noma Hiroshi kenkyū.* Tokyo: Kasama Shoin, 1977.

Yamada Minoru. "Jitsuzon ishiki to naizo kankaku – Noma Hiroshiron." In *Noma Hiroshi kenkyū.* Ed. Watanabe Hiroshi. Tokyo: Chikuma Shobō, 1969. 118–29.

Yamada Teruo. "Watashi shōsetsu no mondai." *Kokubungaku kaishaku to kanshō* 1 (1965): 43–7.

Yamada Yūsaku, Akiyama Shun, Kuritsubo Yoshiki, and Tsuge Teruhiko. "Ōe Kenzaburō no sakuhin wo bunseki suru." *Kokubungaku: kaishaku to kyōzai no kenkyū* 24, 2 (1979): 33–81.

Yamaoka Akira. *Shomin no sengo: fūzoku hen – sengo taishū zasshi ni miru.* Tokyo: Taiheishuppansha, 1973.

Yamashita Minoru. *Noma Hiroshi ron.* Tokyo: Sairyusha, 1994.

Yohana Keiko. "Onna no shintai/onna no ishiki." In *Kōza Shōwa bungakushi.* 5 vols. Ed. Yūseido henshūbu. Tokyo: Yūseido, 1988. 5: 117–29.

Yokote Kazuhiko. *Hisenryōka no bungaku ni kansuru kisōteki kenkyū: ronkōhen.* Tokyo: Musashino shobō, 1996.

Yōrō Takeshi. *Nihonjin no shintaikan no rekishi.* Kyoto: Hozokan, 1996.

———. *Shintai no bungakushi.* Tokyo: Shinchōsha, 1997.

Yoshida Hiroo. "Kindai ni okeru shintai: *Maihime* wo chūshin ni." In *Bungaku ni okeru shintai.* Ed. Satō Yasumasa. Tokyo: Kasama Shoin, 1984. 81–97.

Index

Dante 78, 79
daraku 100–6, 109–10, 112, 115, 118–20,
    123–5, 128, 130, 183n 71; *see also*
    decadence
Dazai Osamu 2, 24, 52, 184n 85
decadence 55, 99–100, 102–4, 106–9, 116,
    120, 124–6, 161; *see also daraku*
democracy 4–5, 13, 16, 69, 126, 134, 143,
    157, 172n 5
domesticity *see* home
Dower, John 44

economy 19, 31, 34, 35, 47, 59, 88, 131,
    148, 160
écriture feminine 32
Edo 12, 121, 126
empire *see* imperialism
Enchi Fumiko 137
enlightenment 16, 40, 105, 109–10, 112,
    152
erotic 1–2, 7, 10, 15, 25–9, 30, 43, 45, 48–9,
    52, 55, 57, 106, 109, 120, 124–5, 172n
    4; *see also* body, carnal
essential 9, 16, 19, 25, 30, 44, 46, 47, 54,
    100, 101, 103, 111, 112, 117–20, 122–4,
    180n 6, 181n 13
ethnicity 62–4, 140
Existentialism 18, 26–9, 95, 107, 110,
    128–9, 162, 165n 3, 169n 60, 178n 48,
    181n 21

Fascism 12, 30, 86, 166n 15, 168n 48,
    177n 17
Feminism 37, 132, 183n 60
feudal 50, 54, 56, 167n 34
"flesh writers" 2–30, 31–42, 65, 73, 76, 118,
    124, 130, 131–2, 137, 139, 160–2,
    167n 36, 180n 4
Foucault, Michel 11, 12, 37, 50, 110, 180n 5
France 24, 27, 163n 4, 168n 56, 180n 5
freedom 4–5, 13–18, 20–3, 26–7, 33–8,
    40–2, 46–50, 61, 65–8, 73–8, 85, 91–2,
    128–9, 138–9, 143–7, 151, 157, 160,
    172n 5
furusato 103–13, 115–17, 124–5,128

gender 5, 14, 16, 31–41, 131–6, 139, 146,
    154–7, 160–1, 173n 34
Gide, André 28–9, 87

Haniya Yutaka 71, 177n 34
Hayama Yoshiki 23
Hayashi Fumiko 32, 135–6, 137
Heidegger 27
Hino Ashihei 18, 22
Hirabayashi Taiko 9, 32, 137
Hirano, Ken 80, 86, 120, 177n 34
Hiroike Akiko 131, 143–5
hiropon (Philopon) 126
home: imagery of private/privacy 32,
    37–9, 71, 121, 137; *see also*
    furusato
Honda Shūgo 3, 21, 86, 93, 177n 34
Hyōdo Masanosuke 127, 129, 185n 88

identity 3–6, 8–10, 13, 14, 16–21, 24, 33–6,
    45, 47, 54–5, 62–3, 72–4, 99–103,
    109, 117–20, 130, 131, 155–6, 160–1;
    cultural 103, 117–20; ethnic 62; female
    33, 57, 135–6; male 14–15, 34, 57, 73,
    76, 80, 100, 130; national 6, 10, 15,
    16–21, 103
ideology 2–3, 17, 18–22, 30, 33, 130, 138,
    173n 30, 180n 4; in Ango 100–1, 104,
    110; of family-state *see kazoku kokka*;
    national 38, 50, 55, 62, 75; in Noma
    75–6, 79–81, 85–9; in Tamura 44–51,
    55, 59, 61–2; of wartime Japan 10, 13,
    18, 23, 31, 47, 108, 129
Igarashi Yoshikuni 10, 15, 45–6, 56
Ihara Saikaku 28
Imperialism 1, 5, 11, 44, 126, 135, 137,
    165n 7, 171 n15
impotence 33–4, 135
individual *see* identity
Irigaray, Luce 5, 38–9
Ishihara Shintarō 43
Ishikawa Jun 52
Isoda Kōichi 1, 14, 17, 24, 28, 30, 41,
    46, 55
Izuma Kyōka 4